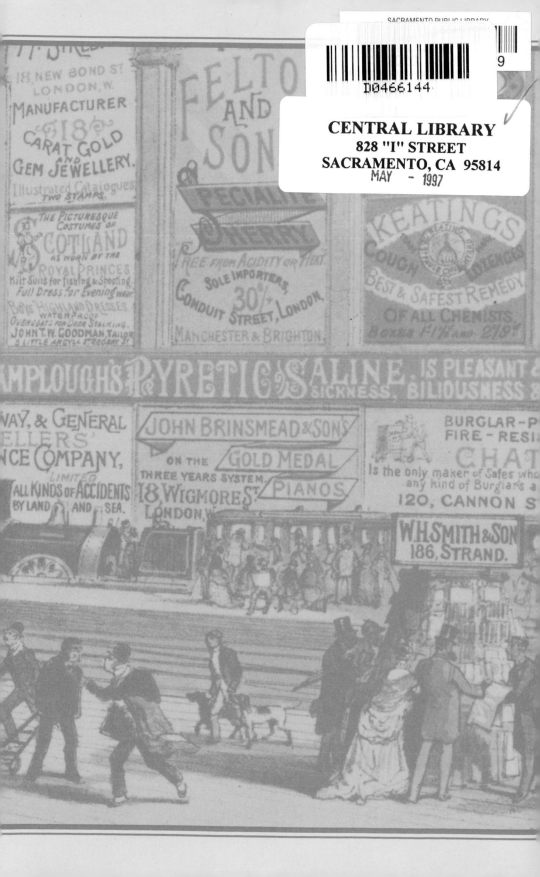

Dickens' Fur Coat and Charlotte's Unanswered Letters

ALSO BY DANIEL POOL

What Jane Austen Ate and Charles Dickens Knew

Dickens' Fur Coat and Charlotte's Unanswered Letters

The Rows and Romances of England's Great Victorian Novelists

Daniel Pool

HarperCollinsPublishers

HarperCollins books may be purchased for educational, business, or sales promotional use. For information please write: Special Markets Department, HarperCollins Publishers, Inc., 10 East 53rd Street, New York, NY 10022.

FIRST EDITION

Designed by Gloria Adelson/LuLu Graphics
Design Assistant: Ruth Lee

Library of Congress Cataloging-in-Publication Data

Pool, Daniel.
    Dickens' fur coat and Charlotte's unanswered letters : the rows and romances of England's great Victorian novelists / Daniel Pool. — ed.
        p. cm.
    Includes bibliographical references (p.   ).
    ISBN 0–06–018365-9
    1. English fiction—19th century—History and criticism. 2. Literature publishing—England—History—19th century. 3. Authors and publishers—England—History—19th century. 4. Authors and readers—England—History—19th century. 5. Literature and society—England—History—19th century. 6. Novelists, English—19th century—Social conditions. 7. Novelists, English—19th century—Economic conditions. 8. Fiction—Authorship—Economic aspects—England. 9. England—Intellectual life—19th century. 10. Books and reading—England—History—19th century. I. Title.
    PR878.P78P66   1997
    823'.809—dc20   96-32521

97 98 99 00 01 ❖/RRD 10 9 8 7 6 5 4 3 2 1

To
Beek and Elizabeth

Children, Charlotte has been writing a book—and I
think it is a better one than I expected.

> —The Reverend Patrick Brontë, upon
> joining his daughters Emily and Anne
> for tea after first reading *Jane Eyre*

Do not speak slightingly of the three-volume novel,
Cecily.

> —*The Importance of Being Earnest*

CONTENTS

PART 4

PART 5

PART 6

ACKNOWLEDGMENTS

The reference staff of the Butler Library at Columbia University were unfailingly helpful and inventive in suggesting how to solve the research problems that a project such as this necessarily entailed. So, too, were the staff members of the reference desk at the New York Public Library. Both Bettina Berch and Jeff Miller read early drafts of the manuscript and provided much needed encouragement. At a later stage, Phillip Mallett gave this manuscript the benefit of his expertise with a close and thoughtful reading that rescued it from numerous errors of fact. Philip Meyler graciously involved himself in various international money transfers of deeply sinister mien in order to promptly pay British institutions for the right to reproduce their photographs and other visual matter herein. Deborah McLauchlan performed prodigious feats of persuasion and scheduling in obtaining those same reproductions and permissions for their use. She also spotted numerous infelicities of style in the manuscript. The usual disclaimer about any remaining errors being the sole fault of the author applies with unusual force in this connection. With no doubt unjustified stubbornness or obtuseness I not only disagreed with some of Phillip and Deborah's suggestions but changed the manuscript more than I would have wished after their final opportunity to review it.

My agent, Malaga Baldi was, as always, unflaggingly enthusiastic, helpful, accessible and tenacious. If doing the rest of the book had been as easy as dealing with her, it would have been a breeze. The book would not exist at all without the enthusiasm and persistence of my editor, Cynthia Barrett. She also gave the book thoughtful editing and made the inexorable demands of the production schedule seem necessary rather than simply unpleasant. Her assistant, Elissa Altman, was efficient and prompt in her help. In addition, the officers and staff of the F. David Korzenik Foundation provided assistance of incalculable value during the preparation of the manuscript. And, last but by no means least, Eileen vastly lightened the drudgery that attends projects of this nature by being so thoroughly wonderful.

Introduction

*V*anity Fair, Middlemarch, Great Expectations, Bleak House, and the other great Victorian classics—we take them to the beach, to the country for long weekends, or to more or less distant locales on those unending plane trips. Why? For pleasure sometimes, perhaps, too, partly out of guilt at the unfinished corners of our liberal education, and no doubt even merely because, like Everest, they are there. They remain touchstones of our sense of literary worth and of what endures in fiction.

The industry that produced the great Victorian novels and the approximately forty to fifty thousand other English novels published during Victoria's reign was a shared business of publishers, writers, and powerful book distributors. This book is the story of how that industry rose from virtual obscurity and, in some respects, ignominy, to dominate English literature and, for a time, world literature as well.

It is an interesting industry, not least because those who worked in it were subject to constraints both of content and format as rigid as today's situation comedy. *Middlemarch*, for example, is divided to this day into eight distinct "books" because George Eliot was tired of trying to fit her novels into the three-volume format dictated by England's leading distributor of novels. Her publisher, John Blackwood, was tired likewise of giving the same distributor discounts of up to 50 percent. *Great Expectations*, similarly, is a relatively brief book rather than a monster on the order of *Bleak House, Little Dorrit*, and numerous other Dickens novels because Dickens had to chop it way down at the last minute to fit it into the small space of a magazine.

But the story is not one merely of economics and literary formats. As in other communities, there was a good deal of interaction, sometimes friendly, sometimes rivalrous, and sometimes downright hostile, between its members, with Dickens in his editorial mode trying to steal George Eliot from another publisher; quiet, retiring Charlotte Brontë being mistaken for Thackeray's mistress (and for the original of Becky Sharp!); Anthony Trollope thoughtfully advising Thomas Hardy on the best way to get paid for his novels; Bulwer Lytton (of "It was a dark and stormy night" fame) allegedly plotting to poison a fellow novelist who happened to be his wife—while all of them tried to figure out how to make a decent living in an era before there were screenplays, creative writing professorships, or much in the way of publishing advances.

The literary environment in which the great Victorian novels were written was fascinating, often difficult, and in some ways only by the purest accident favorable to the production of masterpieces—and yet it produced them, as part of a new, mass phenomenon in the world of publishing.

PART 1

"A Low, Cheap Form of Publication": Charles Dickens, the Coming of *Pickwick*, and Murder by the Book

A figure makes its way rapidly through the sleeping streets of London. There is an east wind, brackish, blowing
up from the Kentish marshes, slicing through his heavy garments as the shop signs creak overhead in the occasional gusts.

March, sometime in the late 1830s.

The vast city lies asleep, the black coal smoke from a few
late-burning chimneys drifting unseen in the dark night overhead, all quiet save for the mews where now and then the
horses turn and paw the ground in their stalls as the coachmen
and grooms snore in their rooms above, or save for the alley
where a drunken reveler staggers home late, or the doorway
where the hurrying man stumbles over a crouching form who
starts up—and, in a greater fright than he—dashes suddenly
away over the cobblestones and mud. There are homeless people sleeping huddled under bridges and stone stairwells as the
figure makes his way through the city, past the wretched match
girls and "mudlarks" (who scavenge the river), old men shivering against the wind—it is, after all, the age of laissez-faire—
and still the figure hurries on, ten, twelve, fifteen miles. On
what lonely mission through the deserted streets of the sleeping metropolis?

On through Hampstead, across the still deserted heath that
lies north of the city, down southward toward Westminster,
through the still rural lanes and orchards of Kensington,

perhaps by the pawnbrokers' shops in the poorer areas and across the river past the ship chandlers to where the old Vauxhall gardens were, he goes. He turns along the river toward Blackfriars or perhaps north toward Bethnal Green or Camden Town, where clerks like Scrooge's Bob Cratchit make their home, as gusts of wind blow leaves cartwheeling through the muddy streets past flickering gas lamps while the great Monument to the fire of 1666 points like a grim finger toward the silent sky overhead.

Restlessly the figure presses on. It hurries through the muddy streets thick with horse manure, past churchyards overflowing with corpses and bones that spill out of the coffins and graves onto the earth (so fast has the city grown of late), past the wretched district of St. Giles, where murder, poverty and disease dwell, on through the wealthy West End and the town houses of the great, the clubs, the shuttered windows of the expensive shops where a garret candle shows a clerk snatching moments to read, past the docks of the East End where the colliers rock at anchor by the silent immensity of Somerset House, past the rag and bone shops, a solitary horseman now and then clip-clopping slowly by him through the frozen stretches of the night—with the solitary walker avoiding only one building, that of a past and hidden shame. There he crosses to the other side of the street, hugging his secret closely, and continues on.

Dawn is beginning to lighten in the east as the muffin vendors sleepily begin their rounds, and an early-rising coffee man sets out his steaming cups, the Billingsgate market opening down by the river as the fishermen bring in their catches and haggle over prices—and still the figure shows no sign of ceasing, no sign of slackening until he rounds a corner suddenly and is brought up short by the startled cry of a man who sees the face and utters the word, curious, unbelieving, not even realizing that what he sees is no aberration but a nightly practice, an all but unshakable habit, almost, one might say, almost an addiction—

"Dickens!" says the startled figure.

* * *

We think of the Victorian novel as the product of a whole group of authors, notable among them Thackeray, the Brontës, George Eliot, and Trollope. But in reality it was at the outset the work of a single, driven, tormented genius, one who brought into the world a whole new way of writing fiction and describing society— Charles Dickens. A man who took the turbulent, changing industrial landscape of nineteenth-century England and distilled it into a series of volumes filled with vengeful beadles, doe-eyed heroines, plucky, abused orphans, and comic figures in settings ranging from the ludicrous to the surrealistically nightmarish. A man who invented a distinctive way of looking at and talking about the world, a way that would be imitated for decades.

The son of an impoverished, improvident clerk for the Navy Pay Office for whom life had at first seemed to go well, Charles Dickens had grown up along the Kentish coast southeast of London. On walks with his father young Charles saw the "hulks," the prison ships where the convicts worked at Chatham, and the great house with the cupola and bow windows at Gad's Hill on the road from Gravesend to Rochester a few miles away. "If you were to be very persevering and were to work hard," his father, John Dickens, told him, "you might some day come to live in it." Young Charles also heard stories, horror stories of little boys whose parents wanted to get rid of them being shipped off to cruel schools in the wilds of Yorkshire, true stories. His nurse, Mary Weller, told him less true but perhaps equally terrifying tales like the one of the captain who baked his wives into pies, ate them, and then, after being poisoned, turned blue and swelled up till he burst, or the tale about the man who sold his soul to the devil and was thereafter haunted by rats, all over him, in his pockets, on his body, scampering demoniacally after him wherever he went, and eventually drowning him. Sprightly, frail, but clever and energetic, Charles would be put up on the table by his father to sing for company. He was destined, the boy knew, for great things and a distinguished career.

And then misfortune began to dog the Dickens family.

The gigantic economic expansion that followed the end of the conflicts with Napoleon culminated in a disastrous crash in 1825. The Dickenses were already in trouble from the free spending of John Dickens, ever ready with a loan, ever willing to pick up the tab at the tavern nearby. Soon they could no longer afford the solid brick middle-class town house in which they had been living. They moved in the spring of 1821 to humbler quarters in a poorer area of town. Then John Dickens was transferred to London, where his finances continued to deteriorate. As the Dickens family sank deeper into debt and Charles was sent to pawn or sell household possessions, Mrs. Dickens desperately determined on that great expedient of so many genteel Victorian women whose families fell into straitened circumstances—she would teach. A brass plate bearing the inscription "Mrs Dickens' Establishment" was made up and put next to the door of a suitable house, and Charles left circulars for the school at neighborhood doors.

No one came.

In February 1824 John Dickens was at last arrested for nonpayment of a debt of £40 upon the suit of a creditor and imprisoned in the Marshalsea prison in Southwark, across the river from London proper. Only two weeks before, his parents had sent Charles to work at a blacking factory at 30 Hungerford Stairs along the Thames. There he pasted labels on bottles of shoe polish. He had been distraught—a promising student, now set to an ignominious trade next to working-class boys who called him, mockingly, the "young gentleman," and all for only six shillings a week. And then the gates of the Marshalsea clanged shut behind his grandiloquent, good-natured father and—so the twelve-year-old Dickens thought—on all *his* dreams and hopes, too. "I know that I have lounged about the streets, insufficiently and unsatisfactorily fed. I know that, but for the mercy of God, I might easily have been, for any care that was taken of me, a little robber or a little vagabond." Not so different from thousands of other children in London or,

A young girl making her way out of a circulating library. Because England lacked public libraries and books were prohibitively expensive until the mid-1800s, books were rented through these privately owned libraries. Then Dickens introduced the cheap "serial" novel, beginning with The Pickwick Papers *in 1836, which people could afford to buy as it appeared in installments.*

indeed, all across England: ill-used, sometimes orphaned, abandoned, poverty-stricken children whom he would make famous in his novels.

Years later Charles would recall his misery when, before the prison gates had swung to behind his father, John Dickens told his young boy how the sun had gone down for him forever. "I really believed at the time," the grown-up Charles later said, "that they had broken my heart."

But then this was not a kind world, this brave new world of large enterprises and bold ventures struggling slowly into existence. A fast-moving and complicated world compared to the one of simple handicrafts that went before, it was a world of steam, calico, Wedgwood pottery, and iron shipped on British vessels to Calcutta, Buenos Aires, Halifax, and Hong Kong; a world that displaced farmers for mines and mills, silenced the traditional village spinning wheels as the giant looms turned all night and all day, sending the artisans they had deprived of livelihoods to the workhouse. It was a world that made orphans at five and six of the sons and daughters of mill or factory "hands" killed by dangerous machinery, unsanitary working conditions, or disease. Children of six and seven, some naked, hauled the coal needed for the steam engines and railroads that powered this new economy, often dragging the carts full of the precious fuel from the mines on their hands and knees through spaces only eight to ten inches deep with the aid of a chain passed around their waist and then between their legs. Rioting engulfed the countryside in 1830, and five hundred people were sent as convicts to Van Diemen's Land and New South Wales. A poor cleric of Irish descent named Patrick Brontë (who changed his last name from "Brunty" after Lord Nelson was created "Duke of Brontë" by a grateful Sicilian monarch, Brontë being a village on Mount Etna) armed to protect himself in the north of England after speaking out against the machine smashers who revolted against the new order.

England was still a backward and undeveloped country in

many ways. In 1830, seven years before Queen Victoria took the throne and Dickens' first novel, *The Pickwick Papers*, appeared, there were only some 1,100 books of all kinds published in England, and the average edition of a novel was only some 750 to 1,200 copies. Only a third of the men and half the women married in Lancashire in 1840 could sign their names. "For the greatest part of the people do not read books, most of them cannot read at all, but they will gather about one that can read, and listen to the Observator or Review (as I have seen them in the streets)," said a writer in 1750; those days were not so distant in 1837. (Indeed, as late as the mid-century, the young Sunday school teacher Thomas Hardy would be writing letters for village girls in rural Dorset to their soldier sweethearts abroad in India.) Literacy was so rare for centuries that it was assumed that one who read must be a man of God. On this assumption, "benefit of clergy" permitted a schedule of lesser criminal penalties, e.g., branding on the thumb instead of hanging, for anyone who could read. Manslaughter was still "clergyable" under this system until 1822 and benefit of clergy was not abolished altogether until 1837.

Before the mass production of books and widespread literacy, limited demand and primitive manufacturing techniques meant that books were so scarce and expensive that they were necessarily luxury items, bought from tony London establishments like Hatchard's, which maintained a bench outside for footmen to sit on while their employers perused volumes in the shop. In 1836 novels, invariably printed in a three-volume format since Sir Walter Scott had made it popular, cost thirty-one shillings six pence at a time when the average rural or urban workingman made between six and twenty shillings a week. The fact that books were luxury items is one reason why so many of the great country houses had huge libraries with books bound in the owner's own private bindings ostentatiously and magnificently on display. And books being objects of conspicuous consumption—"furniture for the rich," poet Robert Southey called them in 1809—gave rise to jokes like the one about the ignorant nouveau riche collector who gave standing orders to his bookseller to send him anything by Milton, Pope, and Shakespeare "and anything new those fellows may produce."

Those with less money than the great lords of the land rented books, like videotapes, from privately owned circulating libraries that for several guineas a year let one borrow the latest volumes. They spread rapidly, these little lending operations, often operated as adjuncts to other small-scale enterprises. In his *Pendennis*, Thackeray wrote of how Fanny Bolton "had the benefit of the circulating library which, in conjunction with her school and a small brandy-ball and millinery business, Miss Minifer kept." Contemplating a second edition of *Mansfield Park*, Jane Austen observed in 1814 that "people are more ready to borrow and praise, than to buy—which I cannot wonder at." A writer in the June 1821 *Monthly* magazine estimated that the country had about 1,500 circulating libraries with 10,000 regular and an equal number of occasional customers. By 1894, when the system was in decline, the Authors' Society estimated that these libraries still had 60,000 subscribers across the country.

What kinds of novels would such a small, luxury market want? The immensely popular Sir Walter Scott had invented and popularized the historical novel with his *Waverley* books like *Ivanhoe* and *Quentin Durward* at the turn of the century. Now came the epigoni, who for the luxury market wrote novels, naturally, about the rising middle class that had made money in the Napoleonic Wars and the aristocrats they emulated, novels rich in the love affairs, social intrigue, and social climbing that their readers delighted in. And so that is what Henry Colburn, England's foremost publisher of novels and a putative bastard of the king's brother, the Duke of York, gave them, beginning in the century's first few decades.

Colburn's so-called silver fork novels told breathless tales, Judith Krantz–style, of the fast, expensive life among the upper crust. The nobility were the movie stars and television personalities of the era, and everyone wanted to emulate them. Hence the novels came complete with product names of fancy items so the reader from that same upwardly mobile middle class that pushed for the Reform Bill of 1832 could also use Colburn's books for purposes of imitative upward mobility. You read such "a Novel," said the essayist William Hazlitt, "and may fancy yourself reading a collection of quack or fashionable advertisements:—Macassar Oil, Eau de Cologne, Hock and Seltzer Water, Otto of Rose, *Pomade Divine*"—for the products used by the upper crust. Colburn naturally sought noblemen for authors. In the case of common-born authors like the ambitious young Benjamin Disraeli, who started his novelistic career writing for Colburn, the publisher often put out their books anonymously with hints that they were titled. "The authorship is a great secret—a man of high fashion—very high," Colburn whispered mysteriously about Disraeli's first novel, "keeps the first society."

As befitted the coming of industrialism and the modern age of mass manufacture, Colburn was the first to introduce advertising in a major way into novel publishing. In addition to buying ads in literary journals (or, sometimes, the journals themselves), he hired people to go to dinner to talk about his books, inserted publicity notices about his authors in the newspapers, and printed "keys" hinting at the identity of the real-life figures from whom the characters in his novels were drawn to titillate the reader. He used his ad budget, too. "I am intimately acquainted with the editors," he oozed of several publications to a prolific author, "and advertising with them a great deal, keeps them in check." He also used tragedy to stimulate sales. When her husband murdered the Duchess de Praslin in her bed in 1847 in a famous French murder case, a bloodstained volume by the felicitously named Mrs. Gore was found in the bed and put in evidence at the trial; Colburn made sure the novel was swiftly republished. He also made use of manufactured news items, having himself brought, amid much hullabaloo, before the police court for failing to return an author's manuscript—

and then publishing the book amid the resultant publicity a few days later.

Such embryonic mass marketing techniques suggested the possibility of mass producing books, manufacturing them on a scale where they were no longer luxuries, too expensive for most to buy, but objects inexpensive enough to buy and not borrow from a circulating library. Archibald Constable, the publisher of Walter Scott, had vowed a few years before to produce novels that people could afford to buy, as he and the great author sat looking out one day from Scott's beloved home Abbotsford onto the Scottish hills and the river Tweed below. "Scott helped him on by interposing, that at that moment he had a rich valley crowded with handsome houses under his view, and yet much doubted whether any laird within ten miles spent ten pounds per annum on the literature of the day." Instead, they borrowed from the circulating libraries, which, of course, wanted to keep prices high so people would continue to rent rather than buy their books. Constable vowed: "But if I live for half-a-dozen years, I'll make it . . . impossible that there should not be a good library in every decent house in Britain . . . I have now settled my outline of operations—A three-shilling or half-crown volume every month, which must and shall sell, not by thousands or tens of thousands, but by hundreds of thousands—ay, by millions!"

Constable's dream was not to be.

In the huge financial failure in 1825, which helped torpedo families like Dickens', Scott's partners Constable and John Ballantyne went under, too, to the then altogether astronomical tune of £250,000.

Were novels therefore destined to remain luxury, elite items, with all the restrictions on subject matter and availability that this would suggest? Or was it possible to devise a way of publishing novels that bypassed the whole stuffy apparatus of small publisher, circulating library, and elite bookshop?

*   *   *

Magazine Day.

In the narrow, dingy street just north of St. Paul's Cathedral in the heart of London the booksellers' reps arrived early on the last day of each month in the mid–1830s, clamoring for copies of the magazines and periodicals to put in their large bags, followed at around ten by the authors anxious to see if they'd been published or reviewed, while the clerks for the wholesalers burrowed away getting the periodicals out to the provinces. Paternoster Row, or, as it was called in "the Trade," simply "the Row," had been the traditional home of the publishing industry almost since the Great Fire of 1666, when the booksellers all moved up out of the churchyard of St. Paul's. The Row was a gloomy, airless cul de sac, home to the wholesalers, who shipped out periodicals all across the country, and a few retail holdouts, like John Murray (at No. 26 under the sign of a ship under sail), bookseller and publisher of Byron and the Hampshire spinster Miss Jane Austen, and the descendants of publisher (Thomas) Longman (since 1724, at the sign of "the Ship and the Black Swan"). And, of course, there was the rather dreary old inn for literary men, the Chapter Coffeehouse at No. 50, where the Reverend Patrick Brontë, now settled with his daughters in the town of Haworth on the edge of the moors in the West Riding of Yorkshire, stayed when in London.

Magazine Day.

A known field day for pickpockets—when the clamoring representatives of booksellers who showed up on the Row could buy any of 220 to 240 periodicals like *Fraser's Magazine* and *Blackwood's Magazine*. "There was once a time when the sun used to shine brighter," wrote that active periodical writer William Makepeace Thackeray wistfully in his novel *The Newcomes* in 1853, "when tavern wines seemed to be delicious, and tavern dinners the perfection of cookery; when the perusal of novels was productive of immense delight, and the monthly advent of magazine-day was hailed as an exciting holiday." Some 400,000 copies of various periodicals would leave the Row on Magazine Day in a distribution as frantic and colorful

Paternoster Row, a dark, gloomy, dead-end street just north of St. Paul's Cathedral in London, and long the center of British publishing. When the Brontë sisters came to London, they stayed at Number 50, the Chapter Coffeehouse.

as it would soon be antiquated. Meanwhile, taxes on newspapers that drove good writers away from journalism and a decline in the theater helped to make magazines an unusually popular form of entertainment and instruction.

In early February 1836, a young stationery store owner named William Hall went to see the now twenty-four-year-old Charles Dickens in the quarters where he lived in "chambers" at No. 13 Furnival's Inn in Holborn in the midst of the old "City." Since the days of the blacking factory, Dickens had grown up, become a clerk in a law office, a parliamentary stenographer, then a reporter for the competition to the *Times*, the *Morning Chronicle*. For the *Chronicle* he had covered various political events, bouncing over England's roads late at night while he scribbled notes on a piece of paper as the motion of the carriage threw candle wax all over his greatcoat; on one occasion he barricaded himself in an inn room to play bagatelle while an election riot complete with gun and clubs belonging to partisans not kindly disposed to *Chronicle* reporters took place outside. Dickens had grown strong, handsome, affable— but underneath it ambitious and determined, very determined. He had never told anyone about the blacking factory, not even his wife, and before his marriage he had also been stabbed to the heart by a four-year love affair that ended with the flirtatious young Maria Beadnell rejecting him.

Would Dickens agree, inquired Hall, acting on behalf of himself and his partner, Edward Chapman, to write the text to accompany some of the comic prints for a monthly, magazine-like issuance to be done by the famous illustrator Robert Seymour? Since Hogarth had invented the sequential "storyboard" panel of prints like the *Rake's Progress* and *Marriage à la Mode* in the mid–1700s and cheap reproductions had become possible, engraved prints had become something of a mania. And while from the *Chronicle* Dickens earned only seven guineas a week, for the text job Chapman and Hall offered him what amounted to fourteen pounds more. So Dickens said he would write for them.

Dickens cranked out twelve thousand words of copy to accompany Seymour's four illustrations. The first printing—four hundred copies—bright and shiny, with a green paper cover bearing decorations of sportive gentlemen, appeared on March 31, 1836—Magazine Day. With a few advertisements—for The Library of Fiction or Family Story Teller ("admirably adapted for fireside reading"), and Mrs. Barwell's *Edward the Crusader's Son*, a helpful depiction of eleventh-century England, for use by "those instructors who disapprove of the too stimulating pages of historical romances." Dickens named the leading character for one Moses Pickwick, who ran a coaching establishment in Bath.

Dickens fortunately did not quit his day job on the *Chronicle*. For *The Pickwick Papers*, as the new serial was called, sold poorly at first, despite advertising in the *Times*, other papers, and Colburn's influential literary journal, the *Athenaeum*. Of the 1,500 copies Chapman and Hall sent out of the next four "numbers," or installments, 1,450 came back.

And to make matters worse Robert Seymour, the *Pickwick* illustrator, shot himself after the second number.

Poor sales. And now the illustrator—and main selling point—was dead. Should they not just drop this serialized set of prints?

Dickens said no. Cut down the number of engraved plates from four to two per installment, he said, as the next Magazine Day deadline loomed. And get another illustrator and expand the text from twenty-four pages to thirty-two. Which meant in effect creating not a magazine exactly—nor merely a set of prints again—but a continuous, periodically issued fictional narrative that now happened to be augmented by engravings. Chapman and Hall took his advice.

There were finally favorable notices after the fourth number of *Pickwick*. Sales picked up—nineteen thousand copies by February 1837, twenty thousand in May. Customers now waited eagerly for each new number, perusing the windows of booksellers—where the prints of each installment were displayed like movie "trailers" to get the crowd outside to come in and buy—to see if a fresh number of *Pickwick* was available yet. In the meantime, as word went out that a new artist to replace Seymour was required, Dickens was visited at Furnival's Inn one day by a six-foot-three, gangling giant with a portfolio of drawings who was seeking the job. The indigent twenty-six-year-old Thackeray, for it was he, had by now lost, through gambling and economic reversals in Anglo-Indian commerce, the £17,000 or so his father had left him. But Dickens hired instead the shy, brown-haired, carelessly dressed Hablot Browne, who agreeably adopted the nickname "Phiz" to match the pseudonym of the author of *Pickwick*—"Boz"—and thereafter illustrated most of Dickens' novels.

Pickwick, meanwhile, became a publishing phenomenon. Doctors chuckled over *Pickwick* in their carriage between patients, boys laughed out loud in church thinking about it, and plagiarists ripped it off for cheap theatrical versions. Pants makers advertised Sam Weller corduroys, linen drapers Pickwick chintzes; waltzes and dogs were named for the book. And it was more than a popular craze. The popularity of *Pickwick* was the sign of a new generation asserting itself— Could she explain the humor? wrote Mrs. Frances Trollope, one of the older generation of writers, a member of the tribe of writing women working to support an ineffectual husband (and, in her case, also an unhappy, lonely son named Anthony), to a friend. Dickens' face now replaced those of Henry Colburn's leading novelists, the celebrated (and dandiacal) Bulwer Lytton and Harrison Ainsworth, which were pasted up in the omnibuses that clip-clopped through the metropolis. He had arrived—which meant that the twenty-five-year-old author of this runaway best seller was about to be caught up in the politics of the London publishing world.

The new publicity-intensive publishing practiced by Colburn was expensive. It cost money to pay for all those ads and run all those magazines, plus Colburn paid his best-selling authors very, very well. Ainsworth got £2,000 for his 1834 novel *Rookwood*, Lady Morgan £2,000 for her *Florence MacCarthy*, and a thousand guineas apiece went to Theodore Hook for his novels. The expense forced Colburn into partnership with his printer, Richard Bentley, a short, bewhiskered man whose appearance Dickens likened to that of a "fraudulent butler."

But the publishing industry hit a slump in the early 1830s. Colburn went to war with one of his writers in an embarrassing set of lawsuits, and Bentley found his partner was untrustworthy and a bad bookkeeper. Colburn was also maddeningly indecisive. Sometimes, an employee said later, Colburn seemed to agonize even over how much sugar to put in his tea. And so in August 1832, Bentley and Colburn split up, with Colburn agreeing not to compete with Bentley within twenty miles of London. Yet Colburn set up shop as a publisher at nearby Windsor, only twenty-three miles from the capital, applying pressure to be bought out of his contract not to compete, and then publishing a naval history in direct competition with a naval history that Bentley had just published. The enraged Bentley asked his lawyer how could he combat this weasel? (Colburn's ads even spoke slyly of how his new "Publishing Establishment at Windsor" was located in "a spot which affords peculiar advantages for an undertaking of this nature.") "For God's sake, sir," Bentley's lawyer begged, "take his money, take his money."

Which Bentley did—but after that it was war.

In the split-up, Colburn had gotten Disraeli, Mrs. Gore, and Bulwer and retained also his magazines, the *Athenaeum* and the *Literary Gazette*, in which to advertise and "puff" his writers. Bentley needed a star. "Is it in your power to lend me any assistance in procuring the insertion of lucubrations of my own in any of the numerous periodical magazines &c which come out in such monthly swarms?" Thus did a rather unprepossessing, tentative offer come to Bentley in May 1835. But it was not from a well-known, or even known, writer who would be useful in the war against Colburn. No, it came, rather, from an appar-

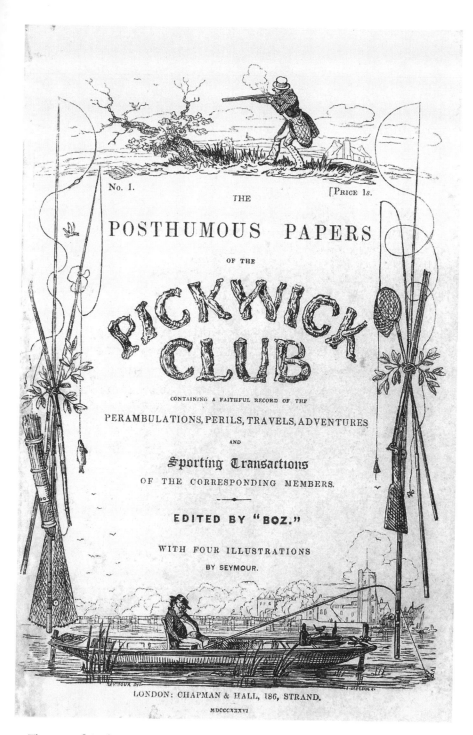

No. 1.

[PRICE 1s.

THE

POSTHUMOUS PAPERS

OF THE

PICKWICK CLUB

CONTAINING A FAITHFUL RECORD OF THE

PERAMBULATIONS, PERILS, TRAVELS, ADVENTURES

AND

Sporting Transactions

OF THE CORRESPONDING MEMBERS.

EDITED BY "BOZ."

WITH FOUR ILLUSTRATIONS
BY SEYMOUR.

LONDON: CHAPMAN & HALL, 186, STRAND.

MDCCCXXXVI

The cover of the first installment of The Pickwick Papers, *published in serial form in April 1836, thereby inaugurating a new publishing format for the English novel.*

ently dismal wannabe who "had not, so far as I am aware, a single friend," as a schoolmate—and subsequent friend—wrote years later of Anthony Trollope during his days at Harrow. He was "without exception the most slovenly and dirty boy I ever met . . . He gave no sign of promise whatsoever." A withdrawn father who had failed at law and farming and had once knocked Anthony to the ground with a large Bible, a scintillating, successful, and overbearing older brother—not a promising family environment. But then, when detailed by his mother, the same Mrs. Trollope who had not "gotten" the humor in *Pickwick*, to deal with Bentley on some business matter on her behalf, Anthony saw his chance and sent the publisher his plaintive request for consideration of his work.

But Bentley was not interested in "lucubrations"; he was in the midst of a battle with his arch rival and former partner. So Anthony, defeated in his first efforts at publication, went back to his work as clerk at the Post Office—and, after witnessing *Pickwick*'s extraordinary popularity in the ensuing months, Bentley approached the hottest young novelist in England.

Yes, said Dickens, he would do a novel for Bentley to appear in his new monthly magazine, except that his price had gone up since the huge success of *Pickwick*—to £500, not unreasonable, he offered, in light of "the rapid sale of *everything* I have yet touched." Bentley accepted—and Dickens began work on a new serial tailored to the small spaces of *Bentley's Miscellany*, as the magazine was called. Bently also hired young Dickens to be the editor of his new monthly.

To a public expecting another jolly novel à la *Pickwick, Son of Pickwick, Pickwick II*, Dickens now offered *Oliver Twist*. The theme of a small boy abandoned in the big city of London obviously drew on his own childhood. But the novel was also full of action and melodrama—robbery, murder, and kidnapping. One reason *Oliver Twist*—and serials to come—were so action-packed was because the serial came out in installments and was bought monthly, like a magazine, unlike the three-volume novels of Colburn's that one bought all at once. So the trick was

Booksellers' representatives swarm out of the storefront of Dickens' publishers, Chapman and Hall, on Magazine Day clutching copies of Master Humphrey's Clock *to distribute to readers awaiting the next installment of* The Old Curiosity Shop *contained therein.*

always to make each month's installment so lively that the reader would come back the following month to buy the next installment. Captain Frederick Marryat, navy man turned nautical novelist, noted that "if there is one good chapter out of three" in a three-volume novel, "the public are generous and are satisfied; but when every portion is serially presented to be analyzed and criticized for thirty days, the author dare not flag. He must keep up to his mark." One needed action. Youth, energy, discipline—with its monthly deadlines of Magazine Day and need for action in each episode to keep the buyer coming back next month, the serial demanded a new kind of writer, as disciplined, ambitious, and driving in his own way as his reader, the new middle-class merchant, shopkeeper, or manufacturer who worked long hours, drove himself ceaselessly, and pushed relentlessly to get ahead of his competition.

Energy, energy, energy. Dickens was doing *Pickwick*, editing *Bentley's Miscellany*, and writing *Oliver Twist*—all at the same time. A family friend visiting one evening found him full of effusive greeting. "'What, you here!' he exclaimed: 'I'll bring down my work.'" He simply moved his writing of *Oliver Twist* down to the fireside where they were gathered and continued writing away, "the feather of his pen still moving rapidly from side to side," and listened attentively, occasionally interjecting a remark as they talked.

He was just one of a whole group of energetic, go-getting new young writers. There was the popular Irish novelist Charles Lever; the well-born, if moody, Edward Bulwer, handsome, intense, accomplished, and heir to a great estate and the peerage; William Harrison Ainsworth, the tall, good-looking dandy who wrote overwrought historical novels (when the nine-year-old Thomas Hardy came to London in 1849 with his mother, he insisted on making a map of the locales mentioned and then retracing all the steps of Ainsworth's clunker *In Old London*); Benjamin Disraeli, the witty, resourceful young man on the make who had written under an assumed name for Colburn; and all the others, including that hapless would-be illustrator

Thackeray. ("He had not the patience," said his former idol and subsequent instructor George Cruikshank, the illustrator of *Oliver Twist*, "to be an artist.") A caller around this time found Thackeray struggling to subsist on dry toast and chocolate in a dressing gown in a garret near Regent Street. Novels? The last thing on Thackeray's mind, although he took periodic shots at the works of Bulwer Lytton, whom he found horrifyingly over-written, in the short pieces Thackeray was beginning to do for *Fraser's Magazine*, one of the periodicals that poured out of Paternoster Row on Magazine Day each month. "Bullwig," Thackeray disrespectfully called the popular novelist.

"Are you aware who are the conductors of that paper, and that they are Chartists, Deists, Anarchists, and Socialists to a man?" Thackeray told of hearing a fierce old man say in a rail-way carriage of another new hard-slugging magazine. In fact, the ascent of Dickens and his contemporaries was emblematic of the rise of a whole new literary culture of ambitious, confi-dent, and iconoclastic young men. "Come to town—here's a man with a notion for a comic paper, & he has £2,000 to lose" was the laconic summons from Henry Mayhew in 1841 to start *Punch* magazine.

The London magazine market was a hard-hitting, confi-dence-boosting business—if you survived. The editor of one magazine was killed in a duel by an angry subscriber. Later, when the Earl of Berkeley published a novel about his family in 1836, the anonymous reviewer in *Fraser's Magazine* wrote that "Mr. Grantley Berkeley's mother lived with Mr. Grantley Berkeley's father as his mistress, and that she had at least one child before she could induce the old and very stupid lord to marry her ... As for the book, it is trash ... stupid, ignorant, vulgar and contemptible," and the writing "horridly vulgar and ungrammatical." Whereupon the earl promptly showed up at the offices of the magazine on Regent Street and when the tiny editor refused to give the name of the anonymous reviewer, the nobleman beat him brutally with the heavy metal end of his whip while a hired thug stood guard outside the door. The editor ultimately died of the effects of the beating.

Rough work for a rough city, in fact, the largest in the world (Paris only a remote second), grown from about a million in 1801 to more than twice that by 1841. No country in the world, in fact, had ever before seen such a large city. A vibrant, growing city—young, like the young men such as Dickens and Thackeray who dined in its rollicking taverns and the clubs springing up along Pall Mall, riding on the city's outskirts, going to whorehouses, and starting more feisty magazines.

They were part of the ascendancy of a newly middle-class London that had demanded novels from Colburn, pushed for the changes that produced the Reform Bill of 1832, and leavened the old division of very rich and very poor. At weekly dinners tendered by the publishing partnership of Bradbury and Evans, the young contributors to the new *Punch*, Thackeray among the foremost, sat around and made up the magazine after ordering in food and drinking heavily, then singing songs, telling ribald jokes, and writing up verbal assaults on perceived idiots of all stripes, like the powerful Lord Brougham—a man, said the magazine in a typical blast, who gave a speech in Parliament "so entirely foolish and unreasonable . . . that it is said he is to be made a Duke." In January 1845 the august Lady Holland noted that when the Irish statesman Daniel O'Connell was condemned to a year in prison, a fellow politician was heard to "say he would much dislike 12 months in Kilmainham Gaol. 'Better,'" came the reply, "'than 6 in *Punch*.'"

Generally, the young iconoclasts stuck together, notably when their friend and riding companion Bulwer Lytton had marital troubles. In 1827 Bulwer had married the beautiful and strong-minded Rosina Wheeler. They had separated by 1836, with Rosina accusing Bulwer of, among other things, kicking her in the side so hard in the spring of 1828 when she was eight months pregnant that she fainted from the pain, threatening her in July of 1834 with a carving knife at dinner ("I'll have you to know," she quoted him as saying, "that whenever *I* do you the honour of addressing you, it requires an answer!") and then biting her in the cheek. He soon got word she intended to publish a novel that harshly caricatured him. "This book must not, and *shall not* be published, or *I will ruin you*," Bulwer wrote her in a frenzy in 1839 as publication became imminent. "I'll say that you have been my mistress, that you drink (a vice not interesting in women), and have forged, with other darker things to which I shall not now allude; which will effectively exclude you from society." And then in prose worthy of one of his novels—"Tremble!" he added, "while I write you are in my power!"

In his power or not, Rosina went ahead.

It was helpful that in so small a literary world, the titled Lytton's publisher, who was, naturally, Henry Colburn, controlled one of the most prestigious literary publications in London. And that John Forster, literary London's Mr. Fix-it, a butcher's son and lawyer who had become friends with Dickens (and handled most of Dickens' negotiations with Bentley), was on the case. He now wrote to Bulwer that he had obtained from the *Athenaeum* "a promise that none of the libels should appear." Forster did more. There was word from the provinces that Lady Rosina had engaged in misbehavior, so Forster took off for Bath in a vain effort to try to uncover compromising evidence about her. "We need not fear the *Times*," Bulwer meanwhile confided to Forster in April 1839. "Barnes has promised me that no notice shall be taken without my consent." In addition, Forster conferred with Charles Dickens' other lawyer friend, Thomas Talfourd. A member of Parliament, he served as the model for David Copperfield's schoolmate Traddles, and Dickens dedicated *Pickwick* to Talfourd because of the latter's efforts to strengthen the copyright laws. Now, consulted about the merits of replying to Rosina's novel, Talfourd advised against any response. Forster agreed. "It is setting the papers that have discreetly refrained from notice . . . a very bad example." It was not the last time that the power of London's literary world would be invoked against Rosina.

*   *   *

A rough world—for defenseless women, for children, for the parish poor like those left to the tender mercies of Mr. Bumble and the Poor Laws—for all those, indeed, without many legal rights or much social standing. *Oliver Twist* could be seen as a crime novel at one level; or at another, as a chronicle of the social ills that dominated England—child abuse, crime, prostitution, or the harsh enforcement of unfair, callous legislation like the Poor Law.

Indeed, with *Oliver Twist* well in hand in the fall of 1837, there came back to Dickens the stories he had heard as a small boy of the horrible boarding schools in the remote north of Yorkshire, not so far either geographically or in spirit from the school for poor daughters of the clergy that the children of the Reverend Patrick Brontë had attended. There were six young children to begin with of the stern man whose wife died so soon in the grim northern industrial town of Haworth to which his ecclesiastical duties as a perpetual curate called him. The elder children had gone off to boarding school so they could one day earn a living as teachers or governesses. The food was poor, the heating and sanitation primitive to wretched, and the younger daughters—Charlotte, Emily, and Anne—of the pistol-toting Reverend Brontë had watched their two elder sisters die from maltreatment, malnutrition and tuberculosis. Later, their younger brother, Branwell, told them of how he could hear the ghost of the eldest sister, Maria, outside on the moors at night, scratching, scratching against the glass of the old parsonage windows. (It would reappear as the young Catherine Linton's ghost, of course, at the beginning of *Wuthering Heights*.)

The schools Dickens now proposed to investigate in the Brontës' part of the country were the boys' schools to which English parents often sent their illegitimate or otherwise unwanted offspring—"No vacations" habitually promised the advertisements—far enough away to ensure no unwelcome visits or inquiring snoopers. One schoolmaster, in particular, interested Dickens: William Shaw. It was alleged in two 1823 court actions brought against him that two boys had gone blind owing to malnutrition and neglect at his Bowes Academy near Greta Bridge.

In late January 1838, accordingly, Dickens departed incognito by stagecoach for the northern wilds of England with his new illustrator, Thackeray's friend the trusty "Phiz," for all the world like a modern-day TV reporter with his cameraman or soundman. They were equipped with a letter from a lawyer in London to a colleague in Shaw's vicinity stating that they were representatives of a poor widow seeking a good school for her son, a journalist's cover story.

Dickens and Phiz traveled northward via the Glasgow mail coach, and the snow grew ever deeper, and the countryside more dreary. "As we crossed the wild heaths hereabout, there was no vestige of a track." They encountered an absurd, dipsomaniacal schoolmistress whose conversation Dickens filed away for later use in his novel. Finally, they reached Shaw, whom they found to be a small, equivocal, suspicious man. Years afterward grown-up former students recalled how teachers, who to parents were all benevolence when they picked up the boys, seized the students' clothes once they arrived at schools like Shaw's, gave them wooden clogs for shoes, and fed them black bread, water, and milk with only a daily ounce of often putrid meat, and how a boy who ran away was stripped naked, tied to the door, and brutally flogged in front of a whole dormitory, the process then being repeated in another dorm.

In the deep snow, Dickens and Phiz visited a churchyard near Shaw's school where some twenty-nine boys who had died at the local boarding schools between 1810 and 1834 had been buried. A laconic entry in the Burial Register concerning the death of an eight-year-old—"supposed a native of Newcastle"—testified not atypically to the evident lack of family interest in the fate of one small victim. Abandonment—the theme of *Oliver Twist*, and, of course, of Dickens's early life.

When they finally met with the jovial, pleasant old lawyer for whom they had been given the cover story, Dickens and

Harrison Ainsworth, author of Jack Sheppard, *was typical of the fast set of young best-selling male novelists to which Dickens, Thackeray, and Bulwer Lytton belonged in the 1830s and 1840s.*

Phiz got their final proof. The three men spent a pleasant evening together, but the Londoners found Mr. Baines reluctant to talk of local schools. They returned to their inn—whereupon Baines burst in on them: "Dinnott let the weedur send her lattle boy to yan o' our school measthers, while ther's a harse to hoold in a' Lunnun, or a goother to lie asleep in," said the old man feelingly. "Ar wouldn't mak' ill words amang my neeburs, and ar speak tiv'ee quiet loike. But I'm dom'd if ar can gang to bed and not tell'ee, for weedur's sak', to keep the lattle boy from a' sike scondrels!"

Out shot the copies of *Nickleby* on Magazine Day, April 1838, when they returned, the Dickens serial settling into its thereafter standard format of twenty monthly issues of thirty-two pages each. Sensational, lurid stuff this new *Nickleby*— "Boy-destroyer," scribbled Charlotte Brontë succinctly when she had read it. Grown up at last, the twenty-year-old Charlotte had sent some of her poems to the venerable, sixty-two-year-old poet laureate Robert Southey in late December 1836 to see if they were good enough to earn a living from. The poems are pretty good, the tired versifier wrote back in March 1837, but "literature cannot be the business of a woman's life, and it ought not to be." No, "the more she is engaged in her proper duties, the less leisure will she have for it." "[I must] thank you for the kind and wise advice you have condescended to give me," Charlotte wrote back gratefully. "I must suppress what I feel, or you will think me foolishly enthusiastic"—and she obediently stopped her writing. No poetry, then. But Dickens' work showed that the door of serious subject matter was opening, as the novel moved beyond Sir Walter Scott's historical romances and the fashionable fluff of Colburn's high-society novels.

One of the clichés about the Victorian novel is indeed how much it became a document of the social abuses of its times— child labor, prostitution, debt, government inefficiency, unsafe working conditions, and so on. In part, this was because the newspapers in Britain that might otherwise have undertaken the investigation and editorial criticism of such evils were by design almost as expensive and unobtainable in Victorian England as Scott's novels. In America newspapers were encouraged and, indeed, celebrated as guardians against government tyranny, especially after the Revolution, and were explicitly protected by the First Amendment. In Britain, however, the government was taxing English newspapers four pence a sheet by 1815, in part to avoid the anticipated contagion from the unrest of the French Revolution. English papers like the *Times* cost seven pence, rendering them so expensive that in Edinburgh in the late 1830s "most people gained their knowledge of what was going on by hiring them at a penny an hour, or by subscribing in groups, the paper passing from hand to hand among neighbours in town and country." Having a rich neighbor helped, too. In *Sense and Sensibility*, Sir John Middleton sends the genteelly poor Dashwoods game, fruit, and vegetables "and would not be denied the satisfaction of sending them his newspaper every day." The *Morning Chronicle*, on which Dickens worked, had a circulation of only about 6,000, the *London Times* (in 1840), the country's leading paper, 18,500 in a city of some two million. The cartoon caricature of old men dozing over their newspapers in men's clubs had a firm basis in the practice of London clubs offering all the newspapers to their members to read because they could not easily afford to buy the expensive papers themselves.

The serial novel could therefore move into a vacuum, where social problems were concerned, that was left by the newspaper as well as by the fashionable, fluffy junk of the three-decker (as the standard three-volume format had been nicknamed after the three-decked ships of the line in the British Navy). And the times seemed increasingly to demand that writers deal with social issues. Child labor, Poor Law abuses, factory deaths—the Reform Act of 1832 and the Poor Law of 1834 had acted not so much to allay demands for reform as to create throughout the country a new hunger for change, a desire to redress the growing inequities of the industrial capitalist system, and a growing realization that those at the bottom of the social and economic heap were suffering intolerably. Speaking to more than forty thousand people at a New Year's Day rally in 1839, the Reverend John Stephens urged reform or else—calling himself "a revolutionist by fire, a revolutionist by blood, to the knife, to the death." In the Hungry Forties, as the new decade came to be called, the Irish famine in 1846 and 1847 would kill almost a million people and send tens of thousands more fleeing to America. Meanwhile, the Chartists gathered to demand universal suffrage and rights for the working man, and riots broke out in the industrial north as an economic crash and rising prices put thousands out of work. Over twenty thousand men marched on Manchester in the summer of 1842, policemen were killed, and troops were called out as the rioting spread. In the backward southwest Dorsetshire of England, where the average wage was nine shillings a week, a mason's young son named Thomas Hardy knew personally a shepherd lad who died of starvation in the 1840s. Hardy in later years also recalled marching around the garden as a child with a wooden sword dipped in pig's blood shouting "Free Trade or Blood" in imitation of adults seeking repeal of the Corn Laws that artificially protected high wheat and grain prices and thereby made bread too costly for the poor.

Novelists sprang to these battles. Anthony Trollope's mother had followed the tradition of fact-based novels, which Dickens had strengthened with *Nickleby*, with on-the-spot research in the industrial north for her 1840 *Michael Armstrong the Factory Boy*. After suffering a setback in the parliamentary career that followed his initial career as an author, Disraeli added his voice to the chorus for reform, turning to his old publisher Henry Colburn for his programmatic *Coningsby*—a far cry from the damasked and ormolued drawing rooms of the silver fork novels. *Sybil, or the Two Nations*, Disraeli titled the second novel in his "Young England" series in 1845; the subtitle ("Two nations between whom there is no intercourse and no sympathy . . . THE RICH AND THE POOR") passed into the language. In Dickens' 1841 *The Old Curiosity Shop* "bands of unemployed labourers paraded the roads, or clustered by torchlight round their leaders, who told them, in stern language, of their wrongs." "Down with everybody," cried an embittered figure in Dickens' *Barnaby Rudge* of the same year, in which the plot centers on the anti-Catholic Gordon riots of 1780, when mobs burnt Newgate prison, "down with everything." And in the 1843 *A Christmas Carol*, there were flying trips by the Ghost of Christmas Present and Scrooge to "a bleak and desert moor . . . where Miners live" and shivering beneath the long robes of the Ghost of Christmas Present, of course, the miserable, childlike figures of Ignorance and Want. "Beware them both," warned the implacable Spirit.

The ideas and incidents described in these novels had a powerful effect. In an era before television, radio, movies, records, compact discs, or even a car to get away from the house, and when newspapers were still expensive, reading novels around the fire at night, as many families did, was often a major source of information as well as entertainment on all kinds of matters. Novels had an impact. Indeed, some came to think, perhaps, too much of an impact.

On the night of May 5, 1840, a valet named B. F. Courvoisier murdered his employer, the seventy-two-year-old Lord William Russell, in Russell's bedroom at the very fashionable address of 14 Park Lane overlooking London's Hyde Park. Horrifying enough, but then Courvoisier confessed on his arrest to having been inspired to commit the murder by reading Ainsworth's *Jack Sheppard*, which had been serialized in *Bentley's Miscellany*.

Uproar! The *Examiner* editorialized that *Jack Sheppard* could "serve as the cut-throat's manual, or the midnight assassin's *vade-mecum* . . . If ever there was a publication that deserved to be burnt by the common hangman it is *Jack Sheppard*." Ainsworth wrote indignantly to the *Times* and to Dickens' old paper the *Morning Chronicle* to protest that apropos of the murderer's statement in the latter paper about wishing he'd never read *Jack Sheppard*, "I have taken means to ascertain the correctness of the report, and find it utterly without foundation. The wretched man declared he had neither read the work in question nor made any such statement."

Not so.

As a crowd of thirty thousand turned out on July 6 to see the man executed, Thackeray and Dickens among them, the sheriff of London and Middlesex wrote back to the *Times* "that Courvoisier did assert to me that the idea of murdering his master was first suggested to him by a perusal of the book called 'Jack Sheppard,' and that the said book was lent to him by a valet of the Duke of Bedford." Dickens was worried. Not only had he been editor of *Bentley's Miscellany* when *Jack Sheppard* appeared in it, but Ainsworth's book had been serialized alongside Dickens' own *Oliver Twist*. *Oliver Twist*, Dickens wrote pleadingly some months later, was aimed not at glamorizing crime but "showing it in its unattractive and repulsive truth."

But fear lingered.

"I have been reading *Jack Sheppard*, and have been struck by the great danger, in these times, of representing authorities so constantly and fearfully in the wrong," Mrs. Mitford, a popular writer of rural sketches, wrote to a friend regarding Ainsworth's new serial. She worried that all those impressionable lower-class people who couldn't read would see *Jack Sheppard* in the rather graphic versions offered at local London theaters, and the lurid actions of the novel would become too vivid for them. "Of course, Mr. Ainsworth had no such design, but such is the effect; and . . . the millions who see it represented at the minor theaters will not distinguish between now and a hundred years back."

Indeed, the new serials seemed to some to be just jazzed-up junk lacking in true literary quality, glorified comics rather than real books. "Pray tell me what you think is the main cause of the great falling off in the sale of books," William Wordsworth wrote anxiously to the publisher Edward Moxon in April 1842. "The young men in the Universities cannot be supposed to be straitened much in their allowance, yet I find that scarcely any books are sold them. Dr Arnold told me that his lads seemed to care for nothing but Bozzy's next No., and the Classics suffered accordingly."

The "Dr Arnold" in question in the great poet's worried communication was none other than the great headmaster Dr. Thomas Arnold (father of Matthew) of Rugby. And, indeed, in preaching to the boys in the chapel at his school, Arnold thundered that they read "a great number of exciting books as *Pickwick* and *Nickleby*" (which latter, after all, was an attack on boarding schools, albeit not the Rugby variety). And he did not use "exciting" as a compliment. Books like Dickens' effectively destroyed the boys' interest, said the good doctor, in "good literature of all sorts, even for History and Poetry."

Not just schoolmasters were disdainful. "All very well," Scott's influential son-in-law John Lockhart had said of *Pickwick*—"but damned low." Dickens smarted under this criticism of his lurid serials. Of *Pickwick*, Dickens later wrote angrily, "my friends told me it was a low, cheap form of publication, by which I would ruin all my rising hopes." But then, by contrast to the windy but high-priced format of the three-decker, the serial was a glorified magazine, an upstart and a demonstrably "cheap" one at that, each "number" being a modest little pamphlet costing only a shilling—and carrying advertising.

The criticisms of the serial continued—and so in *Nickleby* Dickens struck back at the fashionable three-decker (that was, incidentally, also the staple of his publisher Bentley's arch rival, Colburn). Dickens caricatured the absurd circulating library "keeper" Mortimer Knagg, who aspires to write an effete work "in three volumes octavo." Later in *Nickleby* Kate Nickleby reads aloud to her silly employer from "a new novel in three volumes, entitled *The Lady Flabella*," a blast at the typical piece of Colburn junk. *The Lady Flabella*, Dickens observed, has "not a line in it, from beginning to end, which could, by the most remote contingency, awaken the smallest excitement in any person breathing."

Did that mean, then, that the serial novel was condemned to remain beyond the literary pale and, topical though it might be, to treat only of the lurid and the unacceptable?

In November 1846, the prematurely gray-haired Thackeray and his two daughters moved into 13 Young Street in Kensington, just southwest of London's posh Mayfair district. It was an old brick house with a sloping floor in the schoolroom on the top floor (a marble placed on the schoolroom floor would run down to the other side) with a mysterious trap door, a little garden out back with a small greenhouse, and a bow window in front. Staffed by a manservant, a cook, and a maid, the house could boast the Kensington Square constructed in the era of Thackeray's beloved Queen Anne just around the corner. The broken-nosed Thackeray (it had happened in a schoolboy fight at the prestigious Charterhouse school) had no wife to share his home. He had married a young, sweet, if somewhat helpless girl in 1836 when he was twenty-five and she was nineteen—not unlike David's fictitious child-wife Dora Spenlow in *David Copperfield*. Soon Thackeray had two little girls. But then his wife had tragically gone mad in 1840, first trying to drown her eldest daughter on a seaside walk, then throwing herself overboard—undiscovered for twenty minutes—on a Channel crossing. And so Thackeray had reluctantly had her put away.

It was still the London of Dickens' youth, where there was only one railroad station as yet (and where the railroad company uncoupled the cars for the last mile and let them slide downhill under their own power into the station), the city not yet torn up by railroad tracks and great huge vaulted glass and iron stations that would signal the complete takeover of the iron horse and the industrial age. Nearby, too, at 5 Cheyne Row in Chelsea along the Thames lived the acerbic, witty Jane Carlyle and her irascible, talented husband, Thomas, a friend of

Thackeray who had achieved a towering reputation as a critic of the mindless materialism of the new industrial civilization with his *French Revolution* and *Sartor Resartus*. (A reminder of how different it was to write in those days before carbon paper or photocopying: Carlyle gave John Stuart Mill the only copy of the first volume of his *French Revolution* to read—and while he was out, Mill's maid used it to light the fire one afternoon.) Land speculation after 1851 when the Crystal Palace was built in Kensington would finally spur development of the area, but in the meantime, there were birds, greenery, friends came galloping out on horseback along the tree-lined lanes to visit Thackeray, and there was a horse-drawn omnibus that ran to London. After a snowy-weather call on the Carlyles through the rural lanes that later became South Kensington, Jane Carlyle regularly regaled the little Thackeray girls, Anne and Minny, with cups of hot chocolate on their winter visits. Carlyle raved against the evils of the modern world and complained of the noise in London (there was a piano next door) that made writing impossible. "If you wish for a quiet life," Jane would pointedly warn the Thackeray girls, "never you marry a dyspeptic man of genius."

Thackeray had been toying with the idea of doing "A Novel without a Thesis" or a series of "Pencil Sketches of English Society," as he called them, of London life à la Dickens' *Sketches by Boz*. A real novel complete with hero was unthinkable after all the parodies he had recently done in *Punch* of contemporary writers like the overly prolific historical novelist G. P. R. James, a childhood favorite of George Eliot's. He was also not about to write socially conscious novels, a vein never very congenial to him anyway. Thackeray parodied *Coningsby*, the first of Disraeli's politically concerned trilogy, in *Punch* as "Codlingsby." More reflectively, Thackeray wrote in a review of *Sybil* for the *Morning Chronicle* that "Morals and manners we believe to be the novelist's best themes; and hence prefer romances which do not treat of algebra, religion, political economy, or any other abstract science."

So he would write "The Novel without a Hero," as he came to call it. It was his chance for the big payoff, a project, as he wrote to his mother, "of prodigious importance. This is the scheme by wh. I expect to make a great deal of money." It was time to think of making a stab at the top. Thackeray sat down in the study overlooking the garden at the back of the house below which Minny had ranged the saucers of milk on the terrace for her favorite cats and began setting down the first chapters of his new work.

The context of his efforts was significant, for, although Thackeray himself was not socially concerned, he was writing at a time when the Hungry Forties had become concerned with the suffering members of the marginally middle class, as well as the working class. In particular, there was the governess, the poor relative of all middle-class families, educated to a life of ease and comfort, who had then to earn her living in the only occupation respectable for well-bred middle-class single women. Countess Blessington's *The Governess* had begun the genre of "governess" novels in 1839, while in the *Amy Herbert* of 1844 a governess strove to make her young charge a better Christian, as did Caroline Mordaunt in Mrs. Sherwood's 1845 novel of the same name. The situation of the governess could be grim. In "Hints on the Modern Governess System" in the November 1844 *Fraser's Magazine,* a sympathetic writer described at length how a governess, her average salary a mere £35 a year, was forced to deal—alone—with often spoiled children and then retire, still alone, to the schoolroom. Meanwhile, the family and guests enjoyed themselves below in the drawing room, and the writer compared the plight of the governess invidiously to the new penal punishment of solitary confinement. "The statistics touching lunatic asylums give a frightful proportion of governesses in the list of the insane." In 1846 Elizabeth Grey published her *Sybil Lennard* in which a Swiss orphan became an English governess, and was then seduced, the proximate cause as it happened, being the ever-dangerous yellow-covered French novels—("Yes, Felicia, she said . . . those books, that was the poison that destroyed me . . . harmless it all appeared at first.")

For Thackeray, lacking a wife and having two little girls, the need for an adult like a governess to help with the children was self-evident. "I wonder whether I might bring my two girls?" he hazarded in reply to a dinner invitation from the wife of old friend Alfred Tennyson, with whom he would sometimes share a pipe in the backyard. "If you have a party, that of course won't be right: but if only a friend or two—those two young women might have their dinner at home, and would sit quietly upstairs while we had ours." For a man living alone like Thackeray, a governess had to be both plain enough to allay his mother's fears of scandal of a single woman living alone with him ("a nice sober hearty jolly ladylike person—with whom there's no danger of falling in love" he hopefully described one early soon-departing instructress) and smart enough to win the respect of his girls.

Governesses, indeed, seemed to be somewhat on the literary mind just then. A real governess—or rather, ex-governess—was beginning to write a novel about what such work could be like. She lived far from the masculine world of literary London and its fast-paced serials. Nor could she pretend to the ability to write a novel of the fashionable world like a three-decker. "A mere domestic novel will, I fear, seem trivial to men of large views and solid attainments" fretted the anxious little author (she stood all of four foot nine inches) in October of 1848. She had tried governessing, tried, like Mrs. Dickens, running her own school, and finally decided to try to make a living by writing. To her friend Mrs. Gaskell some years later Charlotte Brontë, for the tiny novelist was she, grimly "said that none but those who had been in the position of a governess could ever realize the dark side of 'respectable' human nature." Which was perhaps why she so much admired the writings of the cynical William Thackeray.

But could her dull, mundane story about a governess interest someone like him, she wondered nervously? Ironically, as he was setting down his own tale of a governess, she grew concerned as publication date neared that "Mr Thackeray, Mr Dickens ... possess a knowledge of the world, whether intuitive or acquired, such as I can lay no claim to."

So worried Charlotte Brontë about her first novel to be published, which would soon appear.

It was, of course, *Jane Eyre*.

PART 2

"It Would Never Suit

the Circulating Libraries":

Jane Eyre, Vanity Fair,

and the Three-Volume

Straitjacket

The first Brontë irruption on the literary scene had certainly started oddly.

In June 1847 a number of famous literati across the country—Sir Walter Scott's son-in-law the Dickens critic John Lockhart, Tennyson, and Thomas De Quincey—had received a strangely worded communication accompanied by a book of poetry. "My relatives Ellis and Acton Bell and myself, heedless of the repeated warnings of various respectable publishers, have committed the rash act of printing a volume of poems," said the cover letter signed by "Currer Bell," with mild facetiousness.

With predictable consequences.

"In the space of a year our publisher has disposed of but two copies and by what painful efforts he succeeded in getting rid of these two himself only knows. Before transferring the edition to the Trunk-makers, we have decided on distributing as presents a few copies of what we cannot sell" in acknowledgment of the enjoyment they had gotten over the years from the addressees' works.

And just who were these poets?

None other than Charlotte and Anne Brontë. For some time now, the stationer who lived at the foot of the big hill in Haworth where the parsonage brooded over the village had been receiving orders for large amounts of paper, ink, and other writing supplies from the Brontë daughters. The stationer wasn't sure exactly what they were doing—but sometimes he hiked the eight miles to Halifax to get extra paper for them so they wouldn't be disappointed, and he began keeping a written account of the family's comings and goings. He developed in particular an interest in the middle girl. Once he surprised Emily coming back from the moors: "Her countenance was lit up with a divine light. Had she been holding converse with Angels, it would not have shone brighter. It appeared to me, holy, heavenly."

Well, Emily, Anne, and Charlotte had decided that it was time to forget the Poet Laureate's objurgation to Charlotte that women should not write. They had tried governessing and teaching away from Haworth and disliked it, so they decided to start a school just like Dickens' mother (and countless other impoverished, genteel ladies) had tried to do. Little cards were printed up calling the world's attention respectfully to the institution to be run by the sisters Brontë:

The Misses Brontë's Establishment

For

THE BOARD AND EDUCATION

of a limited number of

Young Ladies

The Parsonage, Haworth

Near Bradford.

———————

Terms

	£	s.	d.
Board and Education, including Writing, Arithmetic, History, Grammar, Geography, and Needle Work, per Annum	35	0	0
French ⎫ German ⎬ each per Quarter Latin ⎭	1	1	0

Music Drawing } each per Quarter	1	1	0
Use of Piano Forte, per Quarter		5	0
Washing, per Quarter		15	0

Each young Lady to be provided with One Pair of Sheets, Pillow Cases, Four Towels, a Dessert and Tea Spoon.

A Quarter's Notice, or a Quarter's Board, is required previous to the Removal of a Pupil.

But, as with Mrs. Dickens' effort, no one came.

How then to earn a living?

One day Charlotte had stumbled over a manuscript of poetry Emily had written; there had then been a struggle to let Emily know that she had read it, perhaps exacerbated by the fact that Charlotte sometimes had a tendency to act the bossy older sister, followed by a further struggle to convince Emily that she should have it *published*. Anne then shyly proffered her poetry. Of the three sisters, Charlotte was perhaps the most impelled toward the outside world, not averse to travel, notably to Brussels, where she had fallen for a (married) teacher at a school she had attended and taught at. She was also, perhaps partly from being the older sister, the bulldozer. But Emily and Anne had long had an informal alliance. Now the two more private sisters would only agree to be published if they could hide behind pseudonyms. Hence they chose the pen names Currer (Charlotte), Ellis (Emily), and Acton, for the youngest, Anne. They selected as publishers Messrs. Aylott and Jones, 8 Paternoster Row.

Their pseudonymity was far from unusual in that day and age. Jane Austen's novels were by "A Lady"or "By the author of ———"; Sir Walter Scott's were anonymous. (Since Scott's first novel was *Waverley* and the sequels, *Ivanhoe*, *Rob Roy*, etc. were all known only as "By the author of *Waverley*," they became known as the *Waverley* novels.) Dickens had used "Boz" in writing both *Pickwick* and *Sketches by Boz*, not writing under his own name until *Oliver Twist* appeared. Why? Apart from the low status of the novel, prose writing was by the standards of the classical education that dominated England always less respectable than poetry. (It was through his sonnets and long poems that Shakespeare sought immortality and which he thought worthy of dedication to titled patrons, not his plays.)

As the eighteenth century wore on, this attitude began to change. "Why should you write a book, print a book, and have everybody read and like your book," said Samuel Johnson's intimate friend Mrs. Thrale to the newly famous Fanny Burney in 1778 about her *Evelina*, "and then sneak in a corner and disown it!" Why, indeed, writers began to feel, most notably Dickens. Not that the stigma still did not linger for some. "I know of no person so perfectly disagreeable and even dangerous as an author," King William IV, whose niece Victoria would succeed him to the throne in 1837, once memorably remarked. Thackeray, especially, who saw himself in some respects as a gentleman reduced by the loss of his father's fortune to the need to work, viewed writing as a low-rent activity. "A literary man (in spite of all we can say against it)," he wrote with his nuanced eye for social distinction, "ranks below that class of the gentry composed of the apothecary, the attorney, the wine merchant, whose positions, in country towns at least, are so equivocal." Thackeray used "M. A. (for "Michelangelo") Titmarsh," "Ikey Solomons" (the name of the real-life "fence" on which *Oliver Twist*'s Fagin was based), and others as pseudonyms, but then again pseudonyms were at least a step away from being anonymous, as Scott had been.

As the novel became more respectable and the nineteenth century progressed, pseudonymity began to serve other purposes. It was not unusual for a woman writer to adopt a masculine pseudonym to get a more respectful hearing than she would have been accorded under her own name. As Henrietta Vaughan, the author of *Cavalry Life*, did, on the advice of her publisher, Chatto & Windus, as late as 1881. "It would never do," it was observed, "to bring out such a book under a woman's name"; so she became "John Strange Winter." In the case of prolific writers like Henry Colburn's Mrs. Gore of the notorious bloodstained novel, pseudonyms kept them from overwhelming the market. (Mrs. Gore once had two different novels published within a few weeks of each other under different names.) There was yet another reason for pseudonymous authorship: the need to conceal the author's real name when he or she had grossly violated the prevailing social code, a factor in Marian Evans' decision to adopt the name "George Eliot" for her fiction when she was "living in sin."

In the Brontës' case, the particular pseudonyms of Currer, Ellis, and Acton Bell were chosen by the sisters, Charlotte later recalled, with "the ambiguous choice being dictated by a sort of conscientious scruple at assuming Christian names, positively masculine, while we did not like to declare ourselves women, because—without at that time suspecting that our mode of writing and thinking was not what is called 'feminine'—we had a vague impression that authoresses are liable to be looked on with prejudice." And perhaps they were influenced in their choice of a pseudonymous surname by the fact that their father's curate was a dull if worthy man by the name of Arthur Bell Nicholls.

But their poetry had been a bust in commercial terms, which had occasioned the gift books to the famous writers and the rueful jokes about the trunk maker. The trunk makers were the ultimate destination of dead books in the nineteenth century, because there discarded pages were used as trunk linings. Dead books were also turned into wrappings for candy and fish; the juvenile George Bernard Shaw was shocked to find the pennyworth of candy he bought in a Dublin shop wrapped in pages from an old Bible. Utterly destroyed books were turned into fertilizer.

After the poetry fiasco, however, the Brontë sisters had been working away for a number of months at pieces of fiction, meeting for that purpose once a week by the big table in the dining room of the old parsonage and walking around it reading aloud the parts they had written that week, asking the others to criticize when they had finished, as they had done since they were children, except that now they were writing novels.

And then they finished the novels. The Messrs. Bell, Charlotte Brontë wrote in April 1846 to Messrs. Aylott and Jones, were accordingly offering to "the Press a work of fiction—consisting of three distinct and unconnected tales which may be published either together as a work of 3 vols. of the ordinary novel size, or separately as single vols. as shall be deemed most advisable." Perhaps understandably, Aylott and Jones were not interested—the books being Charlotte's *The Professor*, the story of a teacher who becomes romantically involved with one of his pupils, Anne's *Agnes Grey*, the story of a governess's trials and eventual marriage—and sister Emily's *Wuthering Heights*. What to do?

Charlotte sent the sisters' manuscripts off to that old master publicist, Henry Colburn, though he was no longer such a dominant figure in novel publishing since the rise of Bentley, Chapman and Hall, and Bradbury and Evans. He liked *The Professor* but said, alas, "such a work would not sell," Charlotte wrote later. The Brontë sisters tried a number of publishers—and then success! The novels were finally taken by Mr. Thomas Newby, 72 Mortimer Street, Cavendish Square, in London, the publisher, inter alia, of Mrs. Grey's governess novel *Sybil Lennard*. Except that he accepted only *Agnes Grey* (one volume) and *Wuthering Heights* (two volumes), which could be done together as a standard three-volume novel. "I tried six publishers in succession," Charlotte recalled later of *The Professor*, "they all told me it was deficient in 'startling incident' and 'thrilling excitement,' that it would never suit the circulating libraries." The circulating libraries! "The Monster-Misery of Literature" Mrs. Gore had called them in a pseudonymous piece a few years before in *Blackwood's Magazine*.

But if books for the circulating libraries did not have to be

He, too, has declined to see his mother, to whom he makes a liberal allowance; and who, besides, appears to be very wealthy. The Baronet lives
entirely at Queen's Crawley, with Lady Jane and her daughter; whilst
Rebecca, Lady Crawley, chiefly hangs about Bath and Cheltenham, where a
very strong party of excellent people consider her to be a most injured
woman. She has her enemies. Who has not? Her life is her answer to
them. She busies herself in works of piety. She goes to church, and never
without a footman. Her name is in all the Charity Lists. The Destitute
Orange-girl, the Neglected Washerwoman, the Distressed Muffin-man, find
in her a fast and generous friend. She is always having stalls at Fancy
Fairs for the benefit of these hapless beings. Emmy, her children, and the
Colonel, coming to London some time back, found themselves suddenly
before her at one of these fairs. She cast down her eyes demurely and
smiled as they started away from her; Emmy skurrying off on the arm of
George, (now grown a dashing young gentleman,) and the Colonel seizing
up his little Janey, of whom he is fonder than of anything in the world—
fonder even than of his "History of the Punjaub."

"Fonder than he is of me," Emmy thinks, with a sigh. But he never
said a word to Amelia that was not kind and gentle; or thought of a
want of hers that he did not try to gratify.

Ah! *Vanitas Vanitatum!* Which of us is happy in this world? Which
of us has his desire? or, having it, is satisfied?—Come children, let us
shut up the box and the puppets, for our play is played out.

London: Bradbury & Evans, Printers, Whitefriars.

Thackeray's illustration for the last page of Vanity Fair, *showing his
two small daughters, who frequently posed for him. The combination
of text and illustration on the same page was unusual before the
1840s, when woodcuts came into wide use.*

positively over the top in each episode like the serial, still, overall, as Mrs. Gore knew, they had to be pretty corny. And if the
Brontës were not going to write serials—which, without connec-
tions in the London literary world, was unlikely—then they had
to write three-volume novels for the circulating libraries. And
The Professor was also rather short to stand on its own as a three-
volume novel. Mrs. Gore had written of how that would be a
problem, too. Said the experienced Mrs. Gore, "This despot of
bookmakers must have length, breadth, and thickness, to fill the
book boxes dispatched to its subscribers in the country." Beyond
simply padding a story with excess description and characters,
mechanical tricks existed for making the three-decker longer,
like adding epigraphs at the start of the chapter, starting a chapter—or ending it—halfway down a page, using larger margins,
and so on. (Short dialogue—"Is he here?" "No." "Where then?"
"In London."—each fragment taking up one line, was also a
favorite trick.) The padding to achieve the obligatory three-volume length was one reason why so many of the three-deckers
were pointless and boring, of course.

Which left Charlotte all by herself.

More or less as a last resort, Charlotte Brontë crossed off the
name of still another publisher who had rejected her novel and,
then, in the summer of 1847, wrapped it up once again—in the
same wrapping paper, simply crossing off the names and
addresses of the publishers who had already rejected it. ("This
was not calculated to prepossess us in favour of the MS.,"
wrote her ultimate publisher dryly later.) She sent out her manuscript to Smith, Elder and Company at 65 Cornhill Street. And
in the meantime Charlotte began work on the novel about a
governess who fell in love with her employer that was to
become *Jane Eyre*.

The established novelists were not idle, either. It was now
four years since Dickens had begun a full-length novel. During
that time, he had become a celebrity. "There never was a king
or emperor upon the earth so cheered and followed by crowds,
and entertained in public at splendid balls, and dinners," he

marveled from America when he went on a tour there in 1842 and did, indeed, receive a reception befitting royalty. He was greeted by the mayor of New York, the president, and the governor of Massachusetts. ("Did they sound *hash*?" asked the governor in response to Dickens' mention of the peculiar Bostonian way of speaking. "I beg your pardon?" said the writer. You know, the governor enlarged, "did the Boston pronunciation sound *hash* to you?") People cut fur off Dickens' coat, by their sheer numbers forced him to barricade himself in his hotel rooms; he hired a secretary to help him sign autographs, gigantic banquets were tendered him—it was all a new and delightful madness. His father and his brother Alfred tried to cash in on his popularity by cadging loans from Chapman and Hall, and the embarrassed Dickens had to relocate his parents to a house near Exeter to get them out of the city.

Like various other media stars in years to come, he quarreled with—and regularly dumped—his publishers, Bentley included, for new ones willing to pay him more and give him greater editorial and artistic freedom. After leaving Macrone for Bentley, he then left Bentley. Then he had again fought with his publishers—this time Chapman and Hall, and so he had now gone off with their old printers, the publishers of *Punch*, Bradbury and Evans.

But for once his petulance made a significant literary difference—one that would influence the development of the serial novel. When Dickens started his new serial at the end of July 1848, it was with a very junior pair of publishers who had seen how this volatile writer could go through publishers like a knife through butter. Bradbury and Evans now agreed to pay him for all his fiction for the next eight years—with the author to get an astounding 75 percent of the profits. And as Dickens now began work on a new novel for Bradbury and Evans to appear in his usual twenty numbers, he would be, they told him, for the first time guaranteed payment for the full twenty.

This was a watershed in the history of the serial. Previously, the serial author had had no incentive to construct an elaborate, long-range plot because a publisher could always stop a serial if public interest failed to develop or diminished after a few "numbers," as, indeed, had almost happened with *Pickwick* and *Vanity Fair*. *The Pickwick Papers* (1837), *Oliver Twist* (1839), *Nicholas Nickleby* (1839), *Barnaby Rudge* (1841), *Martin Chuzzlewit* (1843)—the titles of Dickens' early serials alone all tell the story, which is invariably that of a central character perambulated through a series of rather loosely joined episodes. And it is really the character, rather than any great plot, that links the episodes together. In the preface to *Pickwick*, Dickens revealed that he had been content to have the book seen as "a mere series of adventures."

Serials had also been annoyingly disjointed because all their weekly installments had to be self-contained. "I've just read *Pickwick* by Dickens," Flaubert wrote to George Sand. "Some bits are magnificent; but what a defective structure." Periodical publication, Dickens himself acknowledged in his preface to the collected "numbers" of *Pickwick*, "rendered it an object of paramount importance that, while the different incidents were linked together by a chain of interest strong enough to prevent their appearing unconnected or impossible, the general design should be so simple as to sustain no injury from this detached and desultory form of publication, extending over no fewer than twenty months." That is, "every number should be, to a certain extent, complete in itself."

In the preface to *Martin Chuzzlewit*, however, Dickens said he had tried "to resist the temptation of the current Monthly Number, and to keep a steadier eye up on the general purpose and design." Well now, finally, for the first time Dickens could really do something about this dangling incoherence. Now, instead of starting a book that was merely about a character, like Mr. Pickwick or Martin Chuzzlewit, he began a book about the fate of the Dombey family. With the financial security of knowing the entire serial would be paid for no matter what, Dickens could plan out his whole novel in advance in some detail, as he did, setting out for *Dombey* a long, integrated structure of plot and character development with detailed "mems," as he termed the long slips of paper that were his working notes and outlines.

The new kind of serial called for just as much thought as *Oliver Twist* or *Martin Chuzzlewit*—but of a different kind. "Notice how patiently and expressly the thing has to be planned for presentation in fragments, and yet for afterwards fusing together as an uninterrupted whole," Dickens told Thackeray's friend Mrs. Brookfield some years later when she herself aspired to novelize, telling her to look at some of his own later works like *A Tale of Two Cities*, or *Great Expectations*. Dickens wrote little about his literary techniques, but he once responded briefly to criticisms of how he had allegedly stuck in almost gratuitously the collapse of a house that kills a man in *Little Dorrit* "that the way to the demolition of the man and the house together, is paved all through the book with a painful minuteness and reiterated care of preparation, the necessity of which, (in order that the thread may be kept in the reader's mind through nearly two years), is one of the adverse incidents of that serial form of publication." It was a new combination, in effect, of the serial's episodic nature and the three-decker's long, integrated modes.

As Dickens struggled for the first time with the difficulties of this new kind of composition, he begged off reading some of his fellow writers' new work. He had gotten to know Thackeray after refusing to hire him as an illustrator on *Pickwick*, and after a fashion, they had become friends. The Dickens girls were the same age as Minny and Anny, and the young Thackerays attended the lavish Christmas parties Dickens gave each year. Anny remembered fondly in after years how she and her sister went to the grand-seeming parties and at one in particular were talked to by Mrs. Dickens "as if we were grown-up, which is always very flattering to little girls." Now Dickens told Thackeray placatingly in January 1848, "I am saving up the perusal of *Vanity Fair*" as he worked away on the newly demanding incarnation of the serial, "until I shall have done *Dombey*."

Vanity Fair! For Thackeray now had a title for his new book, he told a woman he met at Brighton where he had gone during the off-season for peace to work. He had given up the title, "The Novel without a Hero," and adopted a more tellingly moralistic one. In the middle of the night, he related, it came to him, and "I jumped out of bed and ran three times round my room, uttering as I went, '*Vanity Fair, Vanity Fair, Vanity Fair.*'"

And Thackeray had more for his new novel than just a title. "One morning a hansom drove up to the front door, and out of it emerged a most charming, dazzling little lady dressed in black, who greeted my father with great affection and brilliancy, and who, departing presently, gave him a large bunch of fresh violets." So wrote Anny Thackeray, years later, of Theresa Reviss, the illegitimate daughter of a friend of Thackeray's named Charles Buller, who was a former tutee of Carlyle's. "This was the only time I ever saw the fascinating little person who was by many supposed to be the original of Becky," Anny continued, "my father only laughed when people asked him, but he never quite owned to it."

"Becky"?

Theresa was, of course, an important inspiration for Becky Sharp, at least in her juvenile incarnation. "She has a splendid voice, and wished to get trained for the opera," reported Jane Carlyle after Theresa paid the Carlyles a visit in 1851. But "her two male guardians, to wash their hands of her, resolved to send her to India, and to India she had to go, to Sir Arthur [*sic*] Buller (whose wife hated her—naturally—being the child of her husband's *ci-devant* mistress), vowing that if their object was to marry her off, she would disappoint them, and return 'to prosecute the artist life,'" Jane continued with wicked delight. (At a ball in India Theresa appeared costumed as the Prince of Darkness—complete with tail.) Indeed, "she produced the most extraordinary furore at Calcutta; had offers every week, Sudar Judges and what not; refused them point-blank; terrified Sir Arthur by her extravagance; tormented Lady Buller by her caprices; 'fell into consumption' for the nonce;

was ordered by the doctors back to England! and, to the dismay of her two cowardly guardians, arrived here six months ago— *with her health perfectly restored!*"

Theresa was clearly the stuff of which dramatic, lively novels could be made, and Thackeray wanted something good. On one occasion he pulled his chair away after hearing someone across the table rhapsodize to Dickens after dinner about his work. "Did you hear that? I go nowhere but I am subject to it. I should not mind to hear Lytton Bulwer praised to the skies," he exploded to his neighbor, "for I own my inferiority, but—" He abruptly fell silent. He was tired of being relegated to minor status behind a prolific, rather excessive writer when Thackeray thought himself a better stylist than Dickens. And the annoyance of Dickens was right in Thackeray's own home, Minny, aged nine, once piping up helpfully during a visit from Tennyson, "Papa, why don't you write books like *Nicholas Nickleby*?" "I like Mr. Dickens's books much better than your books, Papa," he quoted her as saying bluntly on another occasion. Even the Thackeray cats consisted of the great gray tabby cat Nicholas Nickleby, Martin Chuzzlewit, and "a poor little half-starved Barnaby Rudge."

Vanity Fair. Thackeray had a title and a model for its antiheroine, but was at first apparently unable to decide whether to do his new novel as a three-decker or as a serial. He wrote four beginning chapters, and no one wanted it—he took it around to publisher after publisher, three or four at least, including the famous Henry Colburn. At length it occurred to Thackeray— what about the people on whose staff he worked at *Punch*, the same Bradbury and Evans who were Chapman and Hall's old printers and, as it happened, were publishing *Dombey and Son*?

They proved almost as anxious to get him as they had been to get Dickens. "I am deuced sorry I didn't ask them another tenner," Thackeray said thoughtfully to a publishing acquaintance the afternoon he returned from selling his novel. As it was, he had gotten fifty guineas per monthly number—even if Bradbury and Evans did not offer him guaranteed payment for his entire serial the way they had for Dickens. In January 1847, Bradbury and Evans published the first number of *Vanity Fair*, containing what are now the completed book's first four chapters, in a thirty-two-page, yellow-covered shilling serial edition (the bluish green cover first used on *Pickwick* was by now sacrosanct to Dickens' serials).

"PUBLISHED AT THE *PUNCH* OFFICE, 85, FLEET STREET," said the title page. By contrast, their serialization of the celebrated Dickens' *Dombey* bore no such crass advertising. But whereas Dickens' serials usually carried only two full-page engravings per number by way of illustration, *Vanity Fair* sported decorative capitals, end of chapter cartoons, and illustrative woodcuts surrounded by text, as well as full-page illustrations, in a positive explosion of illustration and ornament.

There was even a miniature of a bespectacled, cross-legged Thackeray himself at the end of Chapter IX of *Vanity Fair*, literally obtruding himself into the text, but, characteristically, in a self-deprecating way. (The novel was his first fiction to bear his real name and not a pseudonym.) Minny and Anny were used to Thackeray calling them in from the schoolroom to pose for his drawings. "Well, I see you are going to shut up your puppets in their box," a man observed to the writer as the serial was drawing to a close. "With your permission, I'll work up that simile," said Thackeray. And, lo and behold, the very last illustration in the novel showed the two little girls putting away their puppets, as an indulgent Thackeray bids us—and them—farewell: "Come, children, let us shut up the box and the puppets, for our play is played out." Thackeray at last had a large-scale outlet for both his artistic and literary abilities, and, with his closing depiction of his daughters, his novel interwove text and illustration right to the very end.

This profusion of illustration was made possible by use of woodcuts. Because their ink-bearing lines were raised, like letterpress, woodcuts could be printed on the same page as text, instead of on separate pages, as engravings, like those illustrating *Pickwick* and *Oliver Twist*, had to be, given that all engravings were intaglio. If *Dombey and Son* demonstrated a new structural integrity of the hitherto disjointed parts of the serial achieved by plot development, *Vanity Fair* showed that the serial could be used as a vehicle for a sophisticated, not necessarily "popular" satire of sometimes rather subtle social comedy.

Between *Dombey* and *Vanity Fair*, it was a momentous time for the development of the serial novel.

The publishing houses that Thackeray and the Brontës were dealing with, despite Colburn's leap into the publishing techniques of the 1900s, were by and large small, storefront enterprises that operated with little capital, much like the other shops and stores of early nineteenth-century London. Sometimes they had their own hand printing press in the back of the shop and still sold stationery, books, or had a circulating library as a sideline, like a combination video rental/photocopying/desktop publishing service walk-in store today. (John Newbery, the famous children's book publisher, sold patent medicines on the side; Colburn operated a circulating library; and John Murray in writing to Walter Scott spoke of himself as a "publishing bookseller.") This style of operation suited the small number of books they generally published (and the small editions of such books). The typical bookseller's shop had a counter in front where clerks sold books and screened visitors to the publisher, while the latter worked in a small parlor in the back—often in front of a roaring fire—and often, at least in the early days, slept upstairs.

Given this small-scale, mom-and-pop style of operating, it was not uncommon for a publisher to publish a first book either on some kind of commission or perhaps half-profits basis, or through an arrangement where the author paid all or part of the costs, not unlike contemporary vanity press publishing, the tradeoff being that the author had a correspondingly greater, often exclusive, control over editorial content, layout, binding, and the rest. Jane Austen in publishing *Emma* and the second edition of *Mansfield Park* with John Murray

Haworth, home of the Brontës. The parsonage, where they lived, is the building to the left of the church tower, at the right on the horizon. Rather than the scene of

primitive rural desolation readers inferred from Wuthering Heights, *the town was actually a fast-growing textile manufacturing center.*

thus got all profits after a commission of 10 percent for the publisher, and Thomas Hardy paid the publisher William Tinsley £75 to have his first novel published (the now all-but-forgotten *Desperate Remedies*). The then-unknown "Lewis Carroll" went this route with his *Alice in Wonderland* in 1865, even though it was published by the relatively well-established house of Macmillan. It was thus Carroll who thought of having *Punch* artist John Tenniel illustrate *Alice*; it was Carroll who approached him, and who then paid him for his famous illustrations, not anyone at Macmillan. Indeed, as late as 1890, a representative of the Society of Authors maintained that at least three-quarters of modern fiction was published on commission.

The immediate relevance of all this lay in the fact that although he had accepted Emily and Anne Brontë's books for publication, Mr. Thomas Newby of Cavendish Square had decided for the time being against actually publishing their *Wuthering Heights* and *Agnes Grey*. Before that he had been looking at the manuscript of a first novel submitted to him on her son Anthony's behalf by Mrs. Frances Trollope. Mr. Newby was dubious about the book by the young man who had previously asked Richard Bentley to consider his "lucubrations." "He, like everybody else, gives a most dismal account of the novel-market," Mrs. Trollope told her daughter, but Newby made a typical half-profits offer to young Trollope: four hundred copies to be printed at the publisher's expense, no money up front from Trollope, and half the profits—if any—to go to the novelist after publication.

This particular arrangement for author-subsidized publication—the publisher absorbs all initial costs and gives part of what's left to the writer—was famously open to the criticism that the writer had no real way to verify the publisher's estimates of his costs and expenses. The publisher could thus plead he owed the author nothing. "The publisher pays all the expenses first, and then he and the author divide the profits," remarked a character in Annie Beale's 1864 *Nothing Venture*,

Nothing Have, "but somehow or other there never are any."

But Trollope at this point was still the least distinguished member of his struggling, if valiant, family. He had struck out with Bentley, but he still wanted to write. Reluctantly, he finally agreed to Newby's proposed arrangement. The results were not pleasant. Sales were dismal, and several of Newby's advertisements attributed her son's novel to "Mrs. Trollope." Was it through carelessness or with the design of having people think the novel was by Anthony's celebrated mother and not her as-yet-unknown son? Was Newby just clumsy—or a sharp operator?

At least Trollope had actually gotten his three-decker published. Due to Newby's inaction, Emily and Anne's books were still not on the market. Nor was Charlotte's slim one-volume *The Professor* a good candidate for publication, given its brevity, especially not for the firm of Smith, Elder. Indeed, before George Smith had taken over its direction from his father in 1847, the firm in 1833 had inaugurated The Library of Romance in one volume each in an effort to challenge the circulating libraries' monolithic adherence to the three-decker. With perhaps more courage than reason, the firm's promotional literature ventured the hope that the Library of Romance "will neutralize the mischievous prejudice which prevails in the trade against works in less than three volumes, and this it will do while *increasing* rather than diminishing *the profits of the Circulating Libraries.*" A vain hope, as it turned out. Under pressure from the circulating libraries, who apparently saw things differently, the firm's project rapidly collapsed. The circulating libraries did not want merely to keep prices high and thus encourage people to borrow from them rather than buy. They also specifically favored the three-volume format; if they could split up a novel into three volumes they could make three times as much money renting it out on a per-volume basis as a one-volume work. And it appeared that publishers sided with them. Three volumes, Bentley patiently explained through his representative to one writer thinking of publishing in a two-volume format, could be published almost as cheaply as two and brought in an extra profit for a publisher with the third volume.

But now in the first week of August 1847, a return letter for Charlotte arrived from a Mr. Williams of Smith, Elder at 65 Cornhill Street. Harboring the "dreary expectation of finding two hard hopeless lines, intimating that Messrs. Smith, and Elder 'were not disposed to publish the MS.,'" Charlotte later recalled, she was delighted to find on opening the communication a two-page letter saying that *no*, the firm was not interested in *The Professor*; but *yes*, there was this and this that was good about the work. And if by any chance she could produce a novel in the standard three-volume format used for all novels that were not, like Dickens', serials . . .

Within three weeks of getting the letter from Mr. Williams, Charlotte Brontë finished her new novel *Jane Eyre*, the one about the governess. She sent the manuscript off by railroad to Messrs. Smith and Elder, although not without an apology for sticking them temporarily with the freight charge: "I find I cannot prepay the carriage of the parcel . . . If, when you acknowledge the receipt of the MS, you would have the goodness to mention the amount charged on delivery, I will immediately transmit it in postage-stamps."

Books were evaluated and published fast in those days. The stooping, worried Mr. Smith Williams, the "reader" for Smith, Elder, "in due course" sat down to read the manuscript of *Jane Eyre*. He then brought it to George Smith, who took it home, intending to meet a friend for a ride at midday the next day. The next morning Smith began reading in his study. "Before twelve o'clock, my horse came to the door, but I could not put the book down. I scribbled two or three lines to my friend, saying that I was very sorry that circumstances had arisen to prevent my meeting him, sent the note off by my groom, and went on reading the MS. Presently, the servant came to tell me that luncheon was ready; I asked him to bring me a sandwich and a glass of wine, and still went on with 'Jane Eyre'. Dinner came; for me the meal was a very hasty one, and before I went to bed that night I had finished reading the manuscript.

"The next day we wrote to 'Currer Bell' accepting the book for publication." (Or so, at any rate, he remembered fifty years later. Notwithstanding this charming, romantic account, there was, apparently, some hesitation about the book at Smith, Elder. The old concern was voiced—not enough exciting incidents for the circulating libraries, but whether by Smith, Williams or another we do not know. The decision to publish was taken anyway.)

Charlotte Brontë had sent off the manuscript of *Jane Eyre* to Smith and Elder on August 24, 1847; the novel was published on October 16, 1847. There was even less editing than today—and no legal department, no complex contracts to review or negotiate, no editorial board meetings, no marketing department. The time between manuscript submission and publication was rapid in the days of storefront publishing. A few years later Anthony Trollope sent Longmans the manuscript of *The Warden* in October 1854 and saw it published on January 5, 1855, while the last part of George Eliot's manuscript of *Silas Marner* went to the publisher on March 10, 1861. She received a bound copy of the book on March 25, and publication occurred on April 2.

A memorable year—*Dombey* under way, *Jane Eyre* about to appear, *Wuthering Heights* in the press, to say nothing of *Vanity Fair*. Of course, in true serial fashion, Thackeray's publishers had found themselves wondering whether or not to continue his serial past the third "number," owing to initially poor sales. In October 1847, Thackeray noted dryly of his novel, "it does everything but sell, and appears really immensely to increase my reputation if not my income."

Slowly, at first, and then more rapidly, however, the circulation of *Vanity Fair* began to pick up, talk buzzed, and soon acclaim poured in from all sides. "I am become a sort of great man in my way," Thackeray wrote proudly to his mother in January 1848 as the momentum and excitement were mounting,

Reverend Brontë's Haworth parsonage overlooked the churchyard shown here and also the hills of the moors.

"all but at the top of the tree: indeed there if the truth were known and having a great fight up there with Dickens." Actually, the *Vanity Fair* numbers sold some 10,500 copies monthly, while *Martin Chuzzlewit* reached 23,000 and *The Old Curiosity Shop* 100,000. But still . . . Thackeray was taken up by the nobility and aristocracy. "Isn't that the great Mr. Thackeray?" the silly Lady Chalmer was heard to ask at a dinner party, and Thackeray delighted in the "praise wherever I go." But limner of Becky Sharp that he was, he was fully aware of the ultimate idiocy of Society's acclaim. "This London world is full of a parcel of good-natured tom-fools and directly one begins to cry O all the rest say prodigious." He also detected jealousy and envy. "Jerrold hates me, Ainsworth hates me, Dickens mistrusts me, Forster says I am false as hell, and Bulwer curses me—he is the only one who has any reason," he wrote gloomily to his mother in July 1847. Still, by August of 1848, as the hardcover edition of the complete serial went on sale, he could crow that "*Vanity Fair* is doing very well commercially I'm happy to say at last. They have sold 1500 of the volumes wh. is very well in these times of revolution and dismay."

He was not the only one tasting success. The *Westminster Review* called *Jane Eyre* "decidedly the best novel of the year," and the *Times* was equally enthusiastic. "This indeed is a book after our own heart," wrote a journalist friend of Dickens named George Lewes in the *Fraser's Magazine* for December 1847. He had been so impressed when he received an advance copy of the book that he asked *Fraser's* if he could review it, then had sent the anonymous Currer Bell a fan letter that told "him" not to be so melodramatic next time. ("I restrained imagination, eschewed romance, repressed excitement; over-bright colouring, too, I avoided," Charlotte replied tartly to Lewes in her guise of "Currer Bell" in November 1847, informing him that the publishers before Smith, Elder had turned *The Professor* down because it didn't have *enough* melodrama.)

Charlotte even got a good reaction on the home front. "Papa, I've been writing a book," she said as she cornered her father in his study with a copy of *Jane Eyre* and a few reviews one day as he was reading.

"Have you, my dear?"

He continued to read.

"But Papa, I want you to look at it."

"I can't be troubled to read MS."

Patience—"But it is printed."

This drew a reaction.

"I hope you have not been involving yourself in any such silly expense," he said disapprovingly, evidently assuming that, like Anthony Trollope, Charlotte had had to pay to get such an initial effort published.

"I think I shall gain some money by it," was the reply. "May I read you some reviews."

She then left the book with him.

"Children," he said to Emily and Anne later at tea, "Charlotte has been writing a book—and I think it is a better one than I expected."

To some the novel seemed quite bold as well. In a shrewd review of "Modern Novelists" for *Blackwood's* a few years later, the prolific Mrs. Margaret Oliphant noted that *Jane Eyre* marked the advent of the "fierce incendiary" heroine who would insist, for the first time, on not merely meeting a man as an equal but going *mano a mano*, perhaps almost literally, to insist on her rights if she were not properly treated. "'Let him take me captive, seize upon me, overpower me if he is the better man—let us fight it out, my weapons against his weapons, and see which is the strongest'" was the creed of the *Jane Eyre* heroine, said Mrs. Oliphant breathlessly. "Do you like, it, gentle lover?—would you rather break her head and win, or leave her alone and love her?" Mrs. Oliphant asked her male readers luridly. Many must have shared Mrs. Oliphant's reactions. The young daughter of a widowed estate manager near Coventry named Marian Evans read *Jane Eyre* and admitted that "the book *is* interesting—only I wish the characters would talk a little bit less like the heroes and heroines of police reports." Thus did the future "George Eliot," who had always thought of writing a novel, indeed, had done a corny imitation of G. P. R. James's books as an adolescent, view the work of an important precursor.

In America, some purchasers in Boston returned their copies of *Jane Eyre* to the Old Corner Bookstore because the book was immoral. Lady Herschel reproachfully asked George Smith's mother, "Do you leave such a book as *this* about, at the risk of your daughters reading it?" when she saw the book on Mrs. Smith's drawing room table. "Nice" girls were not allowed to read it, resulting, one guesses, in the usual popularity attendant on such prohibitions. "Miss Maunder had done her best to make us read it by denouncing it as 'quite unfit for any young lady's perusal' so very often," said a character in Francis Paget's 1868 *Lucretia*, "that there was nothing left us but to get hold of it as soon as possible."

In December 1847, two months after *Jane Eyre* had appeared, Thomas Newby quietly published at long last *Wuthering Heights* and *Agnes Grey* together in three volumes. Disguised as a standard three-decker, *Wuthering Heights* made up the first two volumes and *Agnes Grey* the last. The redoubtable Newby, perhaps not surprisingly, made a hash out of it. "The orthography and punctuation of the books are mortifying to a degree," Charlotte angrily noted, "almost all the errors that were corrected in the proof-sheets appear intact in what should have been the fair copies."

Critical reaction centered on *Wuthering Heights*, which, then as now, seemed the more powerful and accomplished novel. Not that the reaction was necessarily laudatory. "*Withering Heights*," said one review, should have been the title, "for anything from which the mind and body could more instinctively shrink than the mansion and its tenants, cannot be easily imagined." Douglas Jerrold's *Weekly Newspaper*, while recommending *Wuthering Heights* for its "great power," nonetheless warned that the reader would be "shocked, disgusted, almost sickened by details of cruelty, inhumanity, and the most diabolical hate and vengeance." The Prince Consort found that the books were lacking in decency, and George Lewes' new magazine *The Leader* was horrified when Charlotte Brontë finally revealed in 1850 that the authors of *Wuthering Heights* and *Agnes Grey* "were two retiring, solitary, consumptive girls! Books, coarse even for men, coarse in language and coarse in conception, the coarseness apparently of violent and uncultivated men—turn out to be the productions of two girls living almost alone, filling their loneliness with quiet studies."

But before the authorship of the "retiring girls" came to light, the unsinkable Mr. Newby came up once again with a plan to make some easy money. In the summer of 1848, he tried to get a shady transatlantic deal going with the American publishers Harper and Brothers along the same lines as the guess-the-author routine he seems to have used on Anthony Trollope's first book. He told Harpers that he was about to publish the next book "by the author of *Jane Eyre*." He was actually offering them the book that became Anne Brontë's *The Tenant of Wildfell Hall*, her second novel, since, of course, he was *her* publisher and not Charlotte's. Would they like the American rights to it?

Harpers was a big player in American publishing. By 1842 it had become America's publishing powerhouse, with nine five-story buildings filled with printing machinery and offices at Franklin Square down near the Battery in New York City. There several hundred employees turned out books and magazines like *Harper's Weekly*, *Harper's Magazine*, and the company's fashion magazine, *Harper's Bazaar*. (James Harper was sufficiently prominent to be elected mayor of New York City in 1844.)

Harpers found Newby's offer of the American rights to what the British publisher claimed was the new work "by the author of *Jane Eyre*" very interesting because they had been informed previously that they were *already* in the midst of negotiations to purchase the next book by "Currer Bell"— except that this book was *Shirley*, a novel about the Luddite riots in the early years of the century, which really *was* Currer

Anne, Emily, and Charlotte Brontë, painted by their brother, Branwell, circa 1834. Not inappropriately, the portrait groups Emily and Anne together; in life they tended to ally informally against their older sister, Charlotte.

Bell's, i.e., Charlotte's, new novel. It was being offered to Harpers by Smith, Elder, which was able to legitimately offer Harpers the right to Charlotte's new book, since, of course, Smith, Elder really was her publisher.

But neither Harpers nor Smith, Elder—nor Newby, for that matter—knew who "Currer," "Acton," or "Ellis Bell" was, nor even if the different names were all pseudonyms for only one person. Was it possible that Newby was telling the truth about having the rights to "Currer Bell's" next novel? The urbane, good-looking, young George Smith grew worried when he got wind of the offer Newby was making to Harpers. Did Newby have the rights to *Shirley*? Smith sent off a letter to "Currer Bell" saying in a diplomatic but self-contradictory clause that after hearing of Newby's statement, Smith, Elder "should be glad to be in a position to contradict the statement, adding at the same time we were quite sure Mr Newby's statement was untrue."

The issue of confused identity was at that moment a sore one with Charlotte. After some rather unenthusiastic reviews of *Jane Eyre*, she had received a wonderful letter from Mr. Williams at Smith, Elder. It relayed the admiring Thackeray's praise of her novel—"It interested me so much that I have lost (or won if you like) a whole day in reading it at the busiest period," Thackeray had written to Williams, "with the printers I know waiting for copy." He had burst out crying in front of the footman over it. "Some of the love passages made me cry—to the astonishment of John who came in with the coals."

Charlotte already liked Thackeray. Indeed, she said, she looked on his works with "reverence"—and now here he was offering his literary support. She felt impelled to reciprocate. "His wit is bright, his humor attractive, but both bear the same relation to his serious genius, that the mere lambent sheet-lightning playing under the edge of the summer cloud does to the electric death-spark hid in its womb." So she viewed the author of *Vanity Fair*, she told her readers in a preface to a new edition of *Jane Eyre*, and he was, she said, greater even than Fielding. And so "to him—if he will accept the tribute of a total stranger," she grandiloquently concluded, "I have dedicated this second edition of *Jane Eyre*. Currer Bell, Dec. 21st, 1847."

But Charlotte, like most people in England, was unacquainted with the facts of Thackeray's private circumstances, or she would, perhaps, have been more cautious. "Of course I knew nothing whatever of Mr Thackeray's domestic concerns," she said later, for if she had—well, if Charlotte had known of Thackeray's insane wife and the two little girls, would she then have known of the endless procession of governesses to and from Thackeray's home as he tried to find one adequate to educate the girls? Governesses ... And wasn't his new bestseller about a scheming, attractive governess who used her charms with her employer's family to advance her fortunes? ("I have found the Prize Governess," Thackeray himself mused the succeeding year, except "if she should turn out to be a Miss Sharp.") But then wasn't *Jane Eyre*, subtitled "An Autobiography" and told in the first person, almost the mirror image of Thackeray's *Vanity Fair*, that is, a novel about a governess who married into the family of her pupil? Moreover, didn't *Jane Eyre* roughly track the facts of Thackeray's domestic situation by depicting the governess marrying a man who had a mad wife locked away—and a little girl? Thackeray was in the same situation as Mr. Rochester in *Jane Eyre*. All very interesting. And now to top it all off here was a still very pseudonymous "Currer Bell" dedicating the second edition of *Jane Eyre* openly and very warmly to Thackeray.

The Thackerays' friend Jane Carlyle was sick in the weeks after the second edition of *Jane Eyre* appeared, and an acquaintance came to visit her in the little room at the Carlyle home at Cheyne Row in Chelsea where she was resting. Well, what did Jane think was being talked about all over London? What, indeed? Off went a letter to Thomas from his maliciously witty, sharp-featured wife, who was so curious about Becky Sharp's original, Theresa Reviss. Her sickroom visitor, Mrs. Carlyle said, "tells me the Town is full of the news that 'Jane Eyre' has been written by Mr. Thackeray's mistress."

The town was indeed full of the news.

Now on top of that here was George Smith writing the Brontës a letter that arrived in Haworth on July 7, 1848, delicately inquiring if "Currer Bell" was double-crossing him by making a deal behind his back for the novel following *Jane Eyre* after he'd already gotten the manuscript for it. Angry with their publisher for evidently distrusting them as well as completely furious by now with Newby (that "shuffling scamp," Charlotte called him), the Brontë women put their heads together. They had no choice, they decided, but to go to London to show George Smith who "Currer Bell" was—and at least two of them would have to go, too, so they could also counter the rumors that there was only one "Bell" who wrote all the books by "Currer, Acton and Ellis."

Anne and Charlotte (the reclusive Emily was not a traveler) finished their chores and sent off a change of clothes by cart to the railroad station at Keighley a few miles away that very day. They had an early tea. Then the two sisters set off on a changeable Friday afternoon in early July to walk to the train. Despite a thunderstorm they pushed on in their four-mile walk across the dreary countryside, not able to afford the luxury of getting out of the rain.

They took the night train to London.

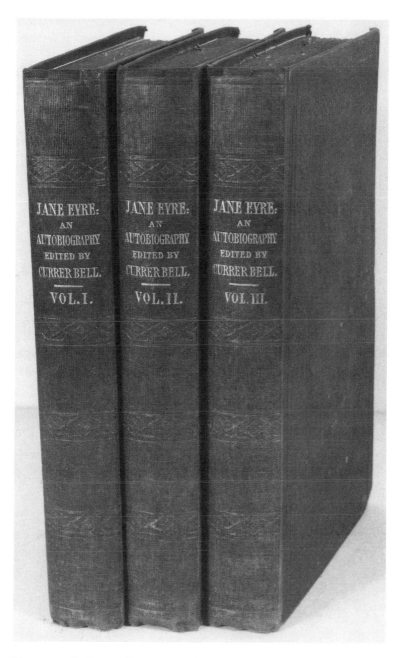

The original edition of Jane Eyre, in the three-volume novel format typical of the era. Charlotte Brontë's use of the pseudonym, Currer Bell, and the subtitle, An Autobiography, led to speculation that she was Thackeray's mistress, so close were the characteristics of Mr. Rochester's household to that of Thackeray.

PART 3

"What Shall I Be Without My Father?": Women Novelists in the London of Dickens and Thackeray, the Coming of Real Money, and the Novel Becomes Respectable

Not so many years before, in 1834, the eighteen-year-old Charlotte had written breathlessly to her close school friend, Ellen Nussey, when Ellen traveled to London, "of that great city, which has been called the mercantile metropolis of Europe." Later she wrote of "the great city which is to me as apocryphal as Babylon, or Nineveh, or ancient Rome"—so unimaginably distant and mysterious did the capital seem. "Few girls would have done as you have done—would have beheld the glare, and glitter, and dazzling display of London with dispositions so unchanged, heart so uncontaminated." The passage caused Charlotte's friend and biographer Mrs. Gaskell to note with gentle amusement in 1857 that "in these days of cheap railway trips, we may smile at the idea of a short visit to London having any great effect upon the character, whatever it may have upon the intellect. But her London—her great apocryphal city—was the 'town' of a century before, to which giddy daughters dragged unwilling papas, or went with injudicious friends, to the detriment of all their better qualities, and sometimes to the ruin of their fortunes; it was the Vanity Fair of the 'Pilgrim's Progress' to her" and, she might have added, the great, glittering city inhabited by rich lords and ladies of the novels of the eighteenth century. But then even as late as the 1770s Edinburgh was still a twelve-day journey from London for young Walter Scott.

The few years between 1834 and 1848 had radically transformed England's society and landscape. In 1829 came the first
public demonstration of a steam-powered railroad; in 1837, the
year of *Pickwick*, the first, halting line connected London with
another part of England. By 1843 there were more than 2,000
miles of railroad track. Twelve years later there were 8,280
miles, and soon the outlines of the modern British rail system
were almost complete, and the Brontës were able to make their
overnight journey to London at a speed of some forty miles per
hour.

The railway was taking over . . .

Aside from their convenience and remarkable ability to put
distant places within rapid reach of any traveler, good, fast predictable trains made travel, well, boring. "The rapidity of railroad communication destroys the Poetry & mystery of distant
places," complained the painter Robert Haydon. "You went to
Windsor as an exploit for two days. Now, down you go in an
hour, see it in another & home in a third." That was bad
enough, but in addition, for the first time in human history,
slow, steady, smooth rides on land made activities like reading
when traveling feasible and enjoyable, as they were not when
riding on or behind a horse. "One of the peculiarities of modern travel," the contemporary comic novelist Robert Surtees
slyly put it, "is the great demand there is for books, a book to
prevent people seeing the country being quite as essential as a
bun to prevent their being hungry."

So in 1848, the same year the Brontës came to London, one
W. H. Smith took the momentous step of opening up a reading
stall of "select" books at London's Euston Station, thus far the
capital's one rail terminus. Railway stalls had previously often
been let to disabled ex-railroad employees, or to the widows of
railroad men. In addition to old muffins, ginger beer, and the
like, the stalls typically carried "cheap French novels," as
Smith's nineteenth-century biographer starchily called them,
"of the shadiest class," mildly off-color novels, and dreary joke-
books, like a *Bowl of Punch*, hawked through the open windows

of departing trains—the latter offering "Why is an umbrella like a Mackintosh? Because it keeps off the wet!" and other similar knee slappers. By the end of 1848, Smith had bought the right to sell to railroad passengers along more than a thousand miles of track. Within a year of opening his bookstall at Euston Station, he also had a stall at Paddington Station with over a thousand books, and by 1851 he had thirty-five shops all over the country.

Smith bought up the copyrights to their best sellers from popular novelists like Ainsworth and the Irish novelist Charles Lever and then had them reprinted by Chapman and Hall in a Select Library of Fiction at two shillings apiece in a convenient one-volume format. To catch the eye of hurrying passengers the new single volumes were decorated with bright colors and then glazed to prevent the covers from getting dirty. Ultimately, patrons of the Smith stalls were able to obtain a "yellow-back," as such a volume came to be called, at the bookstall and read it in the station for a penny while awaiting their train. If they decided to take it with them to finish it, they paid an additional sum, and then dropped it off—rent-a-car fashion—at the end of their trip. The one-volume format was convenient because it was easier to carry on the train and did not take up the storage space in the small railway station stalls that three-deckers would have. More significantly, yellow-backs proved that novels could be made widely available in portable cheap formats that were neither three-deckers nor serials.

Did the Brontës note any of Smith's wares as they entered Euston Station? We do not know, but they surely entered a city that, as Mrs. Gaskell noted, had less about it of the old romance of Miss Burney's *Evelina* and more of the day-to-day energy and bustle brought to it by the new middle class chronicled by Dickens. "Morning in London. Bed-room windows are open; door-steps are drying in patches; and fresh polished brassplates and bell-pulls make your eyes blink in their brightness," wrote a minor novelist of the scene that was London in 1848. "Cattle pervade the thoroughfares; and long barrows of flowers, still wet with country dew, are pushed along the road. Shop-men in shirt-sleeves are arranging their windows; boys in caps are playing fantasias on bits of slate to housemaids at the doors; and governesses, with rolls of music and Berlinwork reticules, are tripping about the pavements near the squares. The Bank-bound omnibuses are crowded, and all with men."

When they appeared in his shop at 65 Cornhill Street that morning of July 8, 1848, George Smith was working away in a back room, the last thing on his mind the possibility of a visit from the mysterious "Currer Bell." Nor had the sisters, acting on the spur of the moment, told Smith they were coming. Refusing to give their names, they told the clerk at the front counter that they wanted to see the publisher on "a private matter." Smith hesitated when apprised of the presence of two mysterious visitors, then went out to see them—and found "two rather quaintly dressed little ladies, pale-faced and anxious-looking" before him.

"Do you wish to see me, Ma'am?"

"It is Mr. Smith?" The Brontës saw facing them a tall, pleasant-looking young man of only twenty-five—but then he had inherited the business at twenty-two when his father died.

"It is."

They proffered a letter addressed in Smith's handwriting to "Currer Bell."

He noticed it had been opened and glanced from the letter to Charlotte suspiciously.

"Where did you get this from?"

"It was addressed to me," Charlotte said.

And then the realization dawned on Smith—"Currer Bell"! At once he took them into the tiny back room with its skylight, three chairs, and desk and fetched "a pale, mild, stooping man"—it was Mr. Williams, who had corresponded with Charlotte in her incognito of "Currer Bell." Williams listened silently as George Smith burbled on eagerly. "Allow me to introduce you to my mother & sisters—How long do you stay in Town? You must make the most of the time—to-night you

George Smith, of Smith, Elder and Company, publisher of Jane Eyre, Villette, *and Mrs.* Gaskell's North and South *and, in his* Cornhill Magazine, *Trollope's* Framley Parsonage *and Hardy's* Far from the Madding Crowd. *Smith was also a friend (and perhaps more) of Charlotte Brontë.*

must go to the Italian opera—you must see the Exhibition." ("I must confess that my first impression of Charlotte Brontë's personal appearance was that it was interesting rather than attractive," Smith later recalled. The heroine of *Jane Eyre* had made it clear in the novel that she was plain, but had Smith perhaps expected, somehow, that the author of the novel would be, well, a bit more glamorous?) Aloud, he was all encomia. "Mr Thackeray would be pleased to see you—If Mr Lewes knew 'Currer Bell' was in town—he would have to be shut up—" Smith rattled on. Charlotte found him attractive, businesslike—and young, she herself being a venerable thirty-two.

The sisters refused many of his offers, though the chance to see her idol tugged at Charlotte. ("I regard Mr Thackeray," she had written Mr. Williams, "as the first of modern masters, and as the legitimate high priest of Truth.") "But when I found in further examination that he could not venture to ask such men as Thackeray etc. at a short notice, without giving them a hint as to whom they were to meet, I declined even this—I felt it would have ended in our being made a show of." They did march over at some point during their visit to confront Mr. Newby in a meeting whose course, alas, has not been recorded. And George and his sister took the Brontës to the opera. (The sisters had put up at the dismal old Chapter Coffeehouse favored by their father.) And then Charlotte and Anne returned to the north, having dipped their toes in the waters of the London literary world.

Some things did not change, of course. Not many weeks after the Brontës' visit to London the execrable Newby advertised the novel *My Sister Minnie* in the *Times* with a quotation from the *Examiner* intimating that the novel's "merits cannot fail to ensure success." Unfortunately, when an interested reader wrote the *Examiner* to ask about the review, the *Examiner* replied that it had never reviewed the book. Hmm. The next week Newby wrote in to apologize for the dreadful mistake (made, naturally, he said, by the printer). The paper, of course, from which the laudatory quote had been taken was the much less prestigious *Glasgow Examiner* (but "a paper of high literary reputation in the north," Newby solemnly observed). Unfortunately, the careless printer had simply omitted the word *Glasgow* from the newspaper's title in composing the ad. Awfully sorry—whereupon the *Examiner* pointed out another ad of Newby's, which had used a warm endorsement by the *Examiner* of Anne Brontë's *The Tenant of Wildfell Hall*—except that the *Examiner* had not reviewed the book until *after* Newby's ad for it had appeared.

Meanwhile the Brontës' private life had suddenly and terribly turned utterly grim. It began with the illness of brother Branwell (of whom so much had been hoped). He had tried painting, writing, and then tutoring—all unsuccessfully. He fell ill and began to waste away, cough, lose weight and lose sleep. The sisters had nursed him, and then he had suddenly taken a turn for the worse and on September 24, 1848, only two months after their trip to London, had died.

A few weeks later, it was Emily's turn to fall ill. She became prey to a persistent cough, then grew emaciated and pale, but, characteristically solitary and independent, refused to see a doctor. On Tuesday, December 19, not yet three months after Branwell's death, Charlotte noted with a chill that Emily no longer recognized the bit of heath Charlotte had gone out to find for her that day on the winter-swept moors that her sister loved so dearly. Emily became more tired and listless, suffered suddenly a great pain, and then, at about two in the afternoon, she died. "It was very terrible," a shaken Charlotte recalled, "she was torn conscious, panting, reluctant though resolute out of a happy life."

Emily was only thirty years old.

And so there was yet another Brontë funeral in the dismal churchyard. Emily's faithful dog, Keeper, howled mournfully day after day at the door of his mistress's room. "Charlotte, you must bear up," begged the old man who had been surprised at the quality of her writing and who had now lost his wife and four children. "I shall sink if you fail me."

And then unbelievably, unbearably, Anne Brontë, too, fell

ill—deadly ill. In January the shy twenty-eight-year-old began losing her appetite and feeling tired and chill, like her brother and sister before her. A specialist saw her and made it clear she would soon die. Surrounded by the moors, rarely traveling, she had only once seen the sea—and fallen in love with it. Now, weakening steadily, daily, was there a chance she could once more view the mysterious waves that stretched away vast and unknowable to the horizon?

A carriage was ordered to take the ailing woman and her older sister on the first stage of the journey to Scarborough on the coast. Carefully, the weakened invalid was made comfortable in the vehicle; they transferred to a train, bystanders springing forward to lift her in and out of the railway carriages when they saw her wasted condition. They arrived on May 25 at Scarborough, where they set up in a small boarding house. By Sunday, two days later, Anne seemed too sick even to go to church. Charlotte offered to stay home to look after her, and that afternoon the two sisters sat and watched as the sun set in spectacular beauty over the ocean. The next day as they carried her to the sofa to make her comfortable, Anne read the anguish on her older sister's face. "Take courage, Charlotte, take courage," she whispered—and then Anne, too, was dead.

Even before these tragedies, Charlotte in her guise of "Currer Bell" and the middle-aged Mr. Williams of Smith, Elder had exchanged gossip, descriptions of the country, literary talk, and advice in their letters. Williams had known Keats, after all, written himself, and worked for the firm that did the lithographs for Darwin's *Voyage of the Beagle*. Charlotte had begun, in fact, to look forward to the letters from London with a good deal of anticipation. "I can give you but a faint idea of the pleasure they afford me," she observed once, "they seem to introduce such light and life to the torpid retirement where we live like dormice," who, of course, spent the winters curled up in hibernation.

Upon Anne's death the sole survivor of the six Brontë children, Charlotte turned unsurprisingly for a measure of comfort and solace to her literary confidant. "A year ago—had a prophet warned me how I should stand in June 1849," she wrote numbly to Williams, "I should have thought—this can never be endured." And now "it is over." "Branwell—Emily—Anne are gone like dreams—gone as Maria and Elizabeth went twenty years ago. One by one I have watched them fall asleep on my arm—and closed their glazed eyes—I have seen them buried one by one—" And yet she had, somehow, endured it. But these tragedies had occurred in a family unusually close-knit and thrown in on itself. "The great trial," she wrote Ellen Nussey, "is when evening closes and night approaches—At that hour we used to assemble in the dining-room—we used to talk." And now? "Now I sit by myself."

She had not wanted to be lionized before—and still didn't. But the incognito of Currer Bell was at last beginning to unravel, and perhaps, too, the unspeakable loneliness of the now desolate Haworth made some company and socializing seem less repellent. George Smith was kind, writing to her to ask how she was and to offer his support. Come to London, he said. She set off for the city at the end of November to visit the Smiths. No more of the forbidding Chapter Coffeehouse of Paternoster Row where the sisters had stayed on their first visit, but instead, the Smiths insisted, she must stay with them. In the pleasant, family atmosphere of their home at Westbourne Place, Paddington, she received the balm of thoughtful, solicitous attention—"Fire in my bedroom evening and morning—two wax candles—"—the most expensive kind—"&c., &c."

Her tiny stature and emotional vulnerability inclined the otherwise watchful Mrs. Smith (who feared unwise entanglements by her son with single females) to collude with him in keeping a harsh review of *Shirley* in the *Times* away from their guest. Even in the midst of all her siblings' illnesses, Charlotte had been able to keep working away at her novel on the subject of the Luddite riots, although she claimed "I have no knowledge of politics." The book had been published not long before she arrived in London, and the Smiths tried in vain to hide the unfavorable article from her. Ever determined to face the worst, however, Charlotte insisted on reading the stinging *Times* review. Through the paper, Mrs. Smith caught a glimpse of "tears stealing down the face" of the tiny woman as she read the review.

Smith determined to get his most celebrated author together with her favorite writer, Thackeray. (Significantly, Charlotte did not like Dickens' writings well enough to want to be presented to him.) Smith, of course, wanted to please Charlotte, but if in the process he could have an excuse to talk to the now increasingly famous author whose work he had in fact once vainly offered to publish when Thackeray was working on *Vanity Fair*—well, what an opportunity for an ambitious young publisher. Thackeray, of course, had thought *Jane Eyre* terrific, so, yes, he would come to dinner to meet "Currer Bell," he said. Smith cautioned the great writer not to do or say anything to anyone else that would blow Charlotte's cover as the author of *Jane Eyre* and *Shirley*. But, of course, said Thackeray to Smith, "you are speaking to a man of the world."

Discretion regarding Charlotte Brontë's identity was perhaps not Thackeray's major concern at the moment, however. He was only some weeks recovered from an almost fatal illness, one that had interrupted serialization of his new novel. In June of 1848, the month *Vanity Fair* concluded, Thackeray had agreed with Bradbury and Evans to do another novel for them, this time an autobiographical work about a young writer, Pendennis. The first of its new yellow-covered serial numbers began to appear in November 1848.

And, of course, Thackeray was also undergoing the torment of the allegations about he and Charlotte Brontë being lovers that gossips like Jane Carlyle found so titillating. Through George Smith, Thackeray had gallantly relayed to Charlotte the information that the two of them were rumored to be lovers to spare her the shock of the story reaching her from some other source. "The very fact of his not complaining at all and addressing me with such kindness," Charlotte wrote in reply to

Mr. Smith Williams of her unwitting faux pas, "increases my chagrin." Little did she know that meanwhile Thackeray was furious. "My friend Gale at a dinner of Winchester big wigs had heard that I was a wretch with whom nobody should associate," he wrote a few years later, as the *Jane Eyre* mistress story continued to circulate, "that I had seduced a governess named Jane Eyre by whom I had ever so many &c." Never mind that it was utterly untrue. "The story of Jane Eyre, seduction, surreptitious family in Regents Park, &c., which you may or mayn't have heard, all grew out of this confounded tradition," he wrote in 1856. "I never spoke 3 words to the lady and had no more love for my Governess than for my grandmother."

And now here they were to have dinner together, at George Smith's. Charlotte had only a small breakfast on the day set for the big dinner with her literary idol, and then, in an attack of nerves at the prospect of meeting Thackeray, ate nothing thereafter. Her imposing literary hero showed up at the Smiths at seven, and Charlotte stayed in the background as the guests foregathered. "When Mr Thackeray was announced and I saw him enter, looked up at his tall figure, heard his voice the whole incident was truly dream-like—I was only certain it was true because I became miserably destitute of self-possession." She and Thackeray were not introduced, and then, as dinner was announced, he went up to her, offered his hand, and said, "Shake hands." And then the four-foot-nine woman and the six-foot-three giant went down to dinner.

Later, when the ladies, following custom, had retired at the dinner's conclusion, Smith offered the famous novelist a cigar, which was then still something of a rare indulgence. The great man puffed away until, after the passage of a suitable interval, he and Smith made their way to the drawing room to rejoin the fair sex. Keep her incognito, Smith had warned. She does not want publicity or notoriety. As they approached the ladies Smith was therefore horrified to hear Thackeray advance on Charlotte—had he had too much to drink?—quoting directly from *Jane Eyre*, "'sweetbrier and southern wood, jasmine, pink

OPINIONS OF THE PRESS

ON MR. BELL'S FIRST NOVEL

"'Jane Eyre' it will be recollected was edited by M
Currer Bell. Here are two tales so nearly related t
'Jane Eyre' in cast of thought, incident and language; a
to excite curiosity. All three might be the work of on
hand."—*Athenæum.*

"The work bears affinity to 'Jane Eyre.'"—*Spectator*

"Written with considerable ability."—*John Bull.*

"A work of very great talent."—*Examiner.*

"The work is strangely original. It reminds us c
'Jane Eyre.' The author is a Salvator Rosa with hi
pen.—*Britannia.*

"We strongly recommend all our readers who lov
novelty to get this story, for we can promise them the
never read anything like it before. It is like 'Jan
Eyre.'"—*Douglas Jerrold.*

"It is a colossal performance."—*Atlas.*

The use by the Brontë sisters of pseudonyms—"Acton Bell" (for Anne), "Ellis Bell"
(for Emily), and "Currer Bell" (for Charlotte)—led some to think Anne's novel
Agnes Grey, *Emily's* Wuthering Heights, *and Charlotte's* Jane Eyre *were*

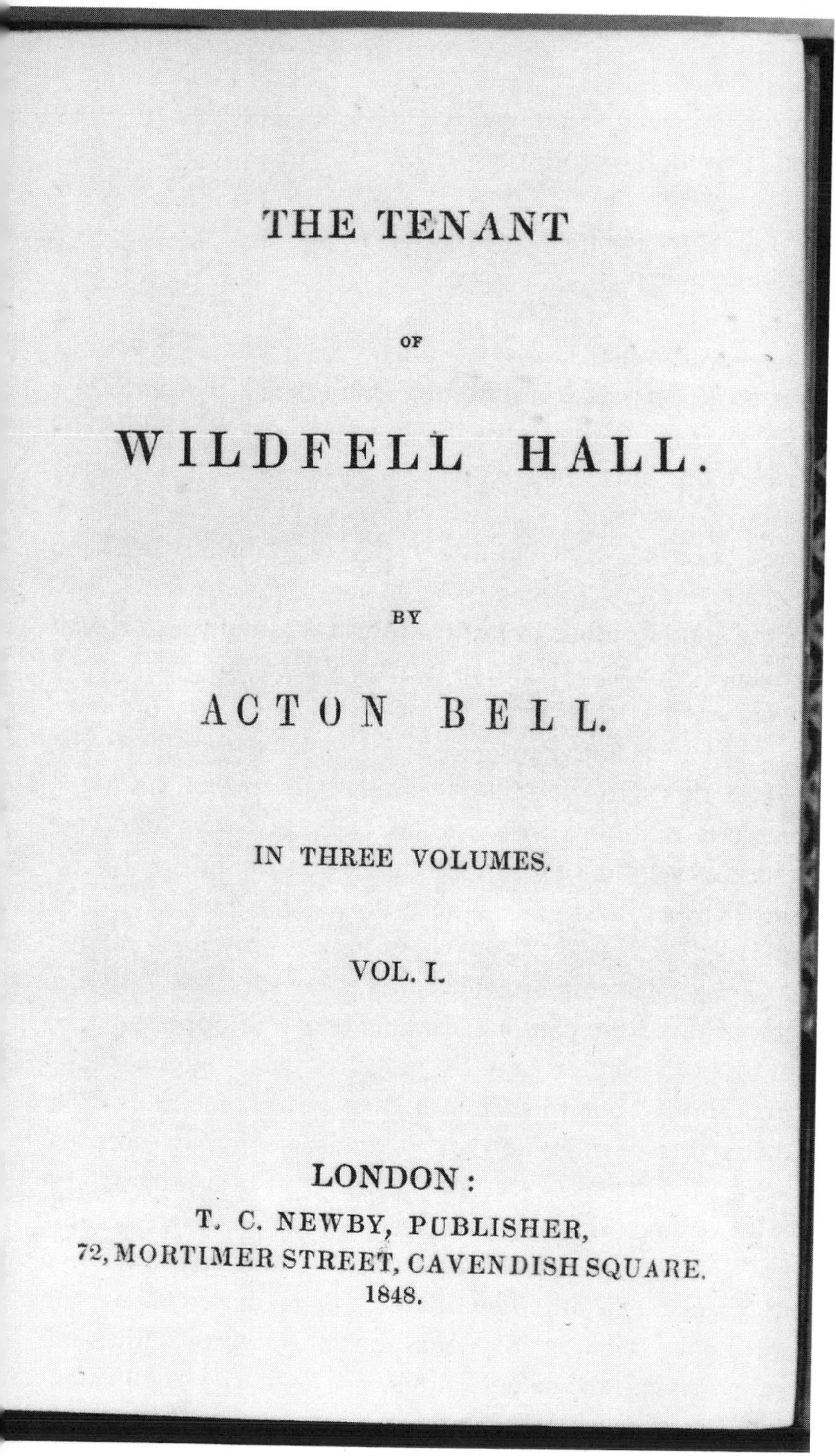

THE TENANT

OF

WILDFELL HALL.

BY

ACTON BELL.

IN THREE VOLUMES.

VOL. I.

LONDON:

T. C. NEWBY, PUBLISHER,

72, MORTIMER STREET, CAVENDISH SQUARE.

1848.

all by the same author. Anne and Emily's unscrupulous publisher Thomas Newby exploited this confusion, as shown here, to promote Anne's second book after Jane Eyre *became a hit.*

and rose, had long been yielding their evening sacrifice of incense. This new scent was neither of shrub nor flower. It was—I knew it well—it was the scent of Mr. Rochester's cigar.'"

Mr. Rochester's cigar?

Smith was appalled. Even in that pre-Freudian era, it was at the very least an astoundingly gauche remark. To those who recognized the passage it hinted ostentatiously at Charlotte's carefully guarded literary identity. In addition, it evoked one of the lushest and most suggestive scenes in her novel, one in which the heavy, deeply scented warmth of an English summer evening—described by Charlotte in ripe, full imagery—set the scene for an erotically charged exchange between the lonely governess and her moody employer. And was not this fictional relationship the very same one in which both the anonymous reviewer in the *Quarterly Review* and countless ordinary Londoners had claimed to have seen depicted the illicit relationship of Thackeray and his governess "Currer Bell"?

Charlotte was horrified—and shot George Smith an accusing glance. What did Thackeray think he was doing?

And yet—and yet—she would be back to London again. She returned to Haworth, but now it was only she and her father of the once numerous Brontës who survived, and she must have found the parsonage wearisome and oppressive. So she returned to London in early June 1850, staying once again with the Smiths, but this time at their new home at No. 76, Gloucester Terrace in Hyde Park Gardens, and the two literary giants tried again. Thackeray paid a two-hour morning call on Charlotte at the Smiths—and, perhaps in revenge for his embarrassment of her on her last visit, Charlotte spent the time calling Thackeray's attention to the things that were wrong with his books (he was frivolous, she said), Smith witnessing Thackeray trying to defend himself in what the publisher termed a "queer scene."

Thackeray was already being arraigned for an irresponsible use of his gifts. In his new serial, *Pendennis*, Thackeray had painted a ludicrous, irreverent portrait of the literary world of his youth, including those colorful old novel publishers Colburn and Bentley, whom he portrayed, respectively, as Bacon and Bungay. "It was at the period when the novel called 'fashionable' was in vogue among us," wrote Thackeray, harking back to the days of the silver fork novel. "Bungay knew no more about novels than he did about Hebrew or Algebra, and neither read nor understood any of the books which he published and paid for; but he took his opinions from his professional advisers and from Mrs. B." Colburn's stand-in, Thackeray made clear, was driven largely by a mindless competition. "Bacon, when he found out Bungay was about to [buy Pendennis's novel], of course, began to be anxious, and curious, and desired to outbid his rival." His ridicule of Bacon and Bungay and more made for a portrait of the literary community sufficiently rancid for the *Morning Chronicle* to remark in January 1850 that *Pendennis* was responsible for "fostering a baneful prejudice" against writers.

Which was all right except that it had seemed that the novel as a genre was finally beginning to become respectable. The publication of *Vanity Fair* plus *Dombey*, *Jane Eyre*, and Mrs. Elizabeth Gaskell's *Mary Barton* was a sign that at last status and respectability had shifted decisively away from poetry, whose prestige had been at its height during the Romantic era. In his 1849 *Outlines of English Literature* Thomas Shaw announced that "the prevailing literary form, or type, of the present age, is undoubtedly the novel—the narrative picture of manners; just as the epic is the natural literary form of the heroic or traditional period." "The novel is now what the drama was in the reigns of Elizabeth and James I," said the *Prospective Review* in 1849. Sure sign: how-to books for the aspiring novelist were now in evidence. The 1842 *Hints and Directions for Authors in Writing and Publishing Their Works* suggested helpfully that for those undertaking a three-decker, three volumes of 300 to 324 pages each with twenty-six lines to a page was the standard; another how-to book pegged the requisite length at 300 pages per volume, with twenty-two lines a page of eight words per line. In a backhanded tribute to the novel's new popularity, the *Dublin Review* in September 1849 even discussed what it called "a strange, but often-repeated, offer 'to make the literary reputation' of any aspirant after fame, by composing, and allowing to be published under his name, any sort of work, from a three-volume romance to a shilling pamphlet." Even poets were trying to climb on the bandwagon. Elizabeth Barrett Browning decided in October 1844 that "a true poetical novel—modern, and on the level of the manners of the day—might be as good a poem as any other, and much more popular besides," and she set to writing the book-length *Aurora Leigh* to translate her insight into action.

Despite novels becoming all the rage, in 1847 *Fraser's* had noted "the unwillingness of literary men to own themselves professional authors; they almost all pretend to be barristers or gentlemen at large." To an author in 1847 who went to get the birth of his child officially registered, the registrar suggested, when filling in the father's occupation, "We'll say Gent." and began to inscribe the abbreviation in the register until he was seized by doubt: "I suppose, sir, authors rank as gents?"

So on January 5, 1850, when *Pendennis* was beginning to appear, Forster leaped in to chastise Thackeray in the pages of the *Examiner* for a "disposition to pay court to the non-literary class by disparaging his fellow-laborers." The *Chronicle* bashed Thackeray, too. Thackeray in return on January 12 wrote in a letter to the *Chronicle* that Forster seemed to suggest that in some of his actions Thackeray might be simply a "rogue and a cheat." Bad feeling all around.

Now, five months later, Thackeray asked Smith and Charlotte to dinner at his home the same day she criticized him at the Smiths', and he invited some of the leading literary lights or hangers-on of the city, including Mrs. Brookfield, a Mrs. Procter, who was married to the poet "Barry Cornwall" to whom Thackeray had dedicated *Vanity Fair*, and her beautiful young daughter, Adelaide. As dinner time drew near, Thackeray paced up and down the room. The Thackeray girls, now aged thirteen and ten, had been allowed to stay up to enjoy the great occasion. When the carriage arrived, their father went out into the hall and fetched in Mr. Smith and Charlotte. Everyone, apparently, was in a serious mood. After they had adjourned to the dining room, Charlotte, her morning anger evidently spent, was mesmerized by her host, gazing at him with a reverent concentration as she answered his remarks, not eating while he murmured to her as he carved the meat.

But as the evening wore on, the crackling, witty, insightful literary conversation that everyone had so anticipated failed to materialize. (Was Charlotte's social unease, in addition to her normal shyness, a factor? Cattily, Mrs. Brookfield noted for future generations that Charlotte was wearing an ill-fitting hairpiece in an effort to conceal her high-domed forehead.) When dinner was finally over and the ladies retreated to the study, Charlotte sank down on the sofa and began a quiet conversation with the Thackerays' aptly named governess, a lady with the Dickensian name of Miss Trulock.

The lovely Mrs. Brookfield finally ventured to say in a desperate conversational gambit that she hoped Charlotte Brontë liked London.

There was a silence.

Did the astute Charlotte pick up on the heavily charged interpersonal tension between the lonely Thackeray and the beautiful Jane Brookfield, flattered at the attention now paid to her by the novelist friend of her, alas, increasingly unsuccessful husband?

"I do and I don't," came back Charlotte's curt reply finally to Mrs. Brookfield's remark about London—which was about as insightful a comment as Charlotte apparently offered that evening.

The dismal tone of the evening was ultimately too much for Thackeray. After Charlotte and her publisher finally said their farewells, Anny flitted through the hall and spotted her father opening the front door with his hat on. When he saw Anny, he silently put his finger to his lips, then stepped out of the house—

and quietly shut the door behind him, leaving a drawing room full of ladies all wondering where was Mr. Thackeray? Where, indeed? "I vaguely answered that I thought he was coming back," said Anny, but he didn't. He had fled, abandoning his sinking, if not sunken, party, for refuge at his club.

Meanwhile Charlotte and George Smith rattled back to his mother's in his carriage. Young Miss Procter was quite good-looking, as Charlotte had noticed—as she had also noticed George Smith's interested appraisal of Miss Procter's charms. In the carriage, Charlotte now leaned forward and in her best take-charge manner put her hands on her young publisher's knees. "She would make you a very nice wife," she said to the startled Smith. Who? "Oh! you know whom I mean," she said knowingly. An interesting interchange, considering the rather familiar nature of such a gesture by an unchaperoned, unmarried woman to a single man in that era when unmarried members of the opposite sex did not even address each other by their first names—unless engaged.

Was it just Charlotte? Was it that publishers were so sexy? Or was it in part a function of the fact that in few other environments in that era did women meet men in the workplace on an equal—or almost equal—footing except in the field of letters? By virtue of her intellectual or literary gifts, a female novelist or writer might be thrown together on a basis of at least some professional equality with a man, if he were her publisher.

The closeness between many publishers and their authors was a function of an old-fashioned gentlemanliness, perhaps, and the small and intimate one-to-one scale of author-publisher relations in those days when publishing was a family affair; publishers like Smith could even put up a visiting author like Charlotte Brontë in their homes. It also doubtless reflected the increasing care that sensible publishers bestowed on their best-selling writers, who were responsible for ever-larger shares of their firms' revenues. Indeed, Smith would later help Mrs. Gaskell buy a house when she switched to his firm from Chapman and Hall; Henry Blackett would offer to personally escort Mrs. Oliphant back from Rome when her husband died there (and the publisher John Blackwood immediately sent her a £200 loan). The Macmillans helped Lewis Carroll to get theater tickets (always on the far right side because he was deaf in the right ear and always at least some rows back so the arm waving of the conductor wouldn't distract him) and even to get his watch repaired. And her faithful publisher John Blackwood purchased a pug on which the childless Marian Evans ("George Eliot") could lavish affection and provided Evans and her companion, George Lewes, with opera tickets.

Which still did not altogether answer the question: What happened when the writers were single, youngish women and their publishers psychologically, as well as legally, available?

After caring for her widowed father for some thirteen years after her mother had died, the twenty-nine-year-old Marian Evans had found herself to all intents and purposes alone in the world upon his death in 1849. She had mended clothes, read him Scott alone in the evenings, and made the household's mince pies and currant jelly while reading and studying intensely. (When it came to writing of rural life, she knew what she was talking about. One of her hands, she told a friend, was wider than the other because of all the butter and cheese she had had to make over the years.)

And now upon her father's death there she was with no dependents and no relatives with whom it would be both convenient and interesting for her to stay. But she had a talent for writing articles and doing translations, including that of a fifteen-hundred-page German life of Jesus, which she did for an energetic and politically liberal, not to say radical, young London publisher named John Chapman (no relation to Dickens' publisher), who had also become the publisher of Carlyle's friend Ralph Waldo Emerson. Evans' father had left her only £2,000, which, with the best management in the world, would not yield her more than £90 a year. She was also, at least in theory, somewhat of a liberal thinker, having to her father's horror broken away from the church when she was a young adult after being earnestly devout. "Our little humbug of a queen is more endurable than the rest of her race because she calls forth a chivalrous feeling," she grumbled during the revolutionary unrest of 1848, "and there is nothing in our constitution to obstruct the slow progress of *political* reform. This is all we are fit for at present."

What a coincidence. In addition to publishing works like the much-praised English translation of Jesus' life that Marian had done, the handsome and charming young John Chapman had taken over a radical quarterly called the *Westminster Review* from John Stuart Mill's father. To a freethinker like Marian (she had changed the spelling of her first name from "Mary Ann" after a trip abroad), the *Review* had the gratifying distinction of being barred by the Merchants Library in Sheffield, banned on the grounds of heresy from the Edinburgh Select Subscription Library, and being unavailable anywhere in the city to the 100,000 inhabitants of Nottingham.

Then why not go to London, where she could perhaps work as a professional writer. The Chapmans' home (for there were a Mrs. Chapman and three children) had been built as a hotel and was too big for the Chapmans alone. The publishing shop was on the first floor of the house and the apartments of the family and boarders above, and, in fact, the Chapmans were in the habit of renting out rooms for forty-five to fifty shillings a week. Notable literary folk, including Horace Greeley and Emerson on an 1848 visit, had stayed there.

She was not altogether at ease, true, about her newfound independence. "What shall I be without my Father? It will seem as if a part of my moral nature were gone. I had a horrid vision of myself last night becoming earthly sensual and devilish for want of that purifying restraining influence." She was earnest, shy, and no beauty, but she had had a crush on her language teacher as a girl, and a young painter had proposed to her in 1845. She was not unduly humble about her abilities. In late 1850, she had met a woman named Eliza Lynn, a writer for

A photograph of Charlotte Brontë taken about 1849. She stood four feet nine inches. Her publisher, George Smith, noted privately at their first meeting that she "had a quaint old-fashioned look" with "but little feminine charm about her."

the *Review* and a former boarder with the Chapmans, who was supporting herself by her writing. Marian found her unimpressive; if Miss Lynn could do it, so could she. Before long Marian had packed up her things and headed for London, where in January 1851, she moved into a distant, tiny upstairs room at the Chapmans'. She had soon agreed to act as Chapman's assistant editor, writing, critiquing, editing, and generally running the *Westminster Review*.

In the process of going to work for Chapman, she stepped into a controversy agitating the literary community that revealed the changing relations of authors and publishers. In the days when presses had been small and publishers' capital limited, publishers sometimes had to not only get authors to pay for publishing, but, in addition, often had to collaborate with one another on the publication of any big projects. The large, multivolume edition of Shakespeare that appeared in 1818 was produced by a consortium of forty publishers, and joint endeavor extended to other areas as well. In a jovial collective get-together called the trade dinner held at the Chapter Coffeehouse where the Brontës had stayed on their trip to London, publishers drummed up orders from booksellers en masse at an auction after a leisurely dinner together. Authors were strategically placed next to booksellers at the congenial meal on the theory that it would be harder for the booksellers not to bid—and bid well—for the latest work of their new acquaintance after dinner if he were sitting right at their elbow.

But joint understandings also extended to remaindering. Any purchaser of remainders, it was generally agreed, would undertake to sell them at full price, even if that sometimes meant destroying half or more of the remainders the purchaser had bought. Discounts in violation of these rules was frowned upon. An ex-shoemaker, one James Lackington, horrified his book business peers in the late 1790s by knocking several houses together in Finsbury Square north of the old City and then putting up a huge sign saying CHEAPEST BOOKS IN LONDON. At his vast "Temple of the Muses," an exuberant dome surmounted by a cheerful flag beckoned customers to examine the riches within, and he sold thousands of remaindered books at, horror of horrors, cut-rate prices. (By 1791, he estimated he was selling more than 100,000 volumes a year.) His fellow book-sellers showed their appreciation of his innovation by trying to drive him out of business. Knowing that good books were all bound in calfskin, he later recalled darkly that "there were not wanting among the booksellers, some who were mean enough to assert that all my books were bound in sheep."

Some years later, the Booksellers Association, formed in 1829, tried to prevent the sale of "under-priced" books by hir-ing spies to find out how some booksellers were managing to avoid their boycott. "By a lucky accident, the spies were sus-pected and apprehended by the police" when the two suspected booksellers they were trailing went by boat to Greenwich in March 1831. A further pursuit by the spies the following month to "Sheerness exhausted the finances of the officials, and they were reduced to the humiliation of asking, from the very men they were pursuing, a loan to enable them to return." And then in 1852, with profits in the publishing industry growing and the stakes becoming commensurately larger, the publishers tried once again to bring recalcitrant booksellers into line, this time under the leadership of a committee that included George Smith, William Longman, Richard Bentley, and John Murray. When John Chapman decided to sell American books at lower rates than the price prescribed by the publishers' committee, the new organization of publishers refused to supply him with any more of their books.

Chapman, being, of course, a good radical, fought back against the oligopolists. He blasted the publishers with an arti-cle written by Marian in the April 1852 *Westminster Review*, bad-gered members of Parliament to intervene on behalf of his stand for free trade, and drummed up support from celebrated literary folk. Enlisting the help of Herbert Spencer, Chapman rounded up a crowd of literary luminaries that included George Lewes, Wilkie Collins, George Cruikshank, Dickens, Dr.

Peter Roget of *Thesaurus* fame, and others. (Bradbury and Evans, perhaps because as the owners of *Punch* they were more involved in magazine publishing or perhaps because their leading author, Dickens, was on Chapman's side, also signed on in opposition to their fellow publishers.) Laissez-faire! It was the high tide of liberalism. William Gladstone, the future Liberal prime minister, even had boycotted booksellers supplied with some of his pamphlets on Italy in defiance of the ban.

The great men came to a meeting at Chapman's on May 4, 1852, with Marian Evans sitting in as unobtrusive acolyte. Speeches were made, proposals were proposed, and a representative of the publishers was duly ridiculed. Dickens, thought Marian Evans, was a good chairman, "preserving a courteous neutrality of eyebrow, and speaking with clearness and decision." As the last impressive guest made his way out the door around midnight, leaving only Spencer, herself, and Chapman behind, Marian sat down at the piano and pounded out "See the Conquering Hero Comes" in acknowledgment of Chapman's triumph. The publishers capitulated—they would, in fact, permit booksellers to give whatever discount they wanted.

So now writers could unite against publishers—and win. If free trade was partly to thank for the victory, one additional reason the writers could pull this off was because the new status of the novel had helped to raise the status of the author. As novels had become respectable, novelists had become figures to reckon with. Dickens, most notably, was now a world-famous figure. In Germany he was already being assigned as a school text, and in Russia the young Feodor Dostoyevsky, who implored his second wife to read Dickens to their children when he was not home, would beseech her to read it on their honeymoon, and, his wife later wrote, to lighten the burden of their poverty, "Feodor Mikhailovich would call himself Mr. Micawber and me Mrs. Micawber." Dickens' picture would hang in Count Leo Tolstoy's study at Yasnaya Polyana. Even when years later Tolstoy would reject the frivolous life he had led for one of ascetic Christianity, Dickens, he would say, had written well. "All his characters are my personal friends," Tolstoy told a visitor in 1903. "I am constantly comparing them with living persons," and he spoke of how "Dickens interests me more and more." In the early 1840s Thackeray even attended a Paris adaptation of *Nicholas Nickleby* (in which the villainous "Monsieur Squarrs" attacked poor "Smeek" in front of "Neeckleby"—"and when Squeers raised his stick to strike— pouf! pif! *un, deux, trois, et la!*—Monsieur Nicholas flanqued him several *coups de poing*, and sent him *bientôt* groveling *à terre*.")

A figure as prominent as Dickens was by now could be pardoned for looking back over his life to contemplate writing it up with confidence the public would be interested. In 1845 Dickens was thirty-three, and sometime between 1845 and 1847 he had written part of an autobiography, only to discard it upon reaching the period in his life when he had suffered his humiliating rejection from Maria Beadnell. He burned the autobiography, in fact, at the bitter memory of her rejection. The recollection of his early consignment to the blacking factory also continued to haunt him. "It is wonderful to me how I could have been so easily cast away at such an age," he wrote in midlife of the unconcern with which, it seemed to him, his parents had abruptly dropped any plans to provide their son with a good education. "Even now, famous and caressed and happy, I often forget in my dreams that I have a dear wife and children; even that I am a man; and wander desolately back to that time of my life." There were the walks in which Dickens haunted the streets of London at night. Perhaps because the sense of abandonment and imagined worthlessness was so great, night alone seemed to alleviate the pain—"In my walks at night I have walked there often, since then, and by degrees I have come to write this." No one—not even his wife and children—had learned of this period except Forster.

Yet the urge to tell his story was still strong.

So, having abandoned an actual autobiography, Dickens in early 1849 went swiftly to work on a fictional one. Significantly, it was his first novel to be written in the first person, and one in which Mr. Micawber, an improvident, self-deluding fool who talks in the long-winded, pompous fashion of Dickens' father, would play a prominent role. Thackeray lauded the new novel into which all Dickens' feelings of being abandoned were now being poured. "Get *David Copperfield*: by Jingo it's beautiful—(it beats the yellow chap of this month hollow)," Thackeray told his friend the Reverend Brookfield—although he then told Jane Brookfield that, of course, one reason *David Copperfield* was so good was that Dickens was finally learning from Thackeray. "It pleases the other Author to see that Dickens who has long left off alluding to his the OA's work has been copying the OA, and greatly simplifying his style and foregoing the use of fine words."

Or was he?

"You said it had affinity to *Jane Eyre*," said Charlotte Brontë to Mr. Smith Williams when Smith, Elder sent her a copy of *David Copperfield*, noting similarities between the two books. "It has now and then—" Was Dickens' use of the first person in *David Copperfield* influenced by Charlotte's publication of the first-person *Jane Eyre* the year before (though Dickens claimed not to have read it), as well as by his destroyed autobiography? Perhaps. But reading *Copperfield* made Charlotte once again realize what a provincial and retiring country person she was. "What an advantage has Dickens in his varied knowledge of men and things!" she marveled of the book.

"The big Babylon," Charlotte Brontë called London. Her admiration for Dickens' wide knowledge and the conflict of Charlotte and Thackeray in some measure reflected differences between the bustling new industrial city versus the country. She was still only a shy country dweller, after all, and Dickens was a world-famous, urban—and increasingly urbane—master of the novel with some half a dozen novels under his belt. And "the Novels of Dickens and Thackeray are, most of them, novels of London," wrote the author of *British Novelists and Their Styles* in 1859. "Dickens and Thackeray might well be consid-

Alexander Macmillan, cofounder with brother Daniel of the publishing house that bore their name. The emphasis of the house was originally on religious and academic books (their first shop was in Cambridge) but in 1865 they published Alice in Wonderland.

ered as the founders of a peculiar sub-variety of the Novel of English Life and Manners, to be called 'The British Metropolitan Novel'." Dickens, a London dweller almost his entire life, knew every inch and street of London virtually by heart and had basically no feel for nor interest in the English countryside. Thackeray rarely set foot in the countryside except to visit and was an inveterate clubman and diner-out. He loved the fact that the capital city "has a tough work-day appearance so much the better—look how every body is pushing forward and looking onward, and anxiously struggling ... O this London is a grand place for scheming, and rare fun for a man with broad shoulders who can push through the crowd." His friend the essayist and statesman Thomas Macaulay, equally, was an urbanist. "Nature holds no allure for me," he wrote at age fifteen, and like Dickens, he loved to take long walks though the city he adored.

Love of the countryside, its flora and fauna and its freedom from the bustle and noise of the city, makes an appearance only in the fiction of the women—like Mrs. Gaskell, the Brontës, and "George Eliot." The countryside, the changing of the seasons, and the flowering of hedgerows and cottage gardens are all depicted with a love and nostalgia that consciously and genially equates the good and the rural. For opportunity, Marian Evans sought out London, but even she never managed to feel altogether at home there. While it would become her companion George Lewes' dream to start his own publishing house, Marian, characteristically, would dream "of a nook quite in the country, far away from Palaces crystal or otherwise, with an orchard behind me full of old trees and rough grass, and hedgerow paths among the endless fields where you meet nobody." Like Charlotte Brontë and Mrs. Gaskell, she remained a country girl at heart. "In the meantime the business of life shuts us up within the environs of London and within sight of human advancement, which I should be so very glad to believe in without seeing," she would write dryly.

Perhaps not altogether coincidentally, the women disliked

the city-based genre of the serial, the offspring of the tavern-based magazine, with its rapid pace, sometimes helter-skelter development, and its need for month-after-month invention on a relentless deadline. It was not a part of the world in which they daily lived and worked, as it was for journalists, magazine writers, and editors like Thackeray and Dickens. Charlotte declined an offer in early 1851 from the *New York Tribune* to do a serial and likewise a suggestion from George Smith later that year that she do a serial novel. No. Unless perhaps you "give Currer Bell the experience of a Thackeray or the animal spirits of a Dickens," she replied, "and then repeat the question. Even *then* he would answer, 'I will publish no Serial of which the last number is not written before the first comes out.'" Likewise, Mrs. Gaskell would find it virtually impossible to write her novel *North and South* serially for Dickens' magazine *Household Words* under the pressure created by the insatiable weekly demand for more, more, more. "I believe I've been as nearly dazed and crazed with this c____, d____ be h____ to it story as can be," she had told a friend frantically as the weeks wore on. It produced, she said, "some of the most felling headaches I ever had in my life." And still the sales of the magazine fell.

There were, in fact, few serialists except Dickens and Thackeray who consistently used the format—Charles Lever tried, as did others—but of the major authors only Dickens stayed the course, book after book, novel after novel. Indeed, at the height of the vogue for serials, in the late 1830s, there were no more than fifteen serials appearing a year. In the 1840s, there were only five a year, and by the late 1860s, the number had shrunk to just one or two annually. But then writing a serial called for a relentless drive, month after month, perhaps only really congenial to someone at the mercy of his own demons, someone not happy unless he walked ten, fifteen, twenty miles a night through the streets of London, as Dickens did, trying to burn off the restlessness in his brain.

The great women writers of Victorian England were never altogether at home in London, despite its many attractions.

And their hesitant attitudes toward the city would show in their writing.

Whether country or city dwellers, however, there were now several novelists who could justifiably count themselves figures of sufficient notoriety and prominence to be veritable celebrities. None equaled Dickens, of course. Still, if not everyone had Dickens' celebrity, there was at least one other author beginning to think himself famous enough that the public would pay to listen to him speak. Making money had been on Thackeray's mind, for himself and to help Minny and Anny. He had tried to wangle an Assistant Secretaryship at the Post Office in 1848 and then unsuccessfully petitioned for a secretaryship to the British Legation in Washington. (What, one wonders, could he not have done with a sequel to *Vanity Fair* that transported Becky Sharp to the United States—and pitted her against Congress?) In a burst of gallows humor, Thackeray in a piece for *Punch* in early 1851 suggested the "advertisement novel," a parody of the mention-the-fancy-accessories silver fork novel. Thackeray created a novelist who tells tradesmen that his new sure-to-be-popular serial novel ("my weekly sale is 281,000") "will be on every table; in the boudoir of the pampered Duke, as in the chamber of the honest artisan. The myriad of foreigners who are coming to London, and are anxious to know about our national manners, will purchase my book, and carry it to their distant homes. So, Mr Tailor, or Mr Haberdasher, or Mr Jeweller—how much will you stand if I recommend you in my forthcoming novel?'" Product plugging, in short, in return for a payoff. "'We are poor, Eliza,' said Harry Hardhand, looking affectionately at his wife,'" Thackeray offered as a sample passage, "'but we have enough, love, have we not, for our humble wants? The rich and luxurious may go to Dillow's or Gobiggin's, but we can get our rooms comfortably furnished at Timmonson's for £20.'"

In the end, Thackeray chose to stick with lecturing instead of shaking down merchants for the carriage trade. In May 1851 it was announced that Thackeray would give six lectures on "The English Humorists" at Willis' Rooms in St. James', an ornate gilded hall with cushioned seats covered in damask, a place eminently suitable for literary presentations to the London gentility and nobility.

The lectures were a great success; not only many of the titled but also Carlyle, Macaulay, Harriet Martineau, Lewes, and Charlotte Brontë attended. Thackeray cleared a tidy £500 for his weekly lectures, helped no doubt by the huge crowds of the curious already in the city to see the Crystal Palace Exhibition. Lecturing was "the easiest and most profitable business" he had tried, he said. Compared to writing novels, it certainly was. By contrast, his initial contract for *Pendennis* (some two years' labor), called for him to be paid just £1,000 a year. Indeed, at the end of his career, Thackeray estimated that about a third of his literary earnings had come from lecturing.

Celebrity writers sometimes agreed to do benefits to help their colleagues who could not make this kind of money. In 1851 and early 1852 Dickens toured a comedy that Bulwer Lytton had written to raise money for a sort of rest home on Bulwer's palatial estate of Knebworth for broken-down writers. And publishers and booksellers, too, were being thrown into what seemed like an increasingly impersonal, increasingly cold marketplace where it was everyone for himself. And at what cost? Alexander Macmillan, a founder of the famous publishing house, wrote Gladstone years after the 1852 discount book battle that the statesman's stance in favor of John Chapman had been a ruinous mistake. Letting booksellers set prices, he said, actually just allowed big booksellers to drive the "independents" out of business by underselling them. Sure, you could throw everything open to the marketplace—but it would destroy the country's intellectual life. Macmillan said sharply,

> Whereas in former years there used to be many booksellers who kept good stocks of solid standard books, one or more in every important town in England,

and these booksellers lived by selling books, the case is now that in country towns few live by bookselling: the trade has become so profitless that it is generally the appendage to a toyshop, or a Berlin wool warehouse and a few trashy novels, selling for a shilling, with flaring covers suiting the flashy contents, and the bookseller who studies what books are good and worth recommending to his customer has ceased to exist.

He continued: "Intelligence and sympathy with literature has gone out of the trade almost wholly. I believe the general intelligence of the country has suffered by it."

But it was not just price cutting that influenced the novel. The high noon of the Victorian era was coming—and with it a growing concentration in the book business. The rise of giant distributors was beginning to affect the novel—and it would soon begin to affect not only the format but also the content of the novel. Ironically, the change came out of that quaintest of eighteenth-century literary institutions, the circulating library.

Marian Evans, age thirty, looking not at all like the scarlet woman to whose home her sometime publisher, George Smith, refused to bring his wife or daughter. Her unmarried cohabitation with George Lewes, who could not get out of a loveless first marriage, put her outside the bounds of respectable society and drove her to adopt the pseudonym George Eliot.

PART 4

"Do Let Me Abuse Mr Newby":

Literary Executors,

Gossip Columnists, and

the Emergence of

the Novelist as

Celebrity

Charles Edward Mudie was born in Chelsea in 1818 to a father who sold secondhand books and newspapers, and lent out books for a penny a volume. The essayist Charles Lamb found the small boy on the floor near the bottom shelves of the alphabetically arranged books—he was making his way through Shakespeare. As Mudie was the youngest of numerous sons, there was no place for him in the family business. In the late 1830s he therefore opened his own bookstore and stationer's shop in the increasingly unfashionable Bloomsbury district on King Street. He published some books, too (ironically, in view of his later career, one-volume novels). Most important: finding that students of the new London University nearby couldn't afford to buy many of the nonfiction books they wanted, one day in 1843 he brought his own personal library down to the shop and put it in the window. According to family legend, every book was out on loan within twenty-four hours—and thus he entered the circulating library business.

Mudie grew fast, buying up surrounding houses into which he expanded in 1852 on New Oxford Street opposite the British Museum library. As his business grew, Mudie began offering publishers a guaranteed advance purchase of some three to four hundred books for their average novel. In a period when the average initial publication was still often only about a thousand books, this was a good deal. In return Mudie got a whopping discount from the publishers—on the order of 50 percent. His library soon became an almost indispensable outlet for publishers eager for guaranteed profit margins, and, thereby, a major player in determining which novels would do well and which badly. "So, *you're* the man that divides the sheep from the goats," Carlyle said to him at a reception in 1850.

Mudie had some things going for him that the ordinary circulating library did not. The first was a cheaper price—only one guinea per year to rent as many volumes as you wanted as compared with the standard six, seven, or eight guineas per annum. In addition, he ran, as he said, a "select" circulating library—by which he meant that his selection was both morally unobjectionable and that it offered nonfiction books as well as junky novels. The tie to London University is significant in this regard. Founded in 1836 as the alternative for Dissenters and other non-Anglicans to Oxford and Cambridge in an effort initiated by John Stuart Mill and others, it represented a new middle-class high-mindedness and soberness of purpose that was then overtaking a host of British institutions. "Novels of objectionable character or inferior ability are almost invariably excluded," Mudie decorously told his subscribers in a somewhat curious but significant turn of phrase.

Historically, indeed, circulating libraries had had a less-than-stellar reputation, owing to the conviction that they stocked trashy romance-style novels read mostly by well-to-do idle women with nothing better to do. "Look at the popular books of a circulating library, and you will find the binding cracked by quantities of powder and pomatum between the leaves" owing to their being read at the hairdresser's, sniffed a contemporary in 1789 in the *Lady's Magazine*. "As an inducement to subscribe Mrs Martin tells us that her Collection is not to consist only of Novels, but of every kind of literature, &, &.," Jane Austen noted dryly of a local circulating library keeper getting into the business in 1798 who sought a respectable clientele. Austen added, "She might have spared this pretension to *our* family, who are great Novel-readers & not ashamed of being so."

Times had changed. The age of fervor for laissez-faire was also one of growing moralism. In 1853 W. H. Smith, the railway book man, got an irate letter attacking Byron's *Don Juan* and asking how he could allow "such a vile book as that to pollute his stalls." Anthony Trollope had had a modest success in 1855 with *The Precentor* (which his publishers insisted on renaming *The Warden*), after leaving Newby for an unimpressive publishing experience with Henry Colburn before ending up at Longmans. But his proposed sequel, *Barchester Towers*, was too racy and immoral, said Longmans' reader, especially the depiction of the wicked, alluring Signora Neroni. (And as Trollope later told George Smith, he had also with respect to *Barchester Towers* had "a terrible & killing correspondence ... with W. Longman because I would make a clergyman kiss a lady whom he proposed to marry.") Likewise, as *Tom Brown's School Days* went to press in 1857, author Thomas Hughes wrote to one of the Macmillans, "When you tell me that you have altered 'beastly' into 'inhumanly' drunk—I suppose etc.—I really think that it is time for me to give up in despair." John Blackwood in the same year would ask Marian Evans to delete from "Janet's Repentance" in *Scenes from Clerical Life* a reference to a minister spitting and a phrase which, after talking of male drinking habits, described how "not more than half a dozen married ladies were frequently observed to become less sure of their equilibrium as the day advanced." The easy days of the 1830s and 1840s just after the notoriously licentious Regency era, when scandal and license were fashionable and amusing, were no longer possible in an era of seriousness and moral rigor.

Of course, the literary atmosphere of London remained strongly masculine. Privately, Thackeray enjoyed the circulation of the bawdy stories and ribaldry that went with male dining out. "'Tis true, tis titty, titty tis tis true," Thackeray noted characteristically on being told at a *Punch* dinner that the rival publication *Fun* was going in for displays of feminine pulchri-

The Reverend Arthur Bell Nicholls, curate to the Reverend Patrick Brontë in Haworth and, ultimately, husband of Charlotte Brontë. His middle name may have inspired the pseudonym Charlotte used when she wrote Jane Eyre.

tude. At another dinner there was mention of a woman having undergone a bladder operation, and Thackeray improvised an obscene limerick, concluding that "They put her to bed/And sewed it with thread/And then the Chirugeon had her!" Beneath the carefully sex-free surface of *Vanity Fair*, Thackeray commented on Becky Sharp's "famous frontal development" and inserted a description of Lady O'Dowd leaving a dance "to retire to the supper-room, *lassata nondum satiata recessit*," a quote from Juvenal's *Satires*, describing the condition of the Roman Empress Messalina ("exhausted but not satisfied") upon returning from a brothel after spending the night there acting as a prostitute.

And it was not just Thackeray, of course. "Boys" would be "boys." In April 1848, Forster had given one of his famous bachelor dinners in his Lincoln's Inn Fields apartments (which Dickens described in his depiction of the chambers of Mr. Tulkinghorn in *Bleak House*) so that Ralph Waldo Emerson could meet Dickens. The former Unitarian minister and sage of Concord now expressed his shock to Dickens and fellow guest Carlyle at the amount of prostitution he had encountered in England. So? Carlyle and Dickens "replied, that chastity in the male sex was as good as gone in our times; &, in England was so rare that they could name all the exceptions," the American recorded. They were perhaps pulling his leg, but if so, Emerson seems not to have realized it. In fact, "Dickens replied, 'that incontinence is so much the rule in England,'" Emerson noted, "that if his own son were particularly chaste, he should be alarmed on his account, as if he could not be in good health."

Which did not mean London had come to seem altogether inhospitable to women writers who were developing ties there.

After returning from the visit to London in late 1849 on which she had first met her publisher George Smith, Charlotte Brontë had grown to rely on the understanding, intelligent man's communications. "I have had no letters from London for a long time," she wrote Ellen Nussey when there was a break in the correspondence, "and am very much ashamed of myself to find, now when that stimulus is withdrawn, how dependent on it I had become. I cannot help feeling something of the excitement of expectation til the post hour comes, and when, day after day, it brings nothing, I get low." Shades of her infatuation at the school with M. Heger in Brussels, when she had first felt an attraction to a knowledgeable, interesting man—and then waited anxiously each day for a communication from her beloved in the mail.

During the summer visit to London in 1850 on which she attended the disastrous dinner party at Thackeray's, Smith invited her to go on an excursion with him and his sister to Edinburgh. Charlotte was beginning to think that possibly, just possibly, it might mean that—or, no, was she just imagining things? "Now I believe that George and I understand each other very well and respect each other very sincerely," she wrote to Ellen. "We both know the wide breach time has made between us—we do not embarrass each other, or very rarely, my six or eight years of seniority"—she was then thirty-four, he twenty-six—"to say nothing of lack of all pretension to beauty &c., are a perfect safeguard." But there it was again—on the one hand, like her talk with Smith in the carriage after Thackeray's party, her words said no—but the putting of her hand on his knee had argued otherwise, and here she was talking of "George" to Ellen at a time when convention permitted the use of first names between unmarried men and women only if they were engaged.

And so Charlotte went to Edinburgh in late June 1850 for two days devoted largely to seeing sights associated with her hero Walter Scott, including the home at Abbotsford where he and Constable had long before planned their unsuccessful assault on the hegemony of the luxury-priced novel, as well as an abbey Scott had restored at Melrose. The day of the literary tourist trade had begun. "Edinburgh compared to London," she wrote, "is like a vivid page of history compared to a huge dull treatise on Political Economy—and as to Melrose and Abbotsford the very names possess music and magic."

And then there was seeing George Smith. A half year later, in January 1851, Charlotte, for all the world like an anxious teenager after a first date, sent a letter she had received from Smith to her friend to say what did she think of the missive?—and, again, in a self-protective disavowal, simultaneously reproved herself for thinking that there was any feeling on Smith's side for her. "—I think the 'undercurrent' amounts simply to this—a kind of natural liking and sense of something congenial. Were there no vast barrier of age, fortune, etc. there is perhaps enough personal regard to make things possible which are now impossible." Indeed. "If men and women married each other because they liked each other's temper, look, conversation, nature and so on—and if besides, years were more closely equal—the chance you allude to might be admitted as a chance—but other reasons regulate matrimony—reasons of convenience, of connection, of money. Meantime, I am content to have him as a friend."

But was she?

She made a further visit to London in the spring of 1851, during which she heard Thackeray lecture and saw the Crystal Palace. There were definitely some giddy moments when she and "George" visited a phrenologist in the giggly guise of "Mr and Miss Fraser" and, literally, had their heads examined. "Temperament for the most part nervous," said the phrenologist of Charlotte. "Is a fair calculator, and her sense of order and arrangement is remarkably good . . . possesses a fine organ of language." These were pretty relaxed encounters. Did it mean something?

Charlotte's next novel, *Villette*, was derived in part from her relationship with George Smith. When it appeared in January 1853, Thackeray was making his way through America on the lecture tour he had prepped for with his talks during the Crystal Palace Exhibition, and he found the New World as lucrative as he had hoped. Trains whisked him about America, and he thanked providence for that necessary instrumentality of the author tour—modern transportation. Thackeray noted of a fast five-hundred-mile rail trip through the snows of an American winter, "20 years ago that journey wd. have taken a fortnight." "Oughtn't I for one to be grateful to railroads, who never could have made all these dollars without 'em?" He was. In America "I," said Thackeray, "agglomerate dollars with prodigious rapidity." "Why a little New England village in the midst of the snow is more ready with its 100$ [sic] than a great bulky Birmingham or Newcastle with its £20 note," he marveled.

Now, after a correspondent told him she was reading *Villette*, he wrote back in March regarding Charlotte that "I can read a great deal of her life as I fancy in her book." He could "see that rather than have fame, rather than any other earthly good or mayhap heavenly one she wants some Tomkins or another to love her and be in love with." An interesting comment. In *Villette*, Charlotte was sure she had painted George Smith in Dr. John Bretton—and the heroine who attracts him, Lucy Snowe, was a plain, intellectual, vibrant woman, a stand-in for herself. Ah, but would she get her Tomkins? No, said Thackeray. "You see she is a little bit of a creature without a penny worth of good looks, thirty years old I should think, buried in the country, and eating up her own heart there, and no Tomkins will come."

No looks, a country dweller, and thirty years old—except that a Tomkins, if not *the* Tomkins, did come.

A new friend, the vivacious forty-two-year-old contemporary novelist Mrs. (Elizabeth) Gaskell visited Charlotte at Haworth in September 1853. In true Gothic novel fashion, Mrs. Gaskell was "half blown back by the wild vehemence of the wind" when she first reached the parsonage gate, and during her visit she had found the Reverend Brontë stern, forbidding, and distant. "I caught a glare of his stern eyes over his spectacles at Miss Brontë once or twice which made me know my man," she noted ominously, finding herself "afraid of him in my inmost soul."

But by chance she had come when Patrick was still angry

that his curate, the Reverend Arthur Bell Nicholls, had dared to propose to Charlotte. Nicholls as a consequence was now an exile from Haworth, and Mrs. Gaskell seems to have found the parsonage dreary and tense with the unspoken conflict between Charlotte, who had begun to look somewhat favorably on Nicholls, and her father; on the Reverend's part, Mrs. Gaskell mistook it for a habitual, oppressive distance toward his daughter. And that dismal parsonage—"The wind goes piping and wailing and sobbing round the square unsheltered house in a very strange unearthly way," Charlotte's visitor wrote feelingly to her friend, John Forster, Dickens' man Friday.

There had, in fact, been other suitors, one a clerk who worked for George Smith who came to Haworth to fetch one of Charlotte's manuscripts for publication whom she tried, vainly, to find acceptable. But then maybe the problem was that all along she was interested in someone else.

Ironically, the success of her novel and others like it had combined to make publishers sufficiently rich and respectable to be perhaps slightly out of reach. Not so many years before, things might have been different. Publishers were then regarded as glorified tradesmen—"I am a mere publishing bookseller" James Murray had written to Sir Walter Scott. They sold things over a counter like common shopkeepers, after all, in addition to running a small publishing operation on the side. In 1836, Harrison Ainsworth had had to assure John Macrone, one of Dickens' early publishers, that "I do not see the slightest reason why the circumstance of your being a publisher should militate against your admission" to a club which Macrone wished to join.

But as the businesses grew they could hire clerks to do the selling for them, and as the novel and novelists gained in prestige so, too, did publishing by association, and, well, that was rather different. From the cheap paper and cardboard covers hitherto standard (except for the calfskin of the rich), the novel now graduated to cloth covers as the nation's textile industry began to provide cheap cloth in quantities sufficient to cover large numbers of books. (The cloth idea came from the Keepsakes, Christmas gift books for young ladies popular in the 1830s that had faux silk covers meant to imitate dresses— Lydgate's wife Rosamond Vincy reads one in *Middlemarch* in what to a contemporary audience would have been an illustration of her shallowness.) As the number of books published grew each year, a need arose for someone who could read incoming manuscripts and recommend or disapprove publication. Hence the "reader," like Mr. Smith Williams, who was not exactly an editor but more of a gatekeeper for incoming manuscripts. Among the ranks of "readers" over the years were George Meredith (whom £250 a year kept alive when his *The Ordeal of Richard Feverel* was rejected by circulating library emperor Charles Mudie as too racy); John Forster; and W. E. Henley, the irascible one-legged author and friend of Robert Louis Stevenson on whom Stevenson modeled *Treasure Island*'s Long John Silver. Indeed, George Smith's firm had come to employ some forty people, a prodigious number in those days, and by 1846 was showing a cash flow of £48,088 a year, even if some of it did come from nonpublishing ventures.

And so when in April 1853, Smith fell in love with a wine merchant's beautiful daughter whom he met at a ball, he proposed. He was accepted in November, and a letter carrying the news from his mother arrived forthwith at Haworth. It was a devastating blow to his most famous author. Charlotte at once canceled a planned visit to London and sent back a load of the books from Smith, Elder that they now often sent her: A few days later she wrote tersely to George, all use of first names forsworn: "My dear Sir. In great happiness, as in great grief—words of sympathy should be few. Accept my meed of congratulation— and believe me Sincerely yours C. Brontë." "Do you think because I am poor, obscure, plain and little, I am soulless and heartless? . . . if God had gifted me with some beauty and much wealth, I should have made it as hard for you to leave me, as it is now for me to leave you." So had spoken the plain and impover-

Mrs. Elizabeth Gaskell, novelist and first biographer of her friend, Charlotte Brontë.
Like other major women novelists, she disliked writing serials but agreed to do so for
Dickens' magazine, Household Words. *The deadlines drove her crazy and*
Dickens, enraged, at one point exclaimed, "O Heaven how I would beat her!"

ished Jane Eyre, of course, when she thought the wealthy and prominent Mr. Rochester was marrying Miss Ingram.

So in April 1854, Charlotte wrote to Mrs. Gaskell that she was, after all, going to marry Reverend Nicholls. "After various visits and as the result of perseverance in one quarter and a gradual change of feeling in others, I find myself what people call 'engaged' . . . My destiny will not be brilliant, certainly, but Mr Nicholls is conscientious, affectionate, pure in heart and life." Not exactly love at first sight.

They were married in June 1854. Before long, Charlotte was pregnant. By January 1855 she was ill. Her illness would not relent and hung on through winter as the wind howled around the old parsonage. She grew weaker and sicker, virtually unable to eat and eventually delirious. She woke one day late in March to find Nicholls by her bed praying that she would recover. Acceptance of the pedestrian man who for so long had sought her hand evidently had finally come to her. "I am not going to die, am I?" she said in a whisper. She could not believe it. "He will not separate us, we have been so happy," she said.

She died early on the morning of March 31, 1855.

Mrs. Gaskell, meanwhile, had not even been aware her friend was sick. She had been slaving away to finish *North and South*, a new novel depicting, like Disraeli's *Young England* trilogy, the gulf between rich and poor.

Mrs. Gaskell, like Thackeray, had been a great admirer of *Jane Eyre*. She had met Charlotte at the home of mutual acquaintances. Soon the two women were sending each other books and warm letters. Charlotte had visited Mrs. Gaskell, who, herself an orphan, was touched at Charlotte's losses and appalled by the melodramatic deprivations breathlessly confided to her by Lady Kay Shuttleworth, at whose home they had met. In January 1853, Charlotte had gone so far as to have George Smith delay publication of *Villette* by four days so that Mrs. Gaskell's new *Ruth* could come out first and get a generous extra amount of publicity.

Mrs. Gaskell had left her home in late 1854, when *North and South* was done, and then fled England altogether for France for a nice two-week vacation in February, as always trying to make herself scarce at review time. (Though she did manage to squeeze in a visit to the Messrs. Hachette, who had started the railway bookstall concession in France equivalent to that of W. H. Smith in England; they bought the right to translate her into French.) Eventually, however, she returned to England and in London a letter reached her in the beginning of April 1855 from Mr. Greenwood, the stationer in Haworth who had supplied the three Brontë sisters with their writing supplies those few short years before—Charlotte was dead.

Mrs. Gaskell was stunned. She had not known of Charlotte's illness. Within weeks she conceived the idea of writing up her recollections of her friend. What a coincidence . . . A June issue of *Sharpe's London Magazine of Entertainment and Instruction* carried "A Few Words About *Jane Eyre*," which recited malicious tales about Charlotte's life. Charlotte's old friend Ellen Nussey was furious and told Reverend Nicholls about it. It needed a good counter-attack, she said, and she suggested Mrs. Gaskell as the counter-attacker.

Mrs. Gaskell was certainly well-known. The lively, sympathetic writer had married William Gaskell, a Unitarian minister whose parish lay in Manchester, the new center of England's textile industry. She had at first been too busy with children to have the will or energy for sustained writing, but the scenes of suffering and hatred she had seen there impressed themselves on her memory, and she was well aware of the demands for rights for the working man that resounded through the fierce political struggles of the Hungry Forties.

After she had lost her beloved, ten-month-old child Willie to scarlet fever in 1845, her husband had encouraged her to write in order to alleviate her loss. Struck by the inequalities of labor and capital, she penned a fiery novel centering on the goading of an honest worker into the murder of a mill owner's son, borrowing from an actual murder that had occurred some ten years before. Through the suggestion of friends it made its way to Dickens' friend and "fixer" John Forster, who had become the reader for Chapman and Hall.

Quite apart from its author's evident talent, *Mary Barton*, as the new book was called, struck a chord because it was so in tune with the whole spirit of revolt now spreading across Europe in 1848 as the culmination of the Hungry Forties. There was revolution in Paris, an uprising in Berlin, disorder in Austria, and in England fears of a mass Chartist uprising in London in mid-April. Would the latter be like Paris all over again? Thousands of dangerous revolutionaries were believed ready to march on London, the Bank of England was barricaded, and the Queen fled to the Isle of Wight. "We were dining at the table of Mr. M.D. Hill, on the 9th of April, 1848, the evening before the expected outbreak of Chartism in London," a contemporary later recalled of a meal he had with Thackeray. "The cloth had scarcely been removed, when he suddenly started up and said, 'Pray excuse me, I must go. I left my children in terror that something dreadful was about to happen.'"

The event proved anticlimactic, but the lines of *Mary Barton* echoed nonetheless: "Carriages still roll along the streets, concerts are still crowded by subscribers, the shops for expensive luxuries still find daily customers, while the workman loiters away his unemployed time in watching these things, and thinking of . . . wailing children asking in vain for enough of food, of the sinking health, of the dying life of those near and dear to him. The contrast is too great." "Times of revolution and dismay"—so had Thackeray described that summer in describing the sales of *Vanity Fair*.

Since then, Mrs. Gaskell had published more novels and stories. Now, in the wake of Charlotte's death, Reverend Nicholls read the article in *Sharpe's* aloud to Charlotte's father. And, as is perhaps not unusual with those who know the actual facts of an event as opposed to how it is reported, the old man found it hilarious—"indeed, I have not seen him laugh as much for some months as he did while I was reading

the article to him," wrote the grieving Reverend Nicholls won-
deringly.

But, on second thought, could one in that day and age
ignore the press? Out of the blue the startled Mrs. Gaskell
received a letter from Reverend Brontë in mid-June of 1855.
Various "articles in newspapers and tracts respecting my dear
daughter Charlotte," he wrote to the minister's wife, stated
"many things that . . . are true, but more false . . . I can see no
better plan, under these circumstances, than to apply to some
established Author, to write a brief account of her life—and to
make some remarks on her works—You, seem to me to be the
best qualified."

Would she write the book?

She would, indeed.

Whether from guilt, business acumen, or plain helpfulness,
George Smith was soon not only supplying Mrs. Gaskell with
correspondence from Charlotte but also agreeing to publish the
book, although, ahem, he would not show her the majority of
the letters Charlotte had written to him on the grounds that
they "contain matter of too purely personal a nature."

Long afterward Mrs. Humphry Ward, when she undertook
to write a preface to *Villette* in 1898 for Smith, Elder, asked
George Smith about his feelings toward his famous author. "I
was amused at your questions," the publisher wrote to Mrs.
Ward after he showed her some letters, perhaps those he had
withheld from Mrs. Gaskell. "No, I never was in the least bit in
love with Charlotte Brontë. I am afraid that the confession will
not raise me in your opinion, but the truth is, I never could have
loved any woman who had not some charm or grace of person,
and Charlotte Brontë had none." But then why did he conceal
the letters if they were so innocent? Or did he perhaps fear
domestic trouble if the exchanges he and Charlotte had had were
revealed? Smith would later recall that his wife repeatedly ques-
tioned his visits to see Marian Evans when the firm was thinking
of publishing her work—until Smith's wife caught a glimpse one
day at the opera of the author's homely appearance.

turn, and pity him. "Poor old boy! Disgusting nonsense! Infernal old pumps," &c. At last one friend descends to particulars.

Friend—"But I say, old fella, what floored you!

Our Swell—Oh! 'ternal history!

Friend—What sort of history? Ancient or modern?

Our Swell—Ah, long before either of 'em! About some swell called William the Conqueror!"

One more example. Our swell weareth a wondrous pair of whitey-brown cool summer trousers, pegtoppian, enormous, magnificent! A friend meeting him attempteth to chaff him.

Friend—"Hallo, old fella! what superb bags! Why are those trousers like the two French towns?"

(It will be perceived that the friend aimeth at the old joke, anent Toulon and Toulouse!)

Our Swell (pondering a minute, then answering dreamily)—"Two French towns! my trousers! Oh, ah! you mean something about Nankin, I suppose!"

LITERARY TALK.

Finding that our pen and ink portrait of Mr. Charles Dickens has been much talked about and extensively quoted, we purpose giving, each week, a sketch of some literary celebrity. This week our subject is

Mr. W. M. THACKERAY.

HIS APPEARANCE.

Mr. Thackeray is forty-six years old, though from the silvery whiteness of his hair he appears somewhat older.

"Yes, yes," broke in the hosier, "of course you will; by all means, do. But first finish the note—"

"If thus my father still continues obdurate, we, who have lived but for each other, at least can die together."

"Certainly; it's the least you can do. A very sensible girl, that."

"I shall be at the Railway Station at nine o'clock to-morrow morning.

"Till death! your own

"JEMIMA."

"Dowse, my friend, wish me joy; I really begin to think the doctors have made a mistake after all."

"So do I," was the brief response.

"Let us go and quaff a bumper to the health of Jemima—tell me, Dowsy, what will you take?"

"Cold, if I stand here much longer, I shall go home."

"Home! and you call yourself a friend—go to Bath!"

Upon that word, the Touters who had come creeping back, spake as with one voice—

"Bath! sir! yes sir! hot bath? cold bath? hip or shower?"

Dowse, who was beginning to shiver in his wet garments, hesitated, and with a Margate Touter, to hesitate was to be lost.

"Well, I think a hot bath might do me good, while you dry my clothes."

"Of course it will, sir; all right sir, this way sir!"

"And the other gent?" said the second Touter, approaching Poppleton.

"No," said that gentleman; "I'll wait."

"This door for the waiting-room."

Poppleton, still in heroics, moved towards the door as directed. Dowse placed his hand upon his arm.

"Poppleton!"

"Jemima!"

This was too much for Dowse's patience, even from a "sick friend;" he, no he did not, bless Jemima—he said something, to blot out which would require from the Recording angel, a tear—and then the friends disappeared in the Margate Bathing Establishment by different doors.

---

publication of the third or fourth number of Vanity Fair, that Mr. Thackeray began to dawn upon the reading public as a great genius. The greatest work, which, with perhaps the exception of The Newcomes, is the most perfect literary dissection of the human heart, done with the cleverest and most unsparing hand, had been offered to and rejected by several of the first publishers in London. But the public saw and recognized its value; the great guns of literature, the Quarterly and the Edinburgh, boomed forth their praises, the light tirailleurs in the monthly and weekly press re-echoed the feux-de-joie, and the novelist's success was made. Pendennis followed, and was equally valued by the literary world, but scarcely so popular with the public. Then came Esmond, which fell almost still-born from the press; and then the Newcomes, perhaps the best of all. The Virginians, now publishing, though admirably written, lacks interest of plot, and is proportionately unsuccessful.

HIS SUCCESS,

commencing with Vanity Fair, culminated with his "Lectures on the English Humorists of the Eighteenth Century," which were attended by all the court and fashion of London. The prices were extravagant, the Lecturer's adulation of birth and position was extravagant, the success was extravagant. No one succeeds better than Mr. Thackeray in cutting his coat according to his cloth: here he flattered the aristocracy, but when he crossed the Atlantic, George Washington became the idol of his worship; the "Four Georges," the objects of his bitterest attacks. These last-named Lectures have been dead failures in England, though as literary compositions they are most excellent. Our own opinion is, that his success is on the wane; his writings never were understood or appreciated even by the middle classes; the aristocracy have been alienated by his American onslaught on their body, and the educated and refined are not sufficiently numerous to constitute an audience; moreover, there is a want of heart in all he writes, which is to be balanced by the most brilliant sarcasm and the most perfect knowledge of the workings of the human heart.

An early example of the literary gossip column—author profile in England. This portrait of Thackeray in the June 12, 1858, Town Talk caused an irrevocable split between Thackeray and Dickens when the latter defended its author.

From the start Mrs. Gaskell did not intend to write an even-handed biography. She meant to cast Charlotte as a noble, wronged Victorian heroine like Mrs. Gaskell's own fictional protagonist Ruth Hilton, a victim of dreadful events who displayed a virtuous and long-suffering resignation. Indeed, as a good Christian (the pseudonym she had originally chosen for *Mary Barton* was "Cotton Mather Mills"), Mrs. Gaskell saw her task not to be that of writing a literary biography but to translate Charlotte's life into an exemplary story of suffering borne with heroic Christian fortitude, to "make the world (if I am but strong enough in expression) honour the woman as much as they have admired the writer." In short, a classic nineteenth-century Victorian biography that pointed a moral lesson.

Which did not mean the whole project couldn't be fun.

"I have three people I want to libel," she told George Smith gaily, proceeding to list the woman who had supposedly seduced the Brontës' brother, England's slipperiest living publisher, and an unkind reviewer of *Jane Eyre*. "Lady Scott (that bad woman who corrupted Branwell Brontë) Mr. Newby, & Lady Eastlake, the first and last not to be named by name, the mean publisher to be gibbeted." And vigorously gibbeted. "*Do* let me abuse Mr Newby as much as I dare, *within the law*. Your legal adviser will I trust keep me from a libel," she wrote engagingly to the publisher a few weeks later.

She collected correspondence from Charlotte's acquaintances and correspondents like Harriet Martineau and Lewes, went to see the Reverends Brontë and Nicholls in Haworth ("No quailing, Mrs. Gaskell!" growled the old parent sternly when she left, "No drawing back!") and drew on the tales Lady Kay Shuttleworth had recounted of how Reverend Brontë had flown into a fury, sawing up chairs and burning hearth rugs when enraged.

Meanwhile, George Smith sent letters to Mrs. Gaskell cautioning her to be sure that these potentially libelous stories she was eagerly gathering about the figures in Charlotte's life were true—or so he later maintained. Mrs. Gaskell forged cheerfully ahead. She had managed to inveigle Reverend Nicholls, much against his will, into giving her his dead wife's letters with the understanding that they were to be used strictly as background. Now she wanted to quote from them. She appealed to George Smith for help, who after some thought wrote Nicholls enclosing a document for his signature that would give the copyright of the letters to Mrs. Gaskell.

Nicholls did not bite. Yes, he had given Mrs. Gaskell the letters, "but never with giving [over] the exclusive right to them." Smith wrote again, apparently suggesting Nicholls was going back on his word. This was too much for the grieving clergyman. He was angry at Mrs. Gaskell—"I never authorized her to publish a single line of my wife's MS correspondence." But finally he caved in and signed, "as it seems to be taken for granted that I am to do so, tho' why it should, I know not, as I never entered into any arrangement with Mrs Gaskell to convey to her the copyright of my wife's MS. for the purposes of the Memoir or any other—"

Finally Mrs. Gaskell completed the biography. Which meant she had only to await publication—and the reviews. "I know it is a weakness, but unfavourable ones depress me very much," she told Smith with publication due in March 1857. "So I plan getting out of England at the time of publication and, if possible [sic], for us to go to Rome for a month." Rome it was. She took off.

And then the biography finally appeared, over the imprint of Smith, Elder, 2,221 copies having been printed on March 25. The critics loved it. (Literary biographies were not new, of course. The nineteenth-century reader could feast on Thomas Moore's 1830 best-selling biography of Lord Byron, and John Lockhart's multivolume biography of his father-in-law, Sir Walter Scott, sold well for decades.) Within a month, 1,500 more copies of Mrs. Gaskell's biography had to be printed while Smith, Elder happily begin issuing "tie-in" reprints of Charlotte's works at six shillings a pop, reissued the Brontë sisters' poems for four shillings, and on May 9 even announced a new edition of the biography.

Alas, the account of Branwell's circumstances that had, so she said, so moved Marian Evans had affected someone else, too—but in a totally different way. Lady Scott, whom Mrs. Gaskell had wanted to "gibbet" as the debaucher of Branwell, discovered the passages about her alleged corruption of Branwell in the *Life* and promptly contacted her lawyers. Before long, all sorts of other people rose up, too, including the man whose school had been identified as the original for the horrible Lowood School attended by Jane Eyre where "Helen Burns" died. Would he, too, threaten legal action? Former Haworth servants complained about Mrs. Gaskell's characterization of "waste" at the parsonage, and Harriet Martineau wrote to Mrs. Gaskell to set her straight on the quarrel she had had with Charlotte over *Villette*. (Though he made no public remark, Thackeray must have winced at being whacked again by Charlotte, this time, of course, posthumously. Mrs. Gaskell had quoted—those letters again—Charlotte's observation that Thackeray was understandably second to Dickens because "Mr. Thackeray is easy and indolent, and seldom cares to do his best." The scene at George Smith's when she had upbraided Thackeray for being frivolous must have been recalled to his mind.)

And as for Reverend Nicholls, who had so resisted letting Mrs. Gaskell quote from the letters—Mrs. Gaskell quoted Charlotte as saying, now for the whole world to hear, about the man who had so humbly and persistently sought her hand, that she was marrying him only as the best of rather poor alternatives. "I have read the work with inexpressible pain," the anguished clergyman wrote George Smith. "It was not without reason that I instinctively shrank from the proposal of a Biography." There was an undercurrent of bitter resentment at the great sensation-hungry beast that had always to be fed. "But I suppose, it matters not, provided the curiosity of the Publick be gratified."

In the face of Lady Scott's ire, Smith's solicitor talked to Mrs. Gaskell's solicitor. The lawyers hired detectives to try to substantiate some of the horrendous tales Mrs. Gaskell had recounted—and, alas, found nothing that would stand up to a courtroom challenge. There was only one option. The Gaskell family solicitor announced under the prominent heading "ADVERTISEMENT *The Life of Charlotte Brontë*" in both the *Times* and the *Athenaeum* on May 30 and June 6, 1857, respectively, that "I am instructed to retract every statement contained in that work which imputes to a widowed lady, referred to, but not named therein, any breach of her conjugal, her maternal, or of her social duties, and more especially of the statement contained in chapter 13 of the first volume, and in chapter 2 of the second volume, which imputes to the lady in question a guilty intercourse with the late Branwell Brontë."

And then there was, oh yes, Charlotte's father, the man who had asked Mrs. Gaskell to write the book in the first place. "I have no objection, whatever to your representing me as a little eccentric," she was told by perhaps her chief victim, "only don't set me on in my fury to burning hearthrugs, sawing the backs of chairs, and tearing my wife's silk gowns—With respect to tearing my wife's silk gown, my dear little daughter must have been misinformed." Upon further examination, in fact, Mrs. Gaskell discovered that there were indeed problems with the colorful tales she had been told about Reverend Brontë: their chief source, the children's mother's nurse, had been fired by him. And the tale of Mr. Brontë allegedly denying his daughters "animal food," i.e., meat, was taken up by partisans of Canorus Wilson, in order to shift the blame away from his school for the death of the two little Brontë girls who had attended it. "Everyone who has been harmed in this unlucky book complains," Mrs. Gaskell wailed, *"and I did so try to tell the truth."*

Yet the overall picture of a grim, dark household with a morbid, withdrawn father and fey, unworldly, or nobly suffering sisters has remained the book's legacy, coloring studies and the popular image alike of the Brontës ever since. Henry Raymond, the editor of the *New York Times*, stopped at the parsonage not long after the *Life* appeared and professed himself "agreeably disappointed in the face of the country and the general aspect of the town, that they were less sombre and repulsive than Mrs. Gaskell's descriptions led me to expect. Mr. Nicholls and Mr. Brontë smiled at each other, and the latter remarked: 'Well, I think Mrs Gaskell tried to make us all appear as bad as she could.'"

As for Charlotte, indeed, she was scarcely in her grave before she became a growth industry, a trade which the growing ease of railway travel vastly facilitated. (Emily and *Wuthering Heights* would take longer to obtain fame and the attentions of literary tourists.) As local hostelries jacked up prices to take advantage of the literary tourist trade, the Haworth sexton displayed Charlotte's signature in the marriage register and hinted that he had photographs for sale. The pharmacist hawked photos of Patrick Brontë in his windows. An American visitor in 1861 bought the lower sash of Charlotte's bedroom window, together with "the wire and crank of Mr. Brontë's bell-pull, which he used daily for 41 years," and wrote home to Mom about it on stationery engraved with a picture of "The Home of Charlotte Brontë" sold by the same Mr. Greenwood who had furnished the sisters with their stationery years before.

And Charlotte was recognized by serious peers as a woman indeed out of the ordinary. "No sooner does a woman show that she has genius or effective talent, than she receives the tribute of being moderately praised and severely criticized ... Harriet Martineau, Currer Bell, and Mrs Gaskell have been treated as if they had been men." So said the October 1856 issue of John Chapman's *Westminster Review* in an attack on a staple of the circulating libraries and the railway stalls. "Silly Novels by Lady Novelists," the author of the article called them, meaning second- and third-rate romantic fiction, such as what she referred to as "the mind and millinery species." In these books, said the author, terrible things happen to "the noble, gifted and lovely heroine ... but we have the satisfaction of knowing that her tears are wept into embroidered pocket-handkerchiefs, that her fainting form reclines on the very best upholstery, and that whatever vicissitudes she may undergo, from being dashed out of her carriage to having her head shaved in a fever, she comes out of them all with a complexion more blooming and locks more redundant than ever."

It was a witty, clever attack, the writer being none other than Marian Evans. Who was thinking about writing a—well, it had "always been a vague dream of mine that some time or other I might write a novel." Certainly there did seem to be a new interest in the female writer, even if it was not always complimentary. "Hundreds of educated ladies have nothing to do, and yet are tormented with a most natural desire, nay are often under a positive obligation, to do something," the author of "False Morality of Lady Novelists" would write in the 1859 *National Review*. "Every educated lady can handle a pen *tant bien que mal*: all such, therefore, take to writing—and to novel-writing, both as the kind which requires the least special qualifications and the least severe study, and also as the only kind which will sell ... the supply of the fiction market has fallen mainly into their hands." "'Shall we write a novel?'" exclaimed Adela in Mrs. Fitzmaurice Okeden's *Felicia's Dowry* in 1866. "'Could we?' replies Kate. 'Oh, yes! Besides, all women write novels now, whether they can or they can't.'"

Naturally, given the limited experience to which society exposed them, women tended mainly to write domestic novels. How could they know about anything else? As Charlotte Brontë's former correspondent George Lewes suggested in his "The Lady Novelists" in the July 1, 1852, *Westminster Review*, "of all departments of literature, Fiction is the one to which, by nature and by circumstance, women are best adapted ... novels are their forte. The domestic experiences which form the bulk of woman's knowledge finds [*sic*] an appropriate form in novels."

Thackeray, in a not uncharacteristically glum moment in later life. He was beginning to doubt his ability to keep writing, physical ailments were crowding in on him, and he never got over the loneliness that resulted from having to commit his insane wife in 1840.

Lewes was a small, vivacious man with a pockmarked face—of "immense ugliness," said Jane Carlyle. From a theatrical family, he had never lost his interest in the theater and once acted in Dickens' theatricals. Like Dickens, Thackeray, and so many others, Lewes wrote, edited, and reviewed, but his interests tended toward the abstract, philosophical, and scientific, and he had an earnest interest in Continental philosophy. (Of Dickens he would later write reprovingly of his sometime friend, "Dickens sees and feels," but "thought is strangely absent from his works.")

Lewes had also, of course, corresponded with Charlotte Brontë, telling her, in fact, to read Jane Austen (whom she didn't like) and had helped to bring *Jane Eyre* to public notice. He had also befriended Herbert Spencer, with whom he often stopped to talk with Marian Evans at John Chapman's. Marian had fallen in love with Chapman—who was simultaneously carrying on an affair with the Chapmans' governess, Elisabeth Tilley, who shared the household downstairs from Marian's rented room with Chapman and his wife, Susanna. Things blew up, and Marian was exiled, literally, to Coventry, Chapman taking her to the train. At the station she asked him how he felt about her, whereupon with a typical tactlessness or honesty, "I told her that I felt great affection for her, but that I loved E. and S. also, though each in a different way. At this avowal she burst into tears"—surprise, surprise.

But her exile proved only temporary. Chapman needed her to help edit the *Review*, and there was a Dorothea Brooke strain in Marian that was still willing to serve—without credit—as the helpmate of intellectually second-rate men. So she came back in September 1851, the women at 142 Strand having somehow been reconciled to her return. Having seen through Chapman, she developed a crush instead on the eminently serious Herbert Spencer, the new subeditor of a young magazine called the *Economist*, which had its offices just across the street from 142 Strand, while her philandering ex-boyfriend John Chapman confronted some acute problems with the solvency of the

Westminster Review. Spencer having in turn proved unrespon-
sive to her attentions, she grew interested in Lewes, though she
had not initially been taken with him on their first meeting
(appropriately, in a bookshop). But as Lewes began haunting
142 Strand where, in her relaxed way, she could often be found,
legs swung up over the arms of a chair, head bent over a manuscript, lost in her editing, they discovered similar interests. She
corrected proofs of his books for him, friendship grew to affection, affection to love—but he and Marian could not marry.

The reason lay in Lewes' involved domestic history. Lewes
had had a wonderful marriage, or so it seemed, to the beautiful,
bright Agnes Jervis, who had been his tutee, "a perfect pair of
love-birds" Jane Carlyle had thought them. And then, after a
period of years, Lewes started spending more time away from
home, doing amateur theatricals in Manchester, until he discovered that Agnes had taken a minor literary figure named
Thornton Leigh as her lover—at about the same time, ironically,
that Lewes and Leigh had agreed to start a new literary magazine called the *Leader* together. Well, but Lewes and his wife
believed in free love and no recriminations. A boy by Thornton
was born to her two weeks after the first edition of the *Leader*
appeared, and Lewes agreed to accept the child as his son,
except that, having condoned this adultery, by law Lewes could
then no longer divorce Agnes.

Those who had heard Marian Evans discourse on political
and social reform might be pardoned for thinking she would
take a relaxed view of participating in an unconventional
domestic arrangement with Lewes. They would have been
wrong. Marian was not a free-love person, and she did not like
having to live "in sin" with Lewes. "One thing I can tell you in
few words," she wrote to her old friend Mrs. Charles Bray in
early September 1855. "Light and easily broken ties are what I
neither desire theoretically nor could live for practically.
Women who are satisfied with such ties do *not* act as I have
done—they obtain what they desire and are still invited to dinner."

THE HOME OF CHARLOTTE BRONTE

J. GREENWOOD, STATIONER, &c., HAWORTH.
[By permission of the Proprietors of the London Journal]

England

At Mrs Gaskell's, Manchester,
Monday Morning, Nov. 11. 1861

Dear Mother — I have been to Haworth,
"the home of Charlotte Brontë" as
you see by this sheet of paper
which I got there. — I had a

The Brontë tourist trade was already in full swing within a few years of Charlotte's death, as is demonstrated by this engraved stationery sold by John Greenwood, the Haworth stationer from whom the Brontë sisters bought the pen and ink to write their novels.

For, indeed, she was not invited to dinner, polite Victorian society being what it was, after she and Lewes traveled on their "honeymoon" to Germany in 1854, and then rented rooms in Richmond near Kew Gardens, not far from London. (Fear of outraging the landlady's sensibilities required Lewes and Evans to impress over and over again on visiting friends that they always "must ask for *Mrs. Lewes* and not for Miss Evans, as a misunderstanding on this point would be very painful.") Even the presumably "radical" patron of her translation of the German life of Jesus, Mr. Joseph Parkes, to whose dinners Marian had once gone in her black velvet gown, flew into a "white rage" on hearing of her moving in with Lewes. Her "husband's" friend William Scott got a letter describing how "blackguard Lewes has bolted with a ____ and is living in Germany with her." Her brother Isaac eventually stopped writing to Evans altogether—and successfully forbade her sisters to—and communicated thereafter with her through his solicitor for the next twenty-odd years.

Lewes and Evans had each other, however, their common interests, and their reading, including the new novel by Charlotte Brontë. "I am only just returned to a sense of the real world about me, for I have been reading *Villette*, a still more wonderful book than *Jane Eyre*. There is something almost preternatural in its power," Evans rhapsodized.

It was such enthusiasm that had led to Marian's praise for Charlotte in her 1856 article on silly woman novelists in the *Review*. (Lewes in September 1856 had dug out his letters from *Villette*'s author for Mrs. Gaskell for use in her biography of Charlotte, and Marian had succumbed to the mania for traffic in Charlotteana. "Shouldn't you like an autograph letter of Currer Bell's?" she wrote to a friend that month. "I hope to get you one bye and bye, when Mrs Gaskell returns the letters that have been sent to her.") Meanwhile, in May 1856, Lewes and Marian took off for Ilfracombe and Tenby on the coast of South Wales for much of the summer. While Lewes researched the seaside and sea creatures with the aim of writing a series of popular science articles for the *Westminster Review*, the couple read aloud to one another at night. Marian had read him an introductory chapter of a fictional work which he thought promising. He encouraged her. While dozing in bed one morning, she found—had she been thinking of the fictional family on whom Mrs. Gaskell's first novel centered?—a title announcing itself to her, "The Sad Fortunes of the Reverend Amos Barton." "O," said the very supportive Lewes when she told him, "what a capital title!"

One night in the fall of 1856 after returning to their home in Richmond she got to the toughest and most pathetic scene of her work, and Lewes considerately went into town so she could write the whole thing without distraction. She was fine on description, he knew, but could she really do dramatic scenes? She read the passage to Lewes when he returned. "We both cried over it, and then he came up to me and kissed me, saying, 'I think your pathos is better than your fun.'" That settled it. Lewes's had published stories and articles in the durable *Blackwood's Magazine*. Now Marian chose for a pseudonym "George Eliot"; "George," she was later to observe, "was Mr. Lewes' Christian name, and Eliot was a good mouth-filling, easily-pronounced word." (Obviously, a female author living in sin could not publish under her own name.) Lewes now submitted Marian's work to the proprietor of *Blackwood's* as being ostensibly the work of an unnamed "friend."

Marian was wise to keep back a bit, for fame, the railroad, and the new prestige of the novel had not only made authors celebrities but were also increasingly turning them into creatures who lacked privacy and, perhaps, the inclination for it as well. Disraeli, for example, certainly received fan mail of an altogether modern nature as he turned out his "Young England" trilogy. One person wanted £5, others help getting a job, still others free copies of his novel. From the secretary of the Leeds Mechanics' Institution came a query asking whether the name of the eponymous heroine of Disraeli's novel was to be "pronounced *SY'*bil or *SIB'* after the Greek. One line from you will allay a fierce contention." Someone else wrote to pour remarks of anti-Semitic abuse upon him, another to ask his help for the Jews, and so on.

Public exposure . . .

Dickens characteristically didn't mind it but in fact wanted to take advantage of it and was threatening, to Forster's unspeakable horror, to undertake a literary road show. Dickens, during a walk one day with Wills, the subeditor of *Household Words*, passed a substantial house at Gad's Hill near Chatham. Dickens told Wills how his father long ago had told him he might someday inhabit the house if he were a success in life. The next night Wills had mentioned this to a dinner partner, the same woman whose negative example had encouraged Marian Evans to write, the former Eliza Lynn, now Mrs. Lynn Linton. But the house was her family's, said Mrs. Linton to Wills—and they were selling it! Dickens purchased the symbolically irresistible trophy in March 1856 for the staggering sum of £1,790— writers had indeed come up in the world. "What do you think," he asked his old friend John Forster, "of my paying for this place, by reviving that old idea of some Readings from my books?" The most famous celebrity writer in the world would now seek to become a performer, too, and not just content himself, as Thackeray had done, with lecturing.

Forster was horrified. The former butcher's son who had so arduously climbed into the middle class through his literary and journalistic efforts still worried about the dignity of the writer. Don't do it, Forster advised; it would degrade literature just as authors were finally beginning to be treated like the meritorious creatures that they were.

But Dickens had already begun to lecture on a pro bono basis in 1853 for worthy organizations, and he was still no multimillionaire despite his immense literary success. And now "I can see no better thing to do," he told Forster, "that is half so hopeful in itself, or"—there was the note of the incessant need for movement again—"half so suited to my restless state."

More prosaically, he had to pay for the new cesspool and remodeling at Gad's Hill, too.

Ah, and his "restless state"? For years, he had been drifting apart from the placid, loving woman he had married when they were both so young. Catherine Dickens remained in love with him, and vaguely good-willed—but as to keeping up with him intellectually or emotionally— In February 1855, the winsome heartbreaker of his youth, Mrs. Henry Winter, the former Maria Beadnell, wrote to Dickens. It was she who had been the cause of so much suffering that he had burned his autobiography rather than write of their relationship. When he spotted her somehow familiar handwriting on an envelope amid some letters, "three or four and twenty years vanished like a dream, and I opened it with the touch of my young friend David Copperfield when he was in love." So did he write back to her eagerly.

It was a sign of how beset by despair he was as his own marriage disintegrated. He ignored Maria's protestations that she was "toothless, fat, old, and ugly" as he pressed for a clandestine meeting. It was a novelist's fantasy come true—an old flame, now chastened by the overwhelming success of the boy she had jilted and humbly petitioning for his attention, their roles at last reversed. They contrived to meet secretly, only for him to find, crushingly, that she had, alas, been all too accurate in her self-description.

Disappointment made him cruel. The Crimean War had spurred him to rare public speech against the government that had blunderingly consigned thousands of soldiers to unnecessary deaths from disease and malnutrition in the Black Sea. The workings of the callous and cynical government bureaucracy accordingly became a central theme of his new novel. But, in addition, as *Little Dorrit* began to appear in December 1855, Dickens' protagonist Arthur Clennam returned after twenty-some years to London to find waiting the Flora Finching who had once been the love of his youthful life now grown silly, fat, and dipsomaniacal, pursuing him with embarrassingly arch and inappropriate effusions of middle-aged ardor. To have spent so many years in heartache, and over such a dreary object of pursuit. "Flora, whom he had left a lily, had become a peony; but that was not much. Flora, who had seemed enchanting in all she said and thought, was diffuse and silly. That was much. Flora, who had been spoiled and artless long ago, was determined to be spoiled and artless now. That was a fatal blow." "We have all had our Floras," Dickens wrote the Duke of Devonshire wanly of the hapless Mrs. Winter, "mine is living and extremely fat."

He was beset by disappointment on all sides; Dickens wrote of his in-laws that "the contemplation of their imbecility" now staggered him. Ominously, he noted, "I find the skeleton in my domestic closet is becoming a pretty big one." "'It is only half an hour'—'it is only an afternoon'—'it is only an evening'— people say to me over and over again—but they don't know that it is impossible to command oneself sometimes to any stipulated and set disposal of five minutes," he wrote now when his former love asked to see him for just thirty minutes. "I am grieved if you suspect me of not wanting to see you, but I can't help it; I must go my way, whether or no."

And in October 1857, Dickens moved out of the bedroom he shared with Catherine and had the open doorway in between closed up with a door and shelves. "The domestic unhappiness remains so strong upon me that I can't write, and (waking) can't rest, one minute," he told a young protégé named Wilkie Collins in March 1858. "I have a turning notion that the mere physical effort and change of the Readings would be good, as another means of bearing it." He decided to move out of their home, and then—catastrophe. A bracelet Dickens had ordered for a young actress named Ellen Ternan, whom he had met and set up in a clandestine suburban house, was mistakenly delivered by the jeweler to Catherine instead. Dickens demanded that Catherine pay a call on Ellen to prove that she believed him innocent. "You shall not go!" So exclaimed Dickens' fierce, red-haired daughter Kate angrily when she came upon her heartbroken, sobbing mother, dutifully putting on her bonnet at her dressing table, as she prepared to pay the call. But, as usual, Dickens was too much for them; Catherine went—and then, at her mother's insistence, Catherine reluctantly moved out. Dickens was finally free of his burdensome companion.

Was he succumbing to the celebrity disease of believing his own press clippings? For Dickens now took the extraordinary step of insisting on printing in the *Household Words* for June 12, 1858, that a "domestic trouble of mine, of long-standing" had, yes, been brought to a satisfactory conclusion, but that "this trouble has been made the occasion of misrepresentations, most grossly false, most monstrous, and most cruel." In addition, he insisted that his separation from Catherine be announced in *Punch*, that jovial organ of his publishers, Bradbury and Evans. When they refused, Dickens was incensed, and so, once again, he broke with a publishing house and headed out for fresh literary territory, returning in the following year to the welcoming embrace of Messrs. Chapman and Hall. Celebrity tantrums. Hall was now dead, and the accommodating, if feckless, Frederic Chapman, whom Dickens privately told Charles Lever was an utter fool, was soon to take up the reins from his cousin, the firm's cofounder, Edward Chapman.

Somehow, by God, though, Dickens would tell the public what was happening with his marriage. In the *New York Tribune* of August 16, sure enough, there appeared a long letter justifying what he had done and remarking, inter alia, that "in the manly consideration toward Mrs. Dickens which I owe to my wife, I will merely remark of her that some peculiarity of her character has thrown all the children on someone else," a cutting and apparently not very colorable claim that she had abdicated her responsibilities as a mother. Dickens also alluded to "a mental disorder under which she sometimes labours." "If this is 'manly consideration,'" said the *Liverpool Mercury* acidly of this airing of domestic dirty linen, "we should like to be favoured with a definition of unmanly selfishness and heartlessness."

The publicizing of celebrity misery had begun.

Mr. THACKERAY's

SENTIMENTS ON THE

Sabbath Question

"I would not only open the Crystal Palace, the British Museum, and the National Gallery but I would go further, and open the CONCERT ROOMS and THEATRES on Sundays."

Vide Report of the Speech delivered by Mr. Thackeray to his Friends at the Mitre Hotel, July 9, 1857.

Thackeray ran unsuccessfully for Parliament from Oxford in 1857 in a demonstration of the new respectability of English novelists. His colorless opponent had the grace to reply "I hope not!" when on meeting him Thackeray sportingly wished that the best man would win. This opposition placard suggested that Thackeray was lax about honoring the sabbath.

It was perhaps no accident that of all writers, this happened to—and was caused by—Dickens. For the curiously modern ring to all this—the airing of intimate problems in public, the use of the press to castigate loved ones, the public appetite for scandal about the notable—should be understood partly as the result of a new kind of quasi-"personal" relationship that serial novelists like Dickens had developed with their reading public. This new sort of relationship was of a kind in which regular, interactive, intimate-seeming contact—as is the case today between a movie or TV star and the public—occurs so as to induce the audience to feel it somehow personally "knows" the distant performer, what Thackeray called a "communion between the writer and the public" that is "continued, confidential, something like personal affection." Dickens called it "that particular relation (personally affectionate and like no other man's) which subsists between me and the public," which is typified, perhaps, by the Irishman who came up to him on the street following a reading to express gratitude "not ounly for the light you've been to me this night, but for the light you've been in mee house, sir (and God love your face!) this many a year!"

In a telling phrase, Dickens hoped in the preface to the collected "numbers" of one of his novels that his readers would "think of the papers which on that day of so many past months they have read, as the correspondence of one who wishes their happiness, and contributes to their amusement." Correspondence: that is, the fact that serials were issued at periodic monthly intervals made for shared reader-author interaction over time. "A sort of confidential talk between writer and reader," Thackeray called it in the preface to *Pendennis.* Just as the serial writer sent out monthly "correspondence" to his readers, they, in turn, wrote to him, and, in fact, because the serials were so loosely plotted, the writer could often respond to requests to change the action or characters. Dickens responded to people asking him to punish the villains and reward the good in *Nickleby* by inserting appropriate incidents as the serial wound on. Or there was the original for the dwarf

Miss Mowcher in *David Copperfield*, who complained that Dickens' fictional caricature of her was deeply cruel. "I have suffered long and much," she wrote him, "from my personal deformities but never before at the hands of a Man so highly gifted as Charles Dickens ... you have made my nights sleepless and my daily work tearfull." The chagrined Dickens accordingly made the character more appealing in a later "number." Perhaps most famously, hints in installments of Dickens' 1840 *The Old Curiosity Shop* made it increasingly clear that Little Nell, as the little heroine was called, would not survive. He was then "inundated with imploring letters recommending poor little Nell to mercy," Dickens wrote to Chapman and Hall, as ominous signs of her impending demise increased. "Six yesterday, and four today (it's not 12 o'Clock yet) already!" And, indeed, hundreds were said to crowd the docks in New York to beg news of the incoming ships from England, "Is Little Nell dead?" In some cases, the feeling of breathless contemporaneity was heightened by the fact that the monthly events of a serial paralleled those in the real world, the *Pickwick* episode dealing with Christmas, for example, appearing as the January 1837 installment of the serial.

Was such intimacy and celebrity transferable to another arena?

Since his days as a parliamentary reporter, Dickens had had an enduring contempt for the windy self-importance of the politicians whose endless speeches he had had to transcribe night after night standing in the galleries of Parliament. No, politics for any reason was out for him. The Liberals had asked him to run for a parliamentary seat in Reading in 1841, and he had said no. Thackeray, however, who had had no such unhappy experiences, took advantage of the new authorial popularity to run for office. He was tiring of writing novels, but did not the popularity of his lectures and the acclaim for Mrs. Gaskell's biography and the like prove that writers were becoming celebrities? In this new age when people voted for men of real accomplishment and not just the man the local landowner told them to, why shouldn't he turn authorial prominence into a means of getting elected to public office?

It was not just glory that he sought. Novelists, even most of the quite successful ones, were not rolling in cash from their literary efforts. And there were no screenplays, no creative writing courses, no professorships to make up the difference. In 1857, Thackeray decided to run for Parliament, in part because it was a position that might in turn open the doors to a permanent sub-cabinet job of some kind. "Just when the novel-writing faculty is pretty well used up here is independence a place in parliament and who knows what afterwards?" he speculated hopefully.

His opportunity came in Oxford, where Thackeray's opponent was a genial nonentity, who responded with a horrified "I hope not" to Thackeray's sportingly expressed wish that the best man should win. This was still the heyday of Trollope's relentlessly Sabbatarian Mrs. Proudie, and the "Sabbath Question." Thackeray favored Sunday opening of "Picture Galleries, Museums, Scientific Collections, and such places as the Crystal Palace," he said, and he would "encourage good Band-Music"—but that did not mean for a moment, he said in response to his opponents, that he "spoke or thought of opening Theatres on Sunday." God forbid.

So what?

"CARDWELL is a man of *Fact*" sneered an opposition broadside.

> "*Thackeray* is a man of *fiction*
> *Cardwell* is a man of Political Renown *Thackeray* is a man of
> *Novel* Greatness
> *Cardwell* helped to give the Poor Man Cheap Bread *Thackeray*
> gave him *Vanity Fair*. "

In the end Thackeray did perfectly respectably (1,005 votes to the winner's 1,070)—but he lost. Yet, realistically, how would the essentially private, sedentary man with the unpredictable sense of humor have made out as a tribune of the people? It was a blessing in disguise, he affected to believe. "If I had won," he wrote, "I should have been turned out, my agents, in spite of express promises to me, having done acts which would have ousted me."

Dickens, of course, ruled out any possibility of becoming a candidate as Thackeray had been. But a public role, trading on his celebrity, why yes! To hell with Forster; he would give readings. Like Thackeray, Dickens sought to trade on his celebrity and pseudo-intimacy with the public in order to get some money by performing for his readers in what he hoped would also be an outlet for his restless unhappiness.

Nowadays readings, even by a world-famous author, might not seem all that sexy, but in an era when there was no television, no radio, no movies, and no evening entertainment, readings could be a big deal, especially because good middle-class people did not go to the theater as a rule. This was partly because the theater had been taken over by the lower classes and crude melodrama and partly because Evangelicalism disapproved of theater. So involved were the stratagems to overcome this prohibition that people flocked to see the Reverend. J. C. M. Bellew declaim *Hamlet* in a concert hall while actors on the stage behind him mimed the action in what was billed as a "recital."

Dickens had long loved the theater, as his amateur theatricals with Bulwer evidenced. Indeed, as a young man he had written briefly for the stage and thought of being an actor. His writing had always had a dramatic quality, and he spoke, conversely, of acting and producing as being "like writing a book in company." There were the famous Dickens amateur theatricals at his home, too, with elaborate costumes and printed playbills. Now he threw himself into preparation for the readings, practicing not only the text itself but the accompanying voices and gestures literally hundreds of times.

And then, in April 1858, he began.

The introductions were deceptively low key, unfussy, as he made his entrance in evening dress—black suit, white shirt, white gloves, and a red geranium in his buttonhole. "Ladies and

Ellen Ternan, Dickens' mistress, whom he met in 1857—he was forty-five, she was eighteen—while touring a play he had co-written with Wilkie Collins. Did she appear in The Mystery of Edwin Drood *as Helena Landless—or as a model for Estella in* Great Expectations?

gentlemen, I have the honor to read from—" and thence into the
two-to-three-hour reading that would follow. A row of special
gaslights that traveled with him spotlighted him from above (in
Ireland during the Fenian troubles the disassembled pipes were
mistaken for a bomb), and advance men helped set up, did publicity, and told him if he was not audible. Bradbury and Evans
printed up reading editions of the selections Dickens was reading to be sold as souvenir programs. He was by turns intimate,
grand, or hypnotic, but always superb at imitating all the different characters as he read aloud. "Charley," said a marveling
Thomas Carlyle to Dickens over a brandy after one performance, "you carry a whole company of actors under your own
hat." His audiences laughed, cried—and applauded wildly.

When the Dickens entourage took off for Scotland, Ireland,
and the provinces, they were constantly on the road. In almost
four months Dickens gave eighty-seven readings—each a two-
to-three-hour solo performance. And he was wildly popular.
"Arthur bathed in checks, took headers into tickets, floated on
billows of passes, dived under weirs of shillings," wrote
Dickens exuberantly of his manager in Liverpool, and "floated
home, faint with gold and silver." Sell-out crowds, fights for
tickets breaking out, people bursting through glass to get to
hear him, throngs sitting on stage at his feet—he was a rock
star—and it was a grueling tour. "Well, the work is hard, the climate is hard, the life is hard," wrote Dickens when he toured
America. His words could equally well have applied to his
British tours, traveling between towns on railroads which as yet
had no sleeping cars. "But so far the gain is enormous." In the
fall of 1858, his tour netted over a thousand pounds a month
while two years before his publishers had initially paid him
only two hundred pounds a month for *Little Dorrit*. His manager fretted that the writer would be booed when he returned to
the lecture stage in mid-June after the appearance of his
Household Words announcement about his separation. But, no.
The audience, like that of a true modern celebrity (it would
prove true of his readers, as well), remained as staunchly loyal

and devoted as ever. In the course of his readings, he was heard, among others, by the young Thomas Hardy and Leo Tolstoy.

With the rise of celebrity it is scarcely surprising that it was about this time that its indispensable medium, the newspaper interview, also came into being. Thackeray had been struck while touring in America, where the interview originated, by the intense attention that newspapers paid to the personal habits of celebrities. "One of his most singular habits is that of making rough sketches for caricatures on his finger-nails," he wrote, parodying an account of himself by a New York reporter. "Besides his novels, he is the author of the *Vestiges of Creation*, the *Errors of Numismatics*, Junius's *Letters* and *Ivanhoe*."

Now the interview moved to England. After writing a gossip column for the *Illustrated Times*, Edmund Yates, the young son of an actor friend of Dickens, did a profile of his fellow Garrick Club member Thackeray for the new *Town Talk* on June 12, 1858. Mild by today's standards, it targeted Thackeray's personal characteristics and demeanor—"his bearing is cold and uninviting, his style of conversation openly cynical or affectedly good-natured and benevolent." In his lectures, his "adulation of birth and position was extravagant . . . here he flattered the aristocracy; but when he crossed the Atlantic, George Washington became the idol of his worship." Cruelly—it was a sore point with Thackeray—"his success is on the wane." And so on.

What Dickens welcomed as attention or a vehicle for closer contact with his public infuriated Thackeray. He was incensed by Yates' piece and its invasion of his privacy. "We meet at a club," he wrote stiffly to Yates, "where, before you were born, I believe, I and other gentlemen have been in the habit of talking without any idea that our conversation would supply paragraphs for professional vendors of 'Literary talk.'" The London clubs were a vital part of the comfortable new middle-class world to which writers like Thackeray belonged. Expanded combinations of the old coffeehouse open to all and the exclusive gambling "hells" of the nobility, the new all-male institutions that had been built along Pall Mall in the first few decades of the century provided places where a bachelor or a man in town could get a decent meal, a place to read the paper, and freedom from his family. The Garrick, in particular, with its small, cozy quarters, was a favorite refuge of Thackeray's. He had, after all, little in the way of adult companionship at home, and now here his sanctuary was being exposed to the world. His father's old friend Dickens helped Yates draft a reply to Thackeray, but the latter demanded that the club consider expelling Yates.

Soon all of London was titillated by the spectacle of the two leading giants of the Victorian literary world going at it hammer and tongs, fed, perhaps, further by the fact that Dickens' son Charles Jr. at one point defended Thackeray in the pages of *Punch*. Dickens finally entered the fray openly on behalf of Yates, but Yates was forced to resign, and so Dickens and Thackeray stopped talking to each other. "It is a quarrel, I wish it to be a quarrel, and it will always be a quarrel," said Thackeray curtly. The dispute surfaced long-smoldering animosity and differences over style, psychology, and Dickens' separation from his wife. "He can't forgive me for my success with *Vanity Fair*," Thackeray had said of Dickens, and he privately thought Dickens' style overblown and his characters not realistic. Then, too, Thackeray had generously received Catherine with professions of his continued fondness after Dickens had brutally rejected her.

So now celebrity disputes were making news, but, of course, nothing so appealed to the penny press as a colorfully disintegrating celebrity ménage. And now that came, too.

That same year, campaigning for Parliament, Dickens' friend Bulwer Lytton, now a baronet, Colonial Secretary, rector of Glasgow University, and with hopes of rising to the very top of the Cabinet, was horrified to see his still unconciliated wife, Rosina, advancing on the speaker's platform at an outdoor rally in Hertford one day, shouting, "Make way for the member's wife" and then shaking her fist at her husband. "How can the people of England submit to have such a man as head of the Colonies, who ought to have been in the Colonies as a transport long ago?"

There was more. Bulwer had left their daughter Emily to die a lonely death in London of typhoid. Then he had her body moved back to Knebworth and told everyone she had died there with him close by. "He murdered my child and tried to murder me," Rosina cried. She suspected him of trying to poison her in 1855. In the face of her denunciations, Bulwer fled—and then consulted with the ever-handy John Forster, now conveniently a member of the Lunacy Commission. Rosina was seized by agents of Bulwer not long after on a London street and then locked up as a lunatic.

The increasingly respectable *Times*, parodied by Trollope as "The Jupiter" and edited by Bulwer's friend John Delane, ignored Lady Lytton's irruption in its coverage of his rally at Hertford—as it had her novel *Chevely*, which had attacked Bulwer twenty years before. The upstart *Daily Telegraph* accordingly took up the cudgels on behalf of Lady Rosina, detailing her abduction. "Upon what authority was Lady Lytton captured and sent to Brentford?" it asked—and proceeded to detail the parties responsible. After the election, in the face of a growing clamor to know whether Rosina had been railroaded, she was released into the custody of one of their children, to whom, in characteristic bursts of spleen, she had purportedly sent letters addressed to "that white-livered little reptile, Robert Lytton."

Life was changing. The concern of the Hungry Forties with social problems was giving way to a preoccupation with scandal and with impropriety in high places that crystallized in the revulsion against the misconduct of the Crimean War. To capitalize on and spread this new concern, penny newspapers now sprang up, for the first time carrying news widely to the working man and woman. Steam presses and stereotypes made multiple copies easier and faster to produce, the telegraph made possible foreign dispatches (the Crimean War in 1855 saw the first foreign correspondent), and the railroads facilitated overnight delivery of newspapers outside London, a franchise handled by W. H. Smith. By 1861 the *Daily Telegraph*, born only in 1855 but priced at only a penny, had over 100,000 readers,

George Lewes, who won Marian Evans's heart after their initial meeting at—naturally—a bookshop. Evans used the first name "George" in her pseudonym "George Eliot" as a tribute to him.

and where the editions were only eight pages before, now they were eighteen, and daily rather than weekly. By the early 1870s Dickens' *Daily News* had a circulation of 150,000, and the *Telegraph* proudly reported that its own 200,000 was the biggest in the world.

What could fill all those pages, though, day after day? As the case of the *Telegraph*'s coverage of Lady Rosina suggests, most of what often fills them today—crime reports, puff pieces, and celebrity gossip. All became increasingly prominent. The passage of the new Divorce Law in 1857 provided heaven-sent copy, as scandalous and copious as one could desire, in the form of the transcripts of the new cases being tried in the divorce courts. They scandalized the Queen, who exclaimed to the Lord Chancellor that such coverage "makes it almost impossible for a paper to be trusted in the hand of a young lady or boy." "Now-a-days," said Trollope in 1855, "a daily newspaper is the only pabulum sufficiently new, and sufficiently exciting for the over-strained public mind."

In the face of these kinds of lurid goings-on was something as mild as the old domestic novel really enough anymore? And, besides, as this new avidity for scandal showed, weren't people really tired of novels about social problems, the horrors of industrialism and starving children?

"I'm sick to death of novels with an earnest purpose," burst out a young woman in Dickens' protégé Wilkie Collins's *The Queen of Hearts* in 1859. "I'm sick to death of outbursts of eloquence, and large-minded philanthropy, and graphic descriptions, and unsparing anatomy of the human heart, and all that sort of thing . . . Why, so far as telling a story is concerned, the greater part of them might as well be sermons as novels. Oh, dear me! what I want is something that seizes hold of my interest, and makes me forget when it is time to dress for dinner; something that keeps me reading, reading, reading, in a breathless state, to find out the end." A real page-turner, in short.

And Collins, in fact, would shortly supply it—

It was time for the "sensation novel."

PART 5

"TERROR TO THE END": THE
SENSATION NOVEL, DICKENS
"DREADFULLY SHATTERED,"
AND ANTHONY TROLLOPE
GETS A TRAVELING BAG
AND AN AUDIENCE

In November 1859, a best-selling serial novel began to appear in Dickens' *All the Year Round*. It described how an evil baronet tried to poison his wife and to lock her up, when she was perfectly sane, in a private lunatic asylum—the year after baronet Bulwer had had his wife seized on the streets of London.

The serial was *The Woman in White*. Mysterious disappearances, an inheritance, smiling villains, insanity, graveyard meetings—the machinations of the dastardly Count Fosco and the nefarious Sir Percival Glyde to seize his wife's inheritance were too convoluted and baroque to be credible anywhere outside a *Masterpiece Theater* production—or the Lyttons' marriage. "I thought the crime too ingenious for an English villain, so I picked upon a foreigner," Collins said impishly. But Rosina Lytton wrote Collins an appreciative note. Her husband's perfidy, Rosina Lytton told Collins, made Count Fosco look like a choirboy. The book made Collins' reputation.

And then, beginning in July 1861, in the magazine *Robin Goodfellow*, came Miss Mary Elizabeth Braddon's runaway best seller *Lady Audley's Secret*. "Wherever she went she seemed to take joy and brightness with her," wrote Miss Braddon of the beautiful governess Lucy Graham. "Every one loved, admired, and praised her ... the vicar who saw the soft blue eyes uplifted to his face as he preached his simple sermon ... her employer; his visitors; her pupils; everybody, high and low, united in declaring that Lucy Graham was the sweetest girl that ever lived." Like Jane Eyre, Lucy married the master and so became Lady Audley, except that she then also tried to murder her first husband (Lord Audley was number two) to conceal her bigamy, then tried to cover up both crimes by burning down an inn with an inconvenient witness in it, and so on. A change from *Jane Eyre*—but then perhaps times were changing. A character in Henrietta Jenkin's 1861 *Who Breaks—Pays* remarked of Mr. Rochester, "If I had been Jane Eyre, I would have killed him."

All these "sensation novels," as they came to be called, were hugely successful. *The Woman in White* raised the circulation of *All the Year Round*, then in a bound edition sold 2,350 copies in two weeks and went through six more editions in six months. Vendors turned out *Woman in White* cloaks, perfume, a waltz—it was a mania. *Lady Audley's Secret* sold some eight editions between October and December 1862, and enabled Miss Braddon's publisher Edward Tinsley to build a magnificent home—which he called Audley Lodge. "Do you know that I am simply steeped in Miss Braddon?" said Tennyson. "I am reading every book she ever wrote," the poet told a young acquaintance in 1868. While staying out of town, Thackeray walked to the railroad station three times in one day to see if Miss Braddon's latest novel had arrived from London.

Charles Reade's *Hard Cash* in 1863 also caused a sensation—with its depiction of a man deprived of his money—and reason—by an unscrupulous banker, whose machinations, when discovered by the banker's own son, lead the villain to imprison his boy in a lunatic asylum, where he is tortured. Well, *Hard Cash* brought Reade £3,000 of that commodity, as well as the annoyance of Dickens. It was serialized in Dickens' *All the Year Round* beginning in March 1863, and its lurid aspects alienated some readers. Reade articulated the creed of the new sensational writer perhaps as well as anyone. "I write for the public," he said, and he saw it as having rather debased tastes. "An aristocratic divorce suit, the last great social scandal, a sensational suicide from Waterloo Bridge, a woman murdered in Seven Dials, or a baby found strangled in a bonnet-box at Piccadilly Circus, interests them."

Perhaps things were getting just a little out of hand. Anthony Trollope, for one, disliked these "trashy" new sensation novels. He had finally been successful, with the publication of *The Warden* in 1855. He sent Marian Evans his new *Rachel Ray* in October 1863, noting that "you know that my novels are not sensational. In *Rachel Ray* I have attempted to confine myself absolutely to the commonest details of commonplace life among the most ordinary people." He and Marian both. In her very first story in *Scenes from Clerical Life* Evans had declared her intent to chronicle "a man whose virtues were not heroic, and who had no undetected crime within his breast; who had not the slightest mystery hanging about him, but was palpably and unmistakably commonplace."

They were both solid chroniclers of normal life, then, upholding the future of decent English life against the new sensationalists. (As Victoria's beloved if somewhat conventional Prince Consort lay dying in December 1861, he asked to be read to from *The Warden* and from *Silas Marner*.) George Smith had instituted monthly dinners at which he had arranged for contributors and editors of his new magazine, the *Cornhill*, to meet convivially at Gloucester Square (no *Punch*-like dirty jokes or stories; in the new era, the ladies were assumed to be present, as Thackeray said of the *Cornhill*). Here Trollope had met George Lewes. Trollope thereafter dined often with Lewes and Evans, at pains, perhaps, from knowing keenly what it felt like to be socially outcast, to see them together when other "proper" people would not, and he also undertook to find Lewes' son by his marriage to Agnes a job at the Post Office.

The *Cornhill* ironically exemplified a new form of publication that contributed to the rise of the sensation novel, as well as the work of Trollope and Evans. Beginning in 1860, the stand-alone serial issuance of novels had been largely replaced by a new genre of magazines that charged a shilling rather than two pence, offered several novels rather than one per issue (as well as poetry and other matter), and also aimed for a higher, better-heeled crowd than the magazines like Dickens' old *Household Words* or *All the Year Round*. Indisputably foremost among them was George Smith's *Cornhill Magazine*, which began publication in January 1860, carrying the first installment of a new Thackeray novel. Both Smith and the Macmillans had seen the coming of a new, prosperous, and perhaps slightly more pretentious middle-class literary market. Macmillan got Thomas Hughes of *Tom Brown's School Days* fame to be editor of his new house publication; Smith got Thackeray.

The *Cornhill* recipe—serials plus something else in a "quality" format—proved thumpingly successful. Before long there were also *Temple Bar* (1860), *St. James's* (1861), *Saint Paul's* (1867), *Belgravia* (1866) and other magazines aping *Cornhill*'s style and even its choice of a title based on London geography. (Longmans followed with a magazine in 1882, Murray's in 1887.) The Virtue brothers, friends of George Meredith and printers for Chapman and Hall, started *Saint Paul's* magazine for Trollope to edit after evidently concluding that the *Argosy*'s publication of Charles Reade's *Griffith Gaunt* in 1865 and 1866 made it too "sensational" for them to acquire. Miss Braddon, meanwhile, after Trollope declined the post, took over the editorship of her husband John Maxwell's *Temple Bar*. It was a small, interconnected, busy world.

Trollope thought that the new magazines spelled the death of the old unaccompanied "part" or "number" serial publication of novels like *Pickwick* and *Vanity Fair*. "The Shilling Magazines had interfered greatly with the success of novels published in numbers without other accompanying matter," he was to write later. "The Public finding that so much might be had for a shilling, in which a portion of one or more novels was always included, were unwilling to spend their money on the novel alone."

He ought to have known. The magazines were a means of publicizing and promoting house authors for the growing publishing houses that put them out, and so it was necessary to get strong writers to attract readers. What was the most he'd been offered for a novel? George Smith asked Trollope. Five hundred pounds, said Trollope. So "I offered him double the amount if he would write one of his clerical novels for the *Cornhill*," Smith later recalled. A dramatic gesture, but Smith knew what he was doing. *Cornhill*, after all, had shot out of the starting gate with 100,000 circulation for its very first issue, which had carried both *Framley Parsonage* and Thackeray's *Lovel the Widower*. (After which the circulation gradually went into a considerable decline—but only George Smith and a few others knew about it.)

Certainly competition from the new magazines might have worried Dickens, although it was Dickens' melodramatic criminality in novels like *Great Expectations* and *Oliver Twist* that had been among the progenitors of the new "sensation novel." Of course, Dickens' *All the Year Round* had benefited enormously from the best-selling publication of his friend Collins' *The Woman in White*. But by the spring of 1860 Collins' serial was coming to an end, and Dickens needed a big-name successor. Dickens wrote Marian Evans asking for the rights to serialize her next book. *Adam Bede*, published the year before, had been an extraordinary success, selling over 10,000 copies in a two-volume reprint edition alone. But Marian said no to Dickens, because of the "terseness and closeness of construction" that serial writing would require, the familiar Gaskell-type complaint. "Adam (or Eve) Bede is terrified by the novel difficulties of serial writing; cannot turn in the space; evidently will not be up to the scratch when Collins's sponge is thrown up," Dickens told Charles Lever in February 1860. Dickens commissioned a novel from Lever instead, which began appearing in *All the Year Round* in July 1860.

Dickens meanwhile "had begun a book which I intended for one of my long twenty number serials." It was to be a long, semiautobiographical tale of lost love, mistaken beliefs, and disappointment, and, at the usual length of twenty numbers, it would have been as long as *Bleak House* or *Little Dorrit*. But

Lever's novel failed to compel the magazine's readership, and Dickens, his money as publisher as well as editor now involved in his editorial efforts, feared the drop in circulation. "I must abandon that design and forego its profits (a very serious consideration, you may believe) and shape the story for these pages. I must get into these pages, as soon as possible," the point being, he said, that Lever's serial, which he allowed him to finish, should not drag the magazine under.

Accordingly, the first episode of Dickens' new novel, vastly shortened from the projected customary length, began appearing in the December 1, 1860 issue of *All the Year Round*. "My father's family name being Pirrip, and my christian name Philip," it began, "my infant tongue could make of both names nothing longer or more explicit than Pip." *Great Expectations*. For the first time—was it a sign of a growing fault line in Victorian fiction?—Dickens had been unable to contrive a happy ending for his hero and heroine at the novel's end.

Thackeray also felt the heat of competition, although more from the new writers, ironically, perhaps, most of all from the one he had helped to boost. "I think Trollope is much more popular with the *Cornhill Magazine* readers than I am," Thackeray noted privately with characteristic glumness as *Cornhill*'s serialization of Trollope's *Framley Parsonage* in 1860 and 1861 proved immensely popular, "and doubt whether I am not going downhill considerably in public favor." "I have told my tale in the novel department," he worried. The years of writing, writing, writing, overindulgence, and loneliness were taking their toll. "I can repeat old things in a pleasant way, but I have nothing fresh to say." The old facility was gone. "I cannot write comfortably in my own room," he complained. "I do most of my composition at hotels or a club. There is an excitement in public places which sets my brain working." And the coolness with Dickens remained. Finding themselves in seats next to one another at the Drury Lane Theater, Thackeray and Dickens shook hands "and didn't say one single word to each other," the former *Cornhill* editor noted.

Lord Lytton

1869

A sinister portrait of Dickens' friend—novelist, member of Parliament, and ultimately peer—Edward Bulwer Lytton. He is chiefly remembered now as the man who wrote the opening line "It was a dark and stormy night" (from his 1833 Paul Clifford) and the fellow author who persuaded Dickens to give Great Expectations a happy ending.

Kate Dickens, Dickens' favorite daughter, who had counseled her mother not to call on the Ternans when Dickens insisted, now incurred her father's wrath by marrying Wilkie Collins' brother, Charley, a dull, and also possibly homosexual man, twelve years her senior. Years later she confided that she had been in love with Thackeray's Garrick Club nemesis, Edmund Yates, but he was, alas, married. However, she was desperate to get out of the house after her parents separated, so impossible and irritable had her father become. "My father was like a madman when my mother left home," Kate recalled later. "He did not care a damn what happened to any of us."

So in July 1860, she and Charley Collins were wed. Dickens had opposed the match but celebrated it with customary grandiosity when it became inevitable, under the pretense that it was all a love match. He put on an elaborate ceremony at the house in Gad's Hill (from which Catherine was conspicuously absent), with a triumphal arch, and guns were fired off the night before by the local blacksmith. But the aftermath of the ceremony suggested that for Dickens, too, the world was beginning to darken. After the great celebration had occurred and the bridal couple and guests not staying in the house had departed, Dickens' daughter Mary went to her sister's old room to find their father on his knees, alone, sobbing brokenly into Kate's wedding dress. "But for me," he said, when he had arisen, "Katey would not have left home."

The newlyweds Kate Dickens Collins and her husband moved in near Thackeray's impressive new house at 2 Palace Green looking out on Kensington Gardens. George Smith's generosity had at last enabled Thackeray to live the life befitting a gentleman. Chatting with Kate one day in the spring of 1863, Thackeray admitted his regret at being alienated from Dickens. She encouraged Thackeray to take the initiative and talk to her father. Mindful of the thin basis on which Dickens's ego rested, she observed, "Perhaps he mightn't know you would be nice to him."

Just as the cozy Garrick Club was the chosen refuge of

those interested in the theater, the imposing Athenaeum Club was a select institution that harbored the nation's elite writers, scientists, and other learned worthies. A short time after Thackeray's conversation with Kate Dickens, he was talking to another man at the foot of the Athenaeum Club's grand staircase, when Dickens made his way out of the morning room after reading the papers. Ignoring Thackeray, he started up the stairs. "It is time this foolish estrangement should cease," said Thackeray, darting after him. "Come; shake hands." Dickens put out his hand, and they chatted briefly. They were to meet once more. Thackeray was suffering one of his increasingly frequent bouts of indisposition and told Dickens illness had kept him from working.

The topic of conversation was significant. Thackeray had never really recovered from his near fatal illness fifteen years before. Meanwhile, the difficulties with his digestive system and his urinary tract, possibly venereal in origin from his days as a young rake in London, got no better. During the rest of the year Thackeray remained ill. And sometimes in pain, once bursting out to his daughters, "Life at this purchase is not worth having. If it was not for you children I should be quite ready to go." He had, he thought, outlived his writing ability, even his interest in life, indeed, perhaps, his era.

At midnight, on December 23, Thackeray's mother heard him retching, a not infrequent symptom occasioned by his attacks, in his room, next to hers. In her room Anny, now twenty-six, dreamt that she and her father were "climbing a very high hill. We went higher & higher so that I had never seen anything like it before and Papa was pointing out something to me wh. I could not see & presently left me & I seemed to come down alone." Going out to the landing the next morning, she found Thackeray's servant: "He is dead, Miss; he is dead." Charley Collins was sent for. They found the novelist, his features by one account "distorted and discoloured," stretched out on the bed, his hands clutching at his nightshirt collar so rigidly he had to be buried that way.

"Thackeray is dead," said Dickens to a family friend who ran into him later that day, the writer's voice breaking. There had been losses untold in the circle of friends that had surrounded him. His friend the painter Augustus Egg had died in April, Dickens' mother in September. "I am in my fifty-second year with a sound of cheering behind me; but my heart faints sometimes under such troubles as I do know, and if it were not for a certain stand-up determination, I should be down. 'Who is hit?' Nelson said, without looking round, when they shot his Secretary," wrote Dickens to Charles Lever. He was separated from his wife, aging, alienated from his favorite child, and his view of English society was growing darker. "'I am hit,' ten thousand of us may cry at once instead, 'in a mortal place,' but our rest is before us, and we will work our way toward it." At Thackeray's grave six days later, 1,500 to 2,000 mourners in attendance, the day beautiful and sunny, Dickens stared into the grave, watching each shovelful of dirt as it fell onto the coffin after everyone else had left. He began to speak with some friends as he made his way from the grave, and then his voice trembled; he shook hands quickly and walked away.

Now of the old giants it was just Dickens, with Marian, Collins, Trollope, and the sensationalists all on his heels, symbolic of the energy and sensibility of the new generation. "He was fortunate," wrote Lever of Thackeray enviously, himself having had so recently and humiliatingly to be rescued by Dickens in *All the Year Round*, "to go down in the full blaze of his genius as so few do. The fate of most of us is to go on pouring water on the lees, so that people at last come to suspect that they have never got honest liquor from the tap at all." The venerable G. P. R. James was also dead, Lytton no longer a novelist of significance. "A strange, forlorn-looking being stopped me today," Robert Browning told John Forster. He'd seen Harrison Ainsworth, the author of that long-forgotten cause célèbre *Jack Sheppard*. Forster was shocked—"Is he still alive?"

And then there was Mrs. Gaskell.

George Smith had never bawled her out for the potentially

disastrous problems she had created with her *Life of Charlotte Brontë*, even though Lady Scott's lawsuit had forced the publisher to withdraw the remaining copies in circulation of a first edition that was selling well, pull an already advertised second edition, and then print a brand-new third edition to comply with Lady Scott's demands.

Mrs. Gaskell had thereafter remained steadfastly loyal to him. "I would much rather have £800 from you than £1,000 from them," she wrote to him glowingly after getting an offer from another publisher. "I mean literally what I say." Whereupon, Smith being Smith of the author-dazzling open pocket, he naturally offered her £1,000. To Smith's *Cornhill Magazine* she contributed *Cousin Phillis* and *Wives and Daughters*. With her earnings she bought (sight unseen) a house and four acres in Hampshire in the summer of 1865 as a surprise for her husband. Smith characteristically helped out with advice, plus, ever the omni-competent merchant, arranged a 22 1/2 percent trade discount on furniture she bought through him and a loan of £1,000 against the £2,600 purchase price. Mrs. Gaskell had managed to keep the house purchase secret from her husband and discussed gaily at tea one afternoon in November 1865 how to make it available to a recently widowed in-law. She was just in the midst of a sentence when she slid into the arms of the person sitting next to her on the sofa. She died almost at once.

A new generation of writers was taking over. There were the chroniclers of everyday life like Marian Evans and Trollope, and also the sensationalists like Collins or Mrs. Braddon. In the case of the latter, there was perhaps a certain literalness about them that hindered them from reaching into the first rank of imaginative work. Reade, for example, kept rows of scrapbooks filled with newspaper and magazine clippings indexed by subject matter for use in his books. "Let us take 'Heroism,'" he told the visiting George Smith and handed down a huge volume and showed the stories therein on the subject to the publisher. "For eighteen years the journal you conduct so ably has been

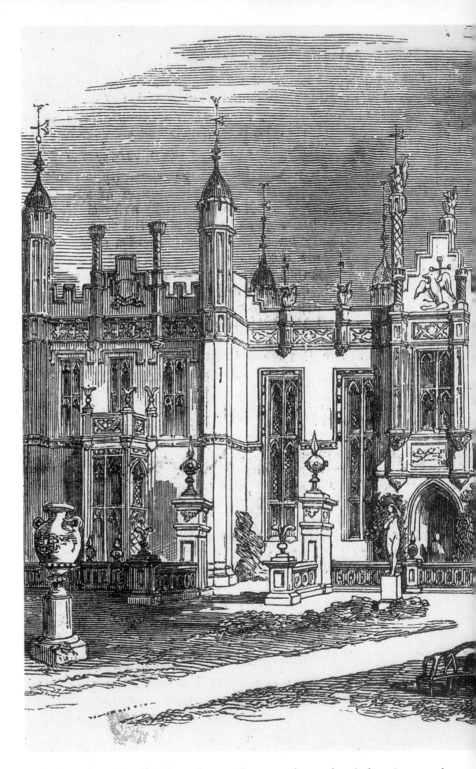

Knebworth, in Hertfordshire, the grand country house that Bulwer Lytton inherited. In 1850 he and Dickens agreed to locate here through their Guild of

Literature and Art rent-free cottages for decrepit writers.

my preceptor and the main source of my works," Reade wrote in an unsolicited letter to the *Times'* editor in 1871. "A noble passage in the 'Times' of September 7 or 8, 1853, touched my heart, inflamed my imagination, and was the germ of my first important work, 'It is Never Too Late to Mend'." Likewise, two scrapbooks of news clippings were found in Wilkie Collins' library after he died, with headings like "Hints for Scenes and Incidents" and "Hints for Character."

But then a certain prosiness seemed to be popular with the reading public. "Mr. Anthony Trollope is, in fact, the most fertile, the most popular, the most successful author—that is to say, of the circulating library sort," said the *Times*, for example, somewhat condescendingly in May 1859. And so he was, and, once he appeared in *Cornhill*, his popularity increased enormously. "You have brought me in contact with readers to [be] counted by hundreds of thousands instead of by hundreds," Trollope wrote gratefully to George Smith, after the latter had characteristically sent him a large fancy traveling bag in celebration of *Framley Parsonage*'s success. "At the beginning of every month the new number of his book has ranked almost as one of the delicacies of the season," said the *Saturday Review* in May 1861, when the book had begun to appear. Mrs. Gaskell had told George Smith that "every one I know is always dreading the *last* number." Even *Sharpe's London Magazine*, which attacked the book, had to concede that Trollope "is now, perhaps, the most popular of our modern novelists."

And Trollope had even come to look successful, having filled out into the tall, loud-voiced, rather heavyset personage with a beard like shredded wheat familiar from his photographs. There was little trace now of the dirty, friendless boy whom everyone at Harrow had taken for a dunce. "A big, red-faced, rather underbred Englishman of the bald-with-spectacles type," James Russell Lowell found him when Trollope visited Boston, "a good roaring positive fellow who deafened me." He was elected to the Garrick Club in the spring of 1862, among whose members—the political series was still in the future—was a man named Palliser. The membership made him almost pathetically grateful. "I have ever had a wish to be liked by those around me . . . In my school-days no small part of my misery came from the envy with which I regarded the popularity of popular boys," the former schoolboy whom no one at Harrow had liked later wrote. "The Garrick Club was the first assemblage of men at which I felt myself to be popular." In August 1869 Trollope even bought for £10,000 a partnership for his son Henry in Chapman and Hall (which needed help after Frederick Chapman took over).

In technique as well as subject matter, Trollope was certainly no rebel. When Thackeray's personal possessions were sold after his death, Trollope had sorrowfully bought a dish to remind him of his friend, whom Trollope called "the greatest master of fiction of this age." Likewise, Trollope's *Barchester* books borrowed from Thackeray the device of using the same characters recurrently in a series of novels. *Pendennis* had interconnected with *Henry Esmond* in this fashion and, in turn, Arthur Pendennis had then supposedly become the narrator of both *Philip* and *The Newcomes*. (Bulwer Lytton had done the same with his 1853 *My Novel*, using a character from his 1849 *The Caxtons*, and there was also a link among the volumes of Disraeli's "Young England" political trilogy.) Trollope was to make use of the device of interrelated novels in his *Palliser* series as well. "If the present fashion continues, and the heroes of one novel reappear so constantly in the next," said a grumpy reviewer of *Framley Parsonage* in 1861, "readers will begin to hope that funerals, and not marriages, may in future be the finale in which all romances terminate."

Trollope was becoming such a prominent figure in the aftermath of Mrs. Gaskell's and Thackeray's deaths that it was now his turn to be imitated. Mrs. Oliphant paid Trollope's 1867 *The Last Chronicle of Barset* the compliment of subtitling her 1876 *Phoebe Junior: A Last Chronicle of Carlingsford*—indeed, her *Carlingsford* series echoed his Barsetshire books. And, like Thackeray before him, the new pillar of English letters felt he had attained sufficient prominence to try for a seat in the House of Commons. Unlike Thackeray, Trollope had a decent income from writing, so he was not hoping to turn political victory into a chance at a good job. Then why do it? Anthony's ambition "to become a candidate," the ever-Parliament-hating Dickens wrote to Anthony's brother, Tom Trollope, "is inscrutable to me."

"I have always thought that to sit in the British Parliament should be the highest object of ambition to every educated Englishman," Anthony later wrote by way of explanation. Characteristically, he was also using his newfound celebrity to battle old slights and insecurities he had suffered as a youth. What do you want to be? his uncle had said when Trollope had been in his early twenties. The boy, already at work in the mail service, replied that he wanted to be in Parliament. Uncle Henry found this risible—how many Post Office clerks became members of Parliament? "It was the remembrance of this jeer," wrote the ever sensitive Trollope years later, "which stirred me up to look for a seat as soon as I had made myself capable of holding one by leaving public service."

Trollope, as it turned out, had decided to run in one of the most thoroughly corrupt electoral districts in the country, namely, the borough of Beverley, the fourteen-thousand-person capital of the East Riding of Yorkshire. "You will spend £1,000, and lose the election," said his campaign agent glumly. "Then you will petition, and spend another £1,000. You will throw out the elected members. There will be a commission, and the borough will be disfranchised," all of which, except for the amount expended and Trollope's role in the petition that was eventually brought, turned out to be largely true. The election proved so crooked that a judicial investigation was ordered, and at a later inquiry by a royal commission, Trollope suffered the indignity of having to testify that "to my knowledge none of the money was used to corrupt the electors, either by money or beer, or any other way, before or after the election." Politics' loss was literature's gain. Trollope's interest in politics had already led him to begin work on a series of "parliamentary novels"; Phineas Finn had begun appearing in *Saint Paul's Magazine* in October 1867. Now "as I was debarred from expressing myself in the House of Commons," he wrote later, "I took this method of declaring myself."

Of Trollope, Evans, Collins, and Reade, it could be said that their careers were all going well. And now, as if in a sort of generational counterpoint, Dickens, the last major representative of the old guard, the man who had started it all, seemed to be failing. John Leech, his illustrator on *A Christmas Carol*, died in late October 1864. After Christmas that year Dickens had terrible gout, and *All the Year Round*, battered by competition from the *Cornhill*-like new magazines, absorbed his attention. Lewes ran into his old friend after Dickens had been caught in a train wreck at Staplehurst while returning from a vacation in Paris in June 1865. Dickens vividly described its horrors. (Three years later Dickens would still suffer "vague rushes of terror, even when riding in a hansom cab.")

He looked sick, worn—there were fewer old friends around to divert him as grim thoughts flooded in. Another of his old illustrators, Thackeray's one-time illustrator, George Cruikshank, who had done *Oliver Twist*, had fallen on hard times. A subscription was taken up for him, Dante Gabriel Rossetti acting as treasurer. *Our Mutual Friend* began appearing in monthly numbers in May, 1864—its themes of the Thames dragged for bodies, murder, betrayal and greed ever darker and less susceptible to the leavening of Dickensian jollity. Meanwhile, Dickens' pulse deteriorated, and his doctor told him he needed a heart exam, yet in April 1866 he embarked on another reading tour.

It was owing to the restlessness and energy that had produced so many characters, so many different endeavors—and that was now wearing him out. He was suffering from insomnia and from pains in his eye, stomach, and chest. He made another tour in January 1867. Then in November he toured America—it was still where the big money was, and he was still big box office. When it was announced that tickets would

Macmillan and Co.'s

ANNOUNCEMENTS.

THIS DAY.

1.

MACMILLAN'S MAGAZINE.

No. XIII. (commencing Vol. III.) for NOVEMBER, 1860, price One Shilling.

Contents.

I. LIFE AND POETRY OF KEATS. By the EDITOR.
II. A DEFENCE OF MOTHERS-IN-LAW. By a SON-IN-DITTO.
III. KYLOE JOCK AND THE WEIRD OF WANTON WALLS. By GEORGE CUPPLES. Chaps. 5 and 6.
IV. THE LOST CLUE.
V. SYSTEMATIZED EXERCISE. By ARCHIBALD MACLAREN.
VI. TOM BROWN AT OXFORD. Chapters 31 and 32.
VII. BLIND! By the Author of 'JOHN HALIFAX.'
VIII. THE GOLDEN ISLAND: ARRAN FROM AYR.
IX. INDIAN CITIES: BENARES.
X. THE NEAPOLITAN REVOLUTION AND THE FUGITIVE SLAVE LAW. By the Rev. F. D. MAURICE.
XI. TORQUIL AND OONA. By ALEXANDER SMITH.
XII. ITALIAN UNITY AND THE NATIONAL MOVEMENT IN EUROPE. By J. S. BARKEL.

VOLS. I. and II. handsomely bound in cloth, price 7s. 6d. each.

2.

LIFE on the EARTH: its ORIGIN and SUCCESSION.

By JOHN PHILLIPS, M.A., F.R.S., F.G.S., Professor of Geology in the University of Oxford, and Rede Lecturer in the University of Cambridge, &c. With Illustrations. Crown 8vo. *[Immediately.*

3.

INTRODUCTION to the STUDY and USE of the PSALMS.

By the Rev. J. F. THRUPP, Author of 'An Investigation into the Topography, &c. of Ancient Jerusalem.' 2 vols. 8vo. 21s. *[This day.*

4.

LIFE of DR. GEORGE WILSON,

F.R.S.E., late Regius Professor of Technology in the

CHEAP NOVELS.

The following Books, withdrawn from Mudie's Library, are offered in Parcels of One Hundred Volumes each, at Five Pounds per Parcel.

G.

	vols.
The Mill on the Floss	3
Castle Richmond, by A. Trollope	3
The Man of the People	3
Almost a Heroine	3
The Voyage of 'The Lady'	2
Stretton of Ringwood Chace	3
The Minister's Wooing	1
The Old Palace, by Julia Tilt	3
Mary Bertrand	2
The Master of the Hounds	3
Maud Skillicorne's Penance	2
Lucy Crofton, by Mrs. Oliphant	1
Against Wind and Tide	3
Ellen Raymond, by Mrs. Vidal	3
Confidences, by Author of 'Rita,'	1
The Wood-Rangers, by Capt. Reid	3
Mr. and Mrs. Asheton	3
Onward! Author of Anne Dysart	3
The Lees of Blendon Hall	3
Every Man His Uwn Trumpeter	3
Hawkview, by Holme Lee	3
The Days of My Life	3
Nelly Carew	3
White Lies, by Charles Reade	3
The Ladies of Bever Hollow	2
Katherine, by Author of 'Clara'	3
The Light of Other Days	2
The Squire of Beechwood	3
Year after Year	1
Grandmamma's Money	3
Seymour and His Friends	3
Life and its Realities	3
Phantastes, by George Macdonald	1
Fellow Travellers	1
Dred, by Mrs. Stowe	3
The Brownrigg Papers	3
Female Influence, by Lady Pepys	1
Round the Sofa, by Mrs. Gaskell	2
Julian Home, by F. W. Farrar	1
What Will He Do with It?	4
Lennox's Story of My Life	3

H.

	vols.
Transformation, by N. Hawthorne	3
The Mill on the Floss	3
The Little Beauty	3
Adele, by Julia Kavanagh	3
Laura Gay	2
Trust for Trust	3
Rita, an Autobiography	1
Debit and Credit	3
Almost a Heroine	3
Cousin Stella	3
Before the Dawn in Italy	2
Say and Seal, by E. Wetherell	1
Creeds	3
The First-Born	3
Cecilia Metella, a Tale of Rome	1
Nelly Carew	3
Wait and Hope, by J. E. Reade	3
Olive Hastings, by Mrs. Parry	2
A Lovers' Quarrel	1
Madelein Clare	3
Every Day	1
Hanworth	3
Extremes	3
The Old Grey Church	3
Diana Wynyard	3
An Old Debt, by Florence Dawson	2
Ordeal of Richard Feverel	3
The Denn; or, Popular Preacher	3
Hinchbridge Haunted	3
Cuthbert St. Elme, M.P.	3
The Ruling Passion	3
The Heirs of Cheveleigh	3
Sir Rohan's Ghost	1
Rank and Beauty	3
Cousin Harry, by Mrs. Grey	2
Deborah's Diary	1
When the Snow Falls	2
Which is Which? by R. B. Brough	1
The Laird of Norlaw	3
The Queen of Hearts	3

I.

	vols.
A Life for a Life	3
Seven Years, by Julia Kavanagh	3
The Man of the People	3
The Mill on the Floss	3
Ursula, by Miss Sewell	1
Father and Daughter	2
The Poor Relation, by Miss Pardoe	2
Edward Willoughby	1
Two Homes, by W. Matthews	2
The Bertrans, by A. Trollope	3
The Earl's Cedars	3
The Day of Small Things	1
Greymore	3
Franklehill Hall	3
Helen Lester	1
Letheller	3
The Rose of Ashurst	3
Tried in the Fire	3
Woman's Temptation	2
Margurite's Legacy	2
The First-Born	3
Freshfield, by W. Johnstone	1
The Cousins' Courtship	2
Henry Clarendon	3
Only a Woman	3
The Reigning Beauty	2
Misrepresentation, by Anna Drury	3
Lord Fitzwarine	3
Anne Sherwood	3
The Way of the World	3
The Tin Box	1
The Land of the Kelt	3
Life's Foreshadowings	3
George Barrington	1
Elfie in Sicily	2
The Eve of St. Mark	2
The Year Nine	1
Kinahan Cornwallis's Adventures	2
A Will and a Way	2
The Lady in Waiting	2
The Fate of Folly	3

The above Books are offered in Parcels (G, H and I), as assorted, for Cash only.—Payment should therefore be made in every instance when the order is given.

CHARLES EDWARD MUDIE, 511, New Oxford-street, London.

A page from the literary magazine The Athenæum. The rapid turnover in novels is indicated by Mudie's Library selling as "cheap novels" in batches of a hundred those that had fallen out of favor. The lefthand column shows the contents of a typical issue of Macmillan's Magazine.

An advertisement for Charles Mudie's "select" library in 1860 shortly before he opened his gigantic store on New Oxford Street.

go on sale at nine in the morning for his lecture in Boston, crowds furnished with blankets began lining up outside the Ticknor & Fields Old Corner Bookstore at ten o'clock the night before. "It is impossible to get tickets," wrote Henry James (still signing himself "Junior"), a young resident of Cambridge, which was across the river, to his brother. "At 7 o'clock A.M. on the first day of the sale there were two or three hundred at the office, and at 9, when I strolled up, nearly a thousand," and $14,000 worth of tickets—reserved tickets were $2 each—were sold in eleven hours. A manufacturer was so moved by the *Christmas Carol* reading that he inaugurated an annual tradition of giving his whole factory Christmas Day off and buying turkeys for all the workers. It was the same in New York, crowds lining up for hours, waiting for the literary superstar despite his growing exhaustion.

But the tour was brutal on Dickens' health. There was the misery of having to travel in upstate and western New York during the winter. By December he had acquired what seemed to be a chronic flu that affected his heart, and he became more pronouncedly lame. At times he was unable to eat; raw eggs beaten in sherry just before the performance and then beef tea at intermission got him through the readings.

When a twelve-year-old admirer named Kate Douglas Wiggin (later to be the author of *Rebecca of Sunnybrook Farm*) materialized beside his seat on the train from Portland, Maine, to Boston, a brief light moment was provided. After rhapsodizing over Dickens' novels, she admitted that she did now and then omit "some of the very dull parts." Dickens roared with laughter and pressed for details as to which parts were the clunkers. She helpfully enumerated them, she later recalled, "dealing these infant blows, under the delusion that I was flinging him bouquets."

And then it was finally over. As Dickens left the United States on April 22, 1868, Trollope came out on a mail tender in New York harbor to bid farewell to Dickens' outbound Cunard line steamer in a symbolic transfer of the literary torch. The younger man was arriving to negotiate a new postal treaty and to try—once again, in Dickens' old dream—to work out a copyright agreement between the United States and Britain.

The five-month tour ended with a net profit to Dickens of over £20,000, but he returned shaky and worn.

He had begun his readings in 1858, just before the great age of the sensational novel. Now he said, perhaps thinking of Collins and Reade, the public needed a new "sensation," so he worked up the murder of Nancy by Bill Sikes from *Oliver Twist* into a forty-minute performance for yet another series of readings, this one beginning in late 1868. Dickens performed both roles, of course; audiences watched in horror as his voice rose to a shout while he enacted the enraged strangler and the desperately pleading doomed woman, with "the blood and the gore flying all over." At Clifton some dozen or so women fainted when he read the murder scene. His friends were horrified at the strain that the tour took on him; slow down, said his readings manager, at which Dickens yelled at the man, threw down his cutlery so violently it smashed his plate—and then tearfully apologized.

Like a superstar ever more driven by the need to perform—and ever more a casualty of the intense round of performances—he was visibly exhausted when not on stage. Dickens toured England again in early 1869 with continuing damage to his health, suffering intestinal bleeding, severe problems with his foot, and weakness on his left side. His doctors called a halt to the readings—to which Dickens reluctantly agreed, turning back to a novel instead, his last, *The Mystery of Edwin Drood*. At Christmas the Dickens family played the old game of Memory in which the players had to make long, unassociated lists of things. When it came Dickens' turn he appended to the long catalog "Warren's Blacking, 30 Strand" in a tone of voice that made his son Henry look at him strangely. Not until after his death would they learn about his humiliation at the blacking factory located there. There was another brief reading tour beginning in January 1870; he all but prostrated himself, his pulse rate, which was 72 when he was not giving a reading, soaring as high as 124 after a performance. "You must be there every night," Dickens' doctor warned the novelist's son, after the physician had ordered steps placed next to Dickens' reading platform—merely climbing to the platform told ever more heavily on the writer's stamina. "And if you see your father falter in the least, you must run and catch him and bring him off with me, or, by heaven, he'll die before them all." Dickens enacted the murder night after night, the gestures vivid, his voice rising to a shout. "I shall tear myself to pieces," he said the last time he performed *Sikes and Nancy*. He was killing himself—literally and figuratively—yet he could not stop. A faithless man murdering his faithful female companion—and enmeshed in guilt. Was there an echo of his abandonment of Catherine? She was never to forget him. One afternoon before her death in 1879, from her sickbed she asked Kate to fetch a package of her now-dead husband's letters to her. Give it to the British Museum, she said: "That the world may know that he loved me once."

But even before meeting Ellen Ternan, Dickens wrote to Forster from France in 1856 that he was always hearing "how odd it is that the hero of an English book is always uninteresting—too good—not natural, etc. I am continually hearing this of Scott from English people here, who pass their lives with Balzac and Sand." A change from this, of course, was one of the things people sought in the sensation novel. Since he had taken up with Ellen, his heroes had passed from the simple, good-natured likes of Nicholas Nickleby, Oliver Twist, and David Copperfield to men haunted by guilt, snobbery, or other often unpleasant impulses, and, like Pip or Sydney Carton, often leading secret or shameful lives. Dickens himself had rented a house for Ellen at Peckham not far from London, which he visited under the surname "Tringham."

In the wake of his affair with Ellen and the collapse of his marriage, was there a self-disillusionment that perhaps made it more difficult to keep turning out those same one-dimensional

" Well, Syusan, 'ow did yer like Aroorer Floyd last night?"
" Oh! so lovely, Jeames—I cried so! that wicked Conyers! . . . Oh, Jeames, you won't desert me for our young Missus, will you, dear?"

Until the coming of playwrights like Shaw and Wilde, the nineteenth-century English theater was notoriously melodramatic and excessive. However, it was often the medium through which the uneducated or illiterate gained access to novels, dramatized for the stage as best sellers are for the movies today. Here, a footman and a maid discuss a dramatization of *Aurora Floyd*, one of the works of the sensational novelist Miss Braddon.

heroes? Perhaps, too, it was a sign of a deeper shift in the course of the novel. Both the deep psychology of Marian Evans and the concealed machinations of the villains in the sensational novels dealt with the difference between outward and inner personality. If one were to press the double-life analogy, one might note that Marian Evans wrote under a pseudonym, Wilkie Collins actually maintained not one but two mistresses surreptitiously, and Miss Braddon lived in a delicate social subterfuge with her "husband," concealing the very *Jane Eyre*–like fact that he was still married to an insane woman whom he could not divorce. (When the servants discovered Miss Braddon's secret, like all good servants, they quit en masse.) But then the staple plot device of the sensational novel was bigamy.

Approaching sixty, worn out from emotional turmoil, disappointment in his family, the constant train rides, the one-night stands, and the guilt and logistics of his double life, Dickens found sometimes when he walked the streets that he could not shake the murder of Nancy from his thoughts—or from his soul—"I am guilty—touched in blood, wreathed in gore."

His children continued to worry or grieve him. Kate had moved out to marry Charley Collins, and Charley Dickens, thirty-one, now married to Bessie Evans and bankrupt to the tune of £1,000, his father had settled with a job (successfully, as it turned out) at *All the Year Round*. And Dickens then sent the almost seventeen-year-old "Plorn" out to join his brother Alfred in Australia—only for the arrangement to collapse. "But he seems to have been born without a groove," his father observed sadly. "If he cannot, or will not find one, I must try again, and die trying." *The Mystery of Edwin Drood*, his bid to write a "sensational" novel, complete, like his protégé Collins', with murder and drug use, began monthly serialization in April 1870. One of the women in it was called Helena Landless, an echo of Ellen Lawless (Ternan)? The echoing *es* and *ls*— Helen, Ellen. How much gratification was the relationship with

"Nelly," as he called Ellen Ternan, providing him? In his only real treatment of adult passion, written three years after he met her, an icy but beautiful young girl torments the hero in *Great Expectations*, her name—"Estella"—again, like Ellen's, a cluster of echoing *es* and *ls*.

Dickens was one of the most distinguished figures in England now. There was an audience with the Queen in March 1870. She stood in apparent deference to his ill health, and they chatted—Dickens must have been compelled by the subject for he spoke of it also to Marian Evans at lunch the same month—of Abraham Lincoln's grim dream before his assassination of drifting alone down a dark river. Former Secretary of War Stanton had told Dickens the story in Washington on his recent American tour. (Evans found Dickens "dreadfully shattered.")

He appeared for one last farewell communion with his beloved public on March 15, 1870, reading from *Pickwick*, with which, so many years before, the interaction with his public had all begun. Then the audience besieged him with applause until he returned, his face streaked with tears, stood one last time before them and put his hands to his lips in a kiss. "Ladies and gentlemen," he said, "I close this episode in my life with feelings of very considerable pain."

He was weakening. One day his son Charles went in to see him in his study in town, spoke to him, and his father continued writing; his son called again, louder—and the novelist looked up—and stared right through him, wordlessly, unseeing. Dickens learned on April 27 of the death of a longtime friend, the artist Daniel Maclise. But that man is killing himself with his work, Prime Minister Gladstone observed after the novelist had left after a breakfast with him. Another old friend, Mark Lemon, the jovial amateur actor and editor of *Punch*, died on May 23, and not many days after in a late-night discussion Dickens talked until the dawn began to break with his beloved Kate of her plans to go on the stage and warned her against it. No, he said, "although there are nice people on the stage, there are some who would make your hair stand on end." He wished, he said, with words that must have had meaning for her even as it now seemed too late, that he had been "a better father—a better man." She left the next morning—and on her way to depart after a quick good-bye to her father, on an unusual impulse she suddenly returned to embrace him, and Dickens rose, also uncharacteristically, to embrace her in turn.

A few days later Dickens and his ever-loyal sister-in-law Georgina Hogarth were at dinner when he announced suddenly that he had to go immediately to London. As he rose from his chair, he almost collapsed. Georgina caught him before he fell to the ground. (Or so the official version had it; there is reason to believe that he was visiting Ellen Ternan at the house he had secured for her in Peckham Rye when he suffered the attack and that she brought the still-living man back to Gad's Hill hurriedly and surreptitiously by carriage.) His doctor was sent for and they made him comfortable, watching through the next day even as it became clear he would not rally. Outside on the steps the children sat amid the scent of early summer flowers. On June 9 around six o'clock he sighed heavily, and a single tear made its way down his cheek. And so he died, on his desk, the installment writer to the end, the unfinished serial manuscript of *Edwin Drood*, three numbers already published, three lying ready to go.

He was the quintessential Victorian self-made man, the hard-working boy from a lower-middle-class origin who had transformed himself from a struggling writer into a wealthy man, famous all over the world, just as the novel had itself gone from being an elite amusement to a new, vibrant mass medium. In the process Dickens demonstrated that novelists could become rich, famous, eminently respectable, figures to be reckoned with. Badgered to run for Parliament, rumored to be offered honors by the Queen, Dickens left an estate of £93,000, unheard of at the time for a writer. The new middle-class culture had demanded new books and new topics and he had provided them.

Many novelists before him had written anonymously, like

Dickens at his most authorial looking. His dress and mien suggest how novelists in general—and he in particular—had gone from being marginal or even socially disreputable figures at the turn of the century to imposing moral and social authorities.

Scott, and even Thackeray's writings were for years pseudonymous, but Dickens used his own name almost from the beginning of his career. He was not only proud of what he did but
sought the limelight. Through his lectures and acting he created
the role of the author as a source of live entertainment. In this
he was distinctly modern, and the nature of Dickens' relationship to his public was modern in still another way. When it
came time for him to split from his wife, he felt the need to jus-
tify this most personal of decisions to his bewildered readers,
most of whom, in that more innocent age, had not a clue that
anything was wrong. In fact, this plea for understanding seems
to have been part of a desperate need Dickens had for his public, as evidenced by how he kept writing serials—and performing his suicidal readings—when there was little or no economic
or literary reason any longer to do so.

At what cost?

Looking back, one sees the hints of violence, the darkness, that
increasingly shadowed the later novels and the restless outlets—
the obsessive walking, the self-destructive readings, the turning
against his family—that he sought for his churning psyche. There
was, of course, the midnight pacing through London. And there is
an early account of him jokingly dragging a girl down a ramp into
the incoming water at the seaside resort of Broadstairs as the terrified girl pleaded with him to let her go as the sea (which figures in
the imagery surrounding Paul Dombey's death in *Dombey and
Son*) reaches out to engulf them both as he chuckled away his family's remonstrations until the girl broke free and fled, terrified,
down the pier. "The great ocean, Death," as Lizzie Hexam had
called it in *Our Mutual Friend*. Was he also one of the first willing
victims of the new celebrity culture that the mass media made
possible? The growing sensationalism of his later performances
and writings perhaps reflected inner tension as well as a desire to
keep up with changing literary tastes. On the next-to-last page of
his reading copy for the hugely successful *Sikes and Nancy* that
helped to kill him there was a large scrawled reminder—"Terror
To The End."

PART 6

"WE ARE A NOVEL-READING COUNTRY": *MIDDLEMARCH* AND MR. MUDIE'S LIBRARY, THE NOVEL APPARENTLY TRIUMPHANT, BUT HENRY JAMES FAILS, OMINOUSLY, TO WRITE A HAPPY ENDING

At Dickens' death, there could of one thing be no doubt. "We have become a novel-reading people," said Trollope in 1870, "from the Prime Minister down to the last-appointed scullery-maid ... Poetry we also read and history, biography and the social and political news of the day. But all our other reading put together hardly amounts to what we read in novels." However you looked at it, the novel had come to dominate. "The list of writers is now swelled to hundreds," said an article in *All the Year Round* on "Novel Names" in December 1871, joking that there were so many novelists that "the difficulty will be to find those who will listen." Some 25 new novels were published in 1820 in Great Britain; by 1850 the total was about 100—and by 1864 it was around 300. And in 1874 no less than 644 adult novels (i.e., not for juveniles) were published. Looking back on the start of his literary career, an Irish literary man who had come to London in 1876 observed that when he first arrived, "I wrote novels because everybody did so then; and the theatre, my rightful kingdom, was outside literature." Thus, George Bernard Shaw, who as a young man wrote no less than five novels, invariably rejected, before turning to playwriting—"five heavy brown-paper parcels," he remembered them, "which were always coming back to me from some publisher, and raising the very serious financial question of the sixpence to be paid to Messrs. Carter, Paterson

& Company, the carriers, for passing them on to the next publisher." "All my life," Gladstone, an inveterate reader and
haunter of Mudie's, confessed to Miss Braddon, author of *Lady
Audley's Secret*, toward the end of the century, "I have known,
and a little fretted, yes wept, under the knowledge that to construct a novel worthy of the name was for me not difficult but
impossible."

The novel, indeed, had come a long way from the harum-
scarum early days when pieces of cheap cardboard and paper
were used to bind novels, the same books that were laboriously
printed a few pages at a time by hand, the air beaten out from
between their pages with special pulpers, and then hand sewn.
Now the beautiful, cloth-bound books that poured from the
presses with embossed covers served notice of the existence of
a new, well-heeled mass market and new, mechanical techniques for meeting its demands. As if providing proof of the
novel's supremacy and respectability, Mudie in December 1860
had opened a gigantic superstore/corporate headquarters
boasting a stock of one million volumes on the site of his old
store. "Do you want me and my daughters to go?" Thackeray
wrote tersely to George Smith about the grand opening.
Mudie's invitation, said the writer, was "bumptious," and
Mudie's behavior objectionable, "but in the way of business, if
you would like me to show—I'm your man."

Entering the big gray building with "high windows and
swinging glass doors," the visitor found himself before a huge
semicircular counter with cards for the store's twenty-five
thousand subscribers. Some of them could be seen on any
given day looking at catalogs or waiting for books they had
requested to be brought by attendants in striped pants from the
main floor or the upper galleries all around in which the most
popular titles were arranged by size and then in alphabetical
order.

Upstairs there was the custom gift department where costly
books suitable for prizes, wedding presents, and the like were
sold, and a bindery where old circulating books could be

repaired or special "prize" books bound in special leather bindings. After a request for books had come in from St. Petersburg
in the 1850s, the overseas division shipped out hundreds of
thousands of volumes a year to remote colonial outposts, all
packed in watertight tin-lined boxes suitable for transport by
rail or sea. (After a shipwreck, the contents of lost boxes of
Mudie's books found at the bottom of the ocean were said to be
in perfect condition when the boxes were opened.)

Before long Birmingham and Manchester also had a
Mudie's, and, as befitted its tony subscription base, the store
branched out into the sale of theater and opera tickets.
(Interestingly, Mudie turned down W. H. Smith's offer to do a
railway circulating library, which, when Smith then undertook
it himself, eventually became a thriving part of his business.)
Carriages lined up outside as subscribers poured through the
doors to seek the latest best sellers, and demand was high, so
much so that clerks unable to find a requested volume often
substituted another. "I don't subscribe to Mudie's," sniffed
Lady Linlithgow in Trollope's *The Eustace Diamonds*, "because
when I asked for 'Adam Bede,' they always sent me the 'Bandit
Chief.'" Still, if a book *was* in stock, a two-guinea subscriber living within twenty miles of London could have it delivered by
one of the nine Mudie vans within a few hours of placing an
order.

Novelists were becoming commensurately prosperous.
Thackeray, after all, had in 1860 bought a new house of dimen-
sions so grand that one relative referred to it as Thackeray's
"Vanity Fair." Trollope had had the Post Office reassign him
from Ireland to England: "A man who could write books ought
not to live in Ireland,—ought to live within the reach of the
publishers, the clubs, and the dinner parties of the metropolis,"
he later said. With his new prosperity in late 1859 he moved to
Waltham House, twelve miles and a half hour's train ride north
of London, "where we grew our own cabbages and strawber-
ries, made our own butter, and killed our own pigs," and
where he added on a drawing room. Friends took the train

The grand opening of Charles Mudie's London "select" circulating library in December 1860. At Mudie's, customers called at the central counter where their selections were entered on borrowing cards, as attendants summoned by elevator

books stored in the "catacombs" below ground or blew whistles to direct the clerks who manned the shelves of the upper galleries. Books were also shipped out to patrons all over the Empire.

down to enjoy six o'clock dinner and the old garden, around which a startled George Smith on arising early one morning "saw Trollope dragging a garden roller at what might be called a canter" for exercise. Meanwhile, in February 1862 Smith offered Marian Evans the unheard of sum of £10,000 for the rights to serialize *Romola* in *Cornhill*. With her profits she and Lewes acquired a long-term lease in August 1863 on the Priory, 21 North Bank, Regent's Park, a little, shabby, two-story building with a brick wall around it and a little garden. The days when Evans and Lewes could remember, after eating a partridge given them by their landlady, such satisfaction that they concluded they had not been eating well enough were finally behind them.

Naturally, the largesse spilled over to their publishers. George Smith had made money since the 1840s—Smith, Elder's cash flow had shot up from £48,088 in 1846 to £627,129 in 1866 as a function both of the revenues from *Jane Eyre* and from a boom in the company's non-publishing business. Smith now entertained friends and writers at his new house in Gloucester Square where he gave the *Cornhill* parties at which Trollope met Thackeray and Lewes. The house, Smith noted, "had been previously occupied by Mr Sadleir, notorious for his frauds, who was found dead on Hampstead Heath with a silver cream-jug by his side which contained prussic acid." (Sadleir, a swindler in the railway business, was a model for the infamous Merdle in *Little Dorrit* and for the crooked Melmotte in *The Way We Live Now*.) Also prospering were the Macmillan brothers, Daniel and Alexander. Their stock-in-trade being religious and academic books, in 1855 they had entered the fiction world, with, not surprisingly, a work by a curate, the up-to-date Charles Kingsley. A first edition of 1,250 copies of his swashbuckling, nationalistic *Westward Ho!* went rapidly, followed by a second edition of 750, and a third—in one volume—of 6,000. Alexander traveled down regularly from the brothers' shop in Cambridge to London on Thursday nights for a "Tobacco parliament" of booze, tea, and smokes with Macmillan authors at a round table that attracted the likes of Tennyson, Herbert Spencer, and Thomas Huxley.

Publishers, indeed, were becoming mighty if they could buy houses in Balham or acquire the dwellings of railway swindlers—even if they could not yet be immune from the subtle gibes of their authors. "By some defect in the construction of the house," Smith recalled of his Gloucester Square House, "when the front door was opened the drawing-room door also slowly opened, and the wind lifted the carpet in slight waves. Thackeray, whose humour was sometimes of a grim sort, was never tired of suggesting that it was Sadleir's ghost come in search of some deeds which had been hidden under the floor."

Still, it all went to show that "it may be the age of anything else people like," wrote poet-novelist Alfred Austin in 1874, "but assuredly it is the age of Novels."

However . . .

With the death of Dickens, the Brontës, and the others, was it also possible that, well, that somehow novels were becoming a little more dull?

Whatever the merits of Trollope and Evans, perhaps the leading novelists of the age, their works in contrast to those of the writers that preceded them had a sober, perhaps at times a somewhat plodding quality. Or so, at any rate, it seemed to some. "I couldn't take to it more than to others I have tried by the Greatest Novelist of the Day," wrote Edward FitzGerald, the dilettante translator of *The Rubáiyát of Omar Khayyám*, after struggling with *The Mill on the Floss*, and *Lorna Doone*'s author R. D. Blackmore rated Miss Braddon's novels higher than those of "George Eliot." Thackeray had written privately in 1861 that "I admire Eliot but can't read *Adam Bede* and the books of that Author."

And as for Trollope himself, "Novelists may be trusted more than poets," harrumphed the *Saturday Review* in 1867 in a perhaps unintentionally backhanded compliment, because "prose fiction is generally written by less morbid people. An ordinary novel is not mere moonshine and dreamland, the production of long hours of seclusion and self-meditation . . . Mr. Trollope is a favourable specimen of the better novel-writers of the day; and if we are to take him as a specimen at all, it may be said that, occasional episodes apart, their tone is natural and sound, and not effeminate." Ahem—take his treatment of love. "The aim and object of such a vocation is, as it should be, to catch passion and tame it down into a domestic kind of creature, synonymous, or nearly synonymous with lively and constant affection. This Mr. Trollope and his followers and rivals do, and do well. Wild passion in his sequels usually goes to the wall, and is led captive in the train of a good sensible conjugal affection of an eminently British kind."

One can, of course, see this new placidity or soberness as a consequence of changing times and tastes, but it may also have been a function of the authors' respective life situations. Neither Marian Evans not Trollope had a real popular success (*Adam Bede* and *The Warden*, respectively) till they were thirty-nine, after all. *Pickwick*, by contrast, appeared when Dickens was in his mid-twenties, *Wuthering Heights* when Emily Brontë was twenty-nine, and *Jane Eyre* when Charlotte was thirty-one. Thackeray, except for Mrs. Gaskell the most middle-aged success of the pre-Trollope-Eliot group, brought out *Vanity Fair* when he was thirty-six. Indeed, its cynicism and rather middle-aged tone of genteel disillusionment somewhat anticipated the tone of Trollope rather than that of his contemporaries. Even today *Jane Eyre* and *Wuthering Heights* find teenage readers readily, *Barchester Towers* rarely.

The influence of the magazines reinforced these tendencies toward a certain placidity. Serial novels like *Pickwick* and *Vanity Fair* were commonly published by themselves and not as part of a magazine. (*Oliver Twist*, which appeared in *Bently's Miscellany*, was, of course, an exception.) If readers did not like some aspect of the serial or found it distasteful, they simply didn't buy any additional installments, and that was that. When serials began appearing as only one element in magazines like the *Cornhill*, however, the novelist had to be conscious of not alienating the magazine's month-in, month-out steady subscribers. And by the time the *Cornhill* came to be published, these subscribers were a self-consciously respectable middleclass. "We shall suppose the ladies and children to be present," Thackeray said when he became the first editor of *Cornhill*, subsequently declining a contribution of Elizabeth Barrett Browning with the observation that "our magazine is written not only for men and women but for boys, girls, infants, sucklings almost." Indeed, he shocked Trollope by sending back a short story that he found objectionable, pointing up still another fact: serials had no editor, i.e., censor; magazines did.

Mudie reinforced the tendency for novels to be respectable to the point of tedium. "They have nothing equivalent to 'Mudie' in Paris," Mrs. Gaskell had lamented by way of contrasting the French lack of respectability, "and the books of their circulating libraries are of so very mixed a character that no careful mother likes to have them lying about on the table." Mudie's, that is, was "select," which meant, among other things, that it screened out books that were morally improper.

Ironically, Mudie was cementing into place the hegemony of the circulating library and so, indirectly, the three-decker, just at the moment when it seemed as if the coming of the sensation and psychological novels, together with new technologies of production and cheaper paper prices, might have shattered the hold of the old three-decker and brought book prices down. Which perhaps would have allowed more innovative approaches to the subject matter and its treatment than marked the late-nineteenth-century English novel. "The Mudie monopoly and the W. H. Smith monopoly are anomalies in a commercial country," growled Wilkie Collins to George Smith in 1871.

But if they were anomalies, they were powerful ones, so powerful that they strengthened the three-volume format of novels. Even Dickens had finally worked out an arrangement with Bradbury and Evans and, later, Chapman and Hall when he returned to them, to package all the "numbers" of his serials together at the end of their run into the standard three-volume format that the circulating libraries demanded. Thus, when it appeared after serialization in book form, *Hard Times* (1854) was split into "Sowing," "Reaping," and "Garnering"; *A Tale of Two Cities* (1859) into "Restored to Life," "The Golden Thread," and "The Track of the Stream"; and *Great Expectations* (1861) into three untitled but significant "stages" of roughly twenty chapters each after being serialized.

Mudie's only real competition, which was the Library Company Limited, through which shareholders could be subscribers and which was capitalized at £100,000, Mudie met with aplomb. Within five years of its creation in the early 1860s it had failed. The other, smaller circulating libraries tried, briefly, to act tough, too. They demanded in 1860 that Wilkie Collins and his publisher give them the same discount as Mudie on the hardcover edition of *The Woman in White*—but to no avail. Only Mudie, it seemed, could dictate terms.

According to the 1849 parliamentary report from the Select Committee on Public Libraries, the British had the worst system of public libraries of almost any major country in the world. This was Mudie's secret weapon. For all the talk of the great literary heritage of England, it was hard for the average Englishman to get to read much of it. France had some 107 public libraries, Austria 48, and the uncivilized United States had 81 public libraries which anyone could use. In England, however, there was exactly one such library (in Manchester), and things did not improve very much until the end of the century.

The three-decker had dominated the novel until Dickens and then the serial had come along, but now Dickens was dead, and Mudie had only strengthened the three-decker's supremacy. Surely not everyone wanted to write novels of that length. But who could challenge the newly reestablished hegemony of the three-decker and so, by implication, Mudie?

One day in early May 1871, John Blackwood opened a letter from George Lewes to find Marian Evans' companion laying

TICHBORNE V. MUDIE'S!
A BAD LOOK-OUT FOR THE CIRCULATING LIBRARIES.

The 1871 Tichborne case, a cause célèbre, *turned on the claims of a self-described long-lost heir to a vast fortune. The widespread newspaper coverage of the trial reflected the new tabloidlike sensationalism of English journalism—which the* Punch *cartoon here suggests was vivid enough to compete with the novels purveyed by Mudie's.*

before him an interesting proposition. Marian had decided to do a panoramic novel about the Midlands countryside that she loved so much and to which, by virtue of her brother Isaac's interdict to her sisters, she could not easily return. It would show the changes that the region, and by extension England, were undergoing. "It will be a frightfully long book," she told a correspondent. "But I wanted to give a panoramic view of provincial life, which could not be done in small space." She ultimately decided to combine her panoramic story with a different kind of work, namely, the story of a modern St. Theresa. Such was the genesis of what she came to call *Middlemarch*.

Mudie, she thought, had a way of seeming less than enthusiastic about taking her books in the customary three-decker format. On the other hand, Marian's serial of *Romola* for *Cornhill* in 1862 and 1863 that George Smith had wangled had been less than enthusiastically received. Critics laid the blame partly on the uncongenial format, advising readers that "as a serial story *Romola* was not attractive." "George Eliot's drawings all require a certain space, like Raffael's cartoons," wrote another critic of *Romola*'s serial format, "and are not of that kind which produce their effect by the reiteration of scenes each complete in itself." In this she joined Charlotte Brontë with her pronounced dislike for the serial and even that relatively cosmopolitan country dweller Mrs. Gaskell as well.

Well, then? Was there some way to get a long, long panoramic novel published—probably more than the standard three volumes permissible by Mudie in length—in a climate where Marian had found the serial format consistently uncongenial and was not very impressed with Mr. Mudie? She had expressed a wish to Blackwood "for trying a new experiment when we publish anything again."

A new experiment . . .

When the circulation libraries took what Blackwood considered insufficient quantities of *Felix Holt* in 1866, he had written to Marian saying that "the next time we take the field together I think we must experiment in a new form." Yes. "This library system I feel to be a false one," he passionately observed to her the succeeding year. "It fosters the production of mediocre novels, but of a really good book each copy is made to do duty some hundred times over."

If Marian disliked Mudie's system, Blackwood, too, was angry with the library giant because Mudie exacted punishing discounts from him by virtue of Mudie's ever more powerful influence over book distribution. When a novel copyright had been purchased for only a few hundred pounds or less, a publisher could afford to give Mudie's a huge discount. This was not true with big-name authors like Marian, however, who in the wake of Dickens' death and the stupendous success of *Adam Bede*, had become the most popular author in England. Blackwood now paid her two shillings of each five shillings that he charged per book, a whopping 40 percent royalty. He therefore could ill afford in addition to give Mudie a 50 percent discount on her books. The economics of the three-decker novel, though it might reward the publisher of the average novel, penalized the publisher of hugely successful writers like Marian.

What to do, then?

"As you have more than once spoken of the desirability of inventing some mode of circumventing the Libraries and making the public *buy* instead of borrowing I have devised the following scheme," George Lewes wrote to Blackwood in early May 1871, "namely to publish it in *half-volume parts* at intervals of one, or as I think better, two months." (Another overlong novel, said Lewes helpfully, namely Hugo's *Les Miserables*, had appeared in such a format not long before.)

The format of *Middlemarch* would thus be that of a four-volume novel—but one sold in bimonthly installments of half a volume each (each bearing a descriptive title, e.g., "Miss Brooke," "Young and Old")—the last two half volumes to be published together just in time for the lucrative Christmas trade. The arrangement was a three-way compromise between Marian's distaste for a serial, Lewes' wish for publication in numbers, and the need to break away from the three-decker.

And such was the plan that was followed.

Then, as now, people goggled at the sheer size of the book. "I hope there is nothing that will be seen to be irrelevant to my design," Marian had worried to her publisher in July 1871, "which is to show the gradual action of ordinary causes rather than exceptional [*sic*]." Evans reported uncomfortably in January 1872 to Blackwood that she "felt something like a shudder when Sir Henry Maine asked me last Sunday whether this would not be a very big book . . . However it will not be bigger than Thackeray's books," she said defensively, "if so long. And I don't see how the sort of thing I want to do could have been done briefly."

It did not matter. A quasireligious status was beginning to attend Marian's work. As the tale of Dorothea Brooke and the withered Casaubon, the hapless Lydgate, Rosamond Vincy, and the steadfast Mary Garth unfolded, the *Telegraph* said in awed tones that it was "almost profane to speak of ordinary novels in the same breath with George Eliot's." Lewes wrote delightedly of how "the book is being talked about in various influential quarters. Thus, one gentleman told me there was an animated discussion in the smoking room of the Athenaeum, and while he was saying this up came Pigott who said he had just left Partridge who had told him that at the Academy dinner Bishops and Archbishops were enthusiastic." Harriet Martineau thought the book remarkable, and in America that other serious-minded woman writer with rural roots, Emily Dickinson, wrote to a cousin, "What do I think of *Middlemarch*? What do I think of glory?"

Of course, although she went outside Mudie's system of distribution and was known for her serious themes, Marian Evans was not immune to popular trends. True, part of Marian's mystique then and now was that she was above it all. "In general," she told a correspondent loftily in 1877, "it is my rule not to read contemporary fiction . . . I daresay you will understand that for my own spiritual food I need all other sorts of reading more than I need fiction." But even in *Middlemarch* Eliot was somewhat more attuned—or susceptible—to currents in contemporary fiction than her grand pronouncements might suggest. Mary Garth's refusal to change old Mr. Featherstone's will and Mr. Bulstrode's dark secret—these strands of *Middlemarch* could have come right from the sensation novels of Collins and Reade. And the incident of Raffles returning to claim a lost fortune sprang surely from the contemporaneous *cause célèbre* in which a butcher returned from Australia had claimed to be the heir to the baronetcy of Tichborne. His sensational trial captivated all England—and was attended by Lewes and Evans in early 1872 when *Middlemarch* was appearing.

In fact, one might wonder if there was not just the slightest bit of envy in Marian's denunciation of the sensation novels. She might sneer at the "merely" popular novel, but she was upset when Mudie's didn't take her books with sufficient alacrity. And so, too, with W. H. Smith. "I suppose the reason my 6/ editions are never on the railway stalls is partly of the same kind [*sic*] that hinders the free distribution of *Felix* [*Holt*]," she mused acidly in 1866. "They are not so attractive to the majority as 'The Trail of the Serpent,'" which, of course, was Miss Braddon's first book. W. H. Smith's railway yellow-backs were junk! "—I suppose putting it in a yellow cover with figures on it reminding one of the outside of a show, and charging a shilling for it, is what we are expected to do for the good of mankind," she mused apropos of *Felix Holt* on being advised to get "greater circulation by cheap sales." "Even then, I fear, it would hardly beat the rivalry of 'The Pretty Milliner,'" or of 'The Horrible Secret,'" she wrote grimly to Blackwood.

Ironically, this high moral and literary tone did not suffice to make her personally respectable. Novelists as a class were much more respected than they had been a half century before—but even the greatest could not openly violate social convention and escape unscathed. Because she was living with a man out of wedlock even George Smith, the same man who had offered her £10,000 in a successful effort to buy her *Romola* in 1862, refused to visit Marian with his wife or his daughter. "Unpleasant social results might have followed," Smith thoughtfully observed, "if young girls had been known as her visitors." His reaction was typical. The admiring Mrs. Gaskell had written Marian to tell her how she had been overcome by the superb writing in *Adam Bede* and *Scenes of Clerical Life* in November 1859: ("I have read them again, and I must, once more, tell you how earnestly, fully, and humbly I admire them. I never read anything so complete, and beautiful in fiction, in my whole life before.") But she could not resist a prim little dig: "I should not be quite true in my ending, if I did not say before I concluded that I wish you *were* Mrs. Lewes." ("Oh, do say Miss Evans did not write it," Mrs. Gaskell had burst out privately to George Smith. *"How came she to like Mr. Lewes so much? . . .* so soiled for a woman like her to fancy . . . ?")

Indeed.

Charles Eliot Norton, on visiting Lewes and Evans in 1869, observed that "she is not received in general society, and the women who visit her are either so emancipée as not to mind what the world says about them, or have no social position to maintain." Lewes and Evans got around the fact of her not being invited anywhere in polite society by having people in to see *them.* "Our day of reception is Sunday, from 2 o'clock till 5. We find it a great economy of time, and a means of saving our friends from calling in our absence, to have a fixed day of reception." On that day the literary great and others (still almost all men, of course, though John Blackwood had loyally taken his wife to meet Evans as early as 1861) regularly repaired to The Priory.

Here the couple regularly received visitors in the drawing room, Lewes chattering away animatedly in his easy chair on the right-hand side of the fireplace, Marian on the left, speaking "in a measured, thoughtful tone which imparted a certain importance to her words," a manner which she had learnt years before at the Miss Franklins' School in Coventry. All topics, consequential or not, were fair game. The poet William

Allingham on an 1873 visit found Lewes arguing amidst a distinguished group "that language makes a irreparable gulf between man and the lower animals, but this does not touch the Darwinian theory." "Make up his . . . *what*?" said the effervescent little essayist and critic on another occasion. "You didn't say mind?" Lewes cheerily observed when told a publisher was taking forever to decide about a manuscript. "I didn't know he had one."

There was something rather old-fashioned and cozily domestic about this scene, and, indeed, the eternal verities— both in publishing and in writing—seemed to be destined to hold for what seemed like a good long time. There were still evidently plenty of eager young writers coming along, willing to play the game and seeking to get published by the big publishers, apparently heedless of the artistic cost to form or substance. "The truth is that I am willing, and indeed anxious, to give up any points which may be desirable in a story when read as a whole," a young architect and would-be novelist wrote to Leslie Stephen, the new editor of *Cornhill*, in early 1874, "for the sake of others which shall please those who read it in Numbers. Perhaps I may have higher aims some day, and be a great stickler for the proper artistic balance of the completed work, but for the present circumstances lead me to wish merely to be considered a good hand at a serial."

Stephen's correspondent was the young Thomas Hardy, a modest man from a rural background with unprepossessing origins, who had started his fiction career with a somewhat formless novel that he wrote after returning to his native Dorchester in 1867 after working in London. Hardy's career represented something rather new, namely, the coming of the working-class author to the "high" English novel. The son of a mason in rural Dorchester, Hardy grew up in a rough village cottage—he was found as a baby with a snake nestling in his cradle, and deer and horses would occasionally poke their heads in the family's window at night. Grown up, he was inspired by his ambitious mother to eventually become an

A railway station in 1874. The W. H. Smith stand at lower right is being besieged for its newspapers, and a row of books is visible near the top of the stand. Note the

ads at lower left for the popular papers like the Daily Telegraph *that had helped create a climate favorable to the sensation novels of writers like* Wilkie Collins.

architect's assistant. He submitted a first, formless novel in the summer of 1868 to Macmillan, who turned it down, recommending that he try Chapman and Hall. Their reader was the tall, unhappy George Meredith, whose *The Ordeal of Richard Feverel* had been turned down for being too racy by Mudie's. But Meredith was always willing to meet with promising young talent (Olive Schreiner, author of *The Story of an African Farm*, and George Gissing being among those whom he encouraged). Over lunch, then, Meredith encouraged the young Hardy to write something with lots of plot and structure instead of the formless mishmash he had submitted.

So Hardy dutifully went home and wrote *Desperate Remedies*, a Collinsesque tale of an actress, murder, and—that standard feature in sensation novels—bigamy. He then submitted it to Macmillan, whose reader found a relatively explicit lesbian love scene "highly extravagant." ("Cytherea stepped out of bed, went to the door, and whispered back 'Yes?' 'Let me come in, darling.' . . . The instant they were in bed . . . she flung her arms around the young girl . . . 'Now kiss me,' she said.") And "the violation of a young lady at an evening party, and the subsequent birth of a child, is too abominable to be tolerated as a central incident," the Macmillan reader went on indignantly.

Too sensational, in short. It was therefore published—anonymously—in March 1871 by the sensation novel specialist William Tinsley, who had made his fortune with *Lady Audley's Secret*. As befitted the somewhat sensational nature of the works he published, Tinsley was not, Hardy felt, a gentleman, and was frequently to be found in a local bar with a black cat. When sufficiently drunk his partner (and brother) would describe how he had first come to London on—shudder—a hay cart. Hardy preferred his contact with Trollope. He heard the great man lecture once and was given advice by him—always hold out for royalties as a means of payment, said the man who had bitter experience with subsidizing publication himself, "if you are not in want of immediate money."

Poor Hardy. Next time out he was not lurid enough, said

editor (and husband of Minny Thackeray) Leslie Stephen when Hardy submitted *Under the Greenwood Tree* to *Cornhill* in August 1871. A subdued tale of love between a rural teacher and a carrier, it faced the old problem of grabbing—and keeping—the serial reader. "There is too little incident for such purposes; for, though we do not want a murder in every number, it is necessary to catch the attention of readers by some distinct and well arranged plot." What could Hardy do? (Though after telling Stephen he was at work on a new book, called *Far from the Madding Crowd*, "I like your proposed title," said Stephen.) His relatively tight focus on a small group of rural characters did not lend itself readily to the expansion and development, week after week, of action-filled plot, subplot and sub-subplot in the way Dickens' and Thackeray's work had.

So it was back to Macmillan—"I read through your story when I was down at Brighton for a short holiday, carefully," Alexander Macmillan wrote Hardy in October 1871. "It is too small for a circulating library and if one makes it a small price to attract sale to the general public," said the head of the firm, "a large number of copies are needed to pay. We could not venture on it now, as our hands are full of Christmas books . . . But if you should not arrange otherwise before the spring . . . "

Serious work like Hardy's or Evans', was never, of course, the norm. There were still plenty of more or less "silly novelists," as Marian might have put it, alive and well in the English literary marketplace. There was, for example, the vaguely Oriental-sounding Ouida. She was the dramatic, glamorous, and controversial author of *Under Two Flags*, a heroic piece of twaddle published in 1867 that went on selling for years (over sixty editions in English alone) and survived in movie form well into the twentieth century. In her novel the unflappable Captain Bertie Cecil of the ultratony Life Guards left London "to protect a lady," signed up with the French Foreign Legion and promptly became beloved of the Legion's mascot, Cigarette. Bertie was then condemned to death for defending the Princess Corona's honor against an evil colonel, and, at the book's climax, Cigarette galloped up with news of a pardon, throwing herself in front of a firing squad just as they opened up—and died, giving her all for the man she loved.

Ouida herself? The small, determined writer "is said to be Miss Evans, the author of 'Adam Bede,'" noted Ouida's mother gravely about one of the more naive efforts to penetrate a pseudonym. Ouida gave parties at which women smoked, but she was basically a nice suburban girl who had fled to London from Bury St. Edmunds in Suffolk. She called it "that slowest and dreariest of boroughs," where "the inhabitants are driven to ring their own doorbells lest they should rust from disuse." (And the vaguely romantic pseudonym of "Ouida" was simply the result of her infant attempt to say "Louise.")

She had stiff competition in the romance department from the redoubtable Rhoda Broughton. A feisty soul, Miss Broughton was a favorite of Gladstone and was perhaps the only Victorian novelist to have a mountain peak—Mount Rhoda—named after her, this courtesy of Captain Clements Markham in 1876, the officers of whose *Alert* were devouring her novels as they mapped part of Ellesmere Island at the North Pole. Her "racy" books raised eyebrows owing to passages like the section in her 1876 *Joan* in which the heroine encounters a noticeably well-equipped rival for the affections of her male. "She is the only décolleté woman in the room; but then, probably, no other woman in the room has such a bust to exhibit. If they had they would possibly be no more backward in advertising it than she ... What shoulders! absolutely unclothed but for the two tiny shoulder-straps, which alone hinder her garment from entirely taking French leave." Miss Broughton could be direct in person as well. "I should like you to know my boy—he's much nicer than I am," boomed a middle-aged pest seated next to her at a dinner party. "Would you like me to say that that's impossible," she said sweetly, "—or that I can quite believe it? Because I'll say either."

Literary "personalities" like Ouida and Miss Broughton were good "copy" and helped to feed the new copy-hungry penny press. The day of anonymity was vanishing, and where authors had previously tried to get men like Edmund Yates kicked out of their clubs, now they flocked to him to have their literary portraits painted. Yates remained bitter at Thackeray for having had him expelled from the Garrick Club years before. "Think that I was then only 27 years old, with wife & three children, supplementing a small Post Office salary by journalistic labour, sitting down at my desk, three or four nights a week, after my day's official grind, sitting down at 8 pm. & steadily writing till midnight. Remember what the social degradation inflicted upon me at Thackeray's instance, not the fury of a moment but deliberately insisted on through six weeks, meant to an unknown man," Yates would, indeed, write bitterly some thirty years after the incident. "Think of being 'expelled' from a club, as tho' one had been a card-sharper, a cheat, a thief, a braggart about women!"

But Yates had a species of revenge. His new magazine, *The World*, was successful to the tune of bringing Yates an annual amount estimated to be in the neighborhood of £10,000. Described in its prospectus as an "amusing chronicle of current history," the weekly began to appear in the summer of 1874 under his direction. *The World* turned Yates' nosiness into a popular feature, "Celebrities at Home," which took the reader to "visit" statesmen and other men and women of the hour, including writers like Yates' friend Wilkie Collins. ("A short man, with stooping shoulders and tiny hands and feet, with bright pleasant face looking out of a forest of light-gray, almost white, hair, greets us as we enter the big double drawing-room in Gloucester-place.")

Yates came from a theatrical family and, as the Thackeray–Garrick Club imbroglio suggested, haunted the clubs and theaters. Now he introduced their gossipy triviality into his literary write-ups, as in the hokey but dramatic description of Collins seeking a title for his new novel as he paced along the sea near a lighthouse. "Savagely biting the end of his last cigar he apostrophized the building, standing coldly and stiffly in the evening light, 'You are ugly and stiff and awkward, you know you are: as stiff and as weird as my white woman. White woman—woman in white! The title, by Jove!"

It is perhaps no accident that writers of sensation novels like Collins and Miss Braddon seemed to feel at home with write-ups in newspapers and magazines like *The World* that mimicked their own sometimes rather breathless tone. Others were less pleased. *Lorna Doone* author R. D. Blackmore fumed that "such is the abundance of demand for little gossip, that I have been asked more than once to jump out (like an owl from his ivy-bush) and blink before the public." Which he refused to do. And "I have neither white hair, 'blue eyes,' nor 'bushy eyebrows,'" he wrote indignantly to the editor who published an erroneous description of him and his house. In fact, as he pointed out, the reporter had actually written up a very nice description of the clergyman who lived a quarter mile down the road from Blackmore. Trollope in the draft of his *Autobiography* called Yates "a literary gutter-scraper" and flatly refused to be a "Celebrity at Home." The *Boston Evening Transcript* had described how Trollope "squeezes his small, well-shaped hand into a very small pair of coloured kids"; "I never wear gloves," Trollope observed contemptuously of the article. "What fools people are."

Newspapers, however, continued to spread their influence in the 1870s and 1880s. The Elementary Education Act of 1870 finally made elementary education in England compulsory, and reading audiences grew in size and diversity of socioeconomic background in the decades that followed. As the number of English papers multiplied, William Tillotson's Fiction Bureau began to subsidize serial fiction whose cost it then spread among the subscribing newspapers. The work of Rhoda Broughton, Bret Harte, Mrs. Oliphant, Charles Reade, and Thomas Hardy appeared in Tillotson syndication. (*Tess of the d'Urbervilles* was in fact originally commissioned by Tillotson's, which backed off when they saw how unconventional it was.)

Perhaps the growing vitality and number of newspapers,

so lacking in Dickens' day, eased the pressure on the novel to deal with immediate topical concerns. With the notable exception of Reade, whose books attacked the misconduct of prisons and insane asylums, the sensation novel was largely content to pander to tastes for rather lurid fiction. Nor were the "domestic" writers any more reformist. Evans and Trollope contemplated society through the lens of the individual psyche, principally concerned to determine how one could work out his or her destiny within the existing social structure, not to change it. In *The Warden*, Trollope had caricatured Dickens as "Mr Popular Sentiment," a mindless popular writer who recklessly inflamed public opinion. After *Little Dorrit* came out, Trollope violently protested Dickens' portrayal of the nepotistic Circumlocution Office as an indirect slur on his beloved Post Office. He even added a long laudatory chapter on "The Civil Service" in his new novel *The Three Clerks* while *Little Dorrit* was still being serialized that was so embarrassingly irrelevant that it was taken out of subsequent editions. "The popular newspaper, the popular member of Parliament, and the popular novelist,—the name of Charles Dickens will of course present itself to the reader who remembers the Circumlocution office,—have had it impressed on their several minds," Trollope snarled in his 1879 *John Caldigate*,"—and have endeavoured to impress the same idea on the minds of the public generally,—that the normal Government clerk is quite indifferent to his work."

Lengthy description and analysis, not judgment, was the order of the day, then. So much was certainly true of the new admirer of Evans who came to Europe in 1875 in search of a literary home. Significantly, he did not think much of Dickens, whom he called merely "the greatest of superficial novelists," because "he has added nothing to our own understanding of human character" and "is nothing of a philosopher." "I regard the march of history very much as a man placed astride a locomotive," Henry James told Charles Eliot Norton in 1873, "without knowledge or help, would regard the progress of that vehicle. To stick on somehow, and even to enjoy the scenery as we pass, is the sum of my aspirations." Such fatalism was anathema to can-do Victorianism and the social concern of, say, a Dickens or a Gaskell. But then James had grown up as a peripatetic tourist, traveling around Europe with his itinerant family before they finally settled in Cambridge, Massachusetts. Looking abroad for models, James had been much taken with the urbane but detached Turgenev, who insisted that the writer must stay out of his writing—and let the story appear simply to tell itself. This comported with James' view of the writer as a detached observer.

But then where was the best observation point? He had tried Rome and tried Paris. Then in December 1876 the thirty-three-year-old James acquired a bachelor apartment for which he paid two and a half guineas a week on the first floor of a Georgian house at 3 Bolton Street just off Piccadilly. "My interest in London is chiefly that of an observer in a place where there is most in the world to observe." True, the English had printed *The American* in 1877 in a (pirated) railway stall yellow-back edition with, he told his mother ironically, "a wonderful picture on the cover." And they were so impossibly atheoretical not just about their novels but about everything. "They live wholly in the realm of the cut and dried. 'Have you ever been to Florence?' 'Oh, yes.' 'Isn't it a most peculiarly interesting city?' 'Oh. yes, I think it's so very nice.' 'Have you read *Romola*?' 'Oh, yes, I think it is so very clever.'"

But James liked the British. He even liked writers like Miss Braddon after a fashion, and was to befriend the somewhat prickly Miss Broughton. (Ouida's latest book he reviewed in 1875 with the comment: "Let no man hereafter despair of anything; even Ouida improves! She began several years ago with writing unmitigated nonsense, and she now writes nonsense very sensibly mitigated.") There were other compensations for an American author living in England, who hoped, as James did, to see his books published in both countries. In the absence of any American-English copyright agreement (which would not come until 1891), American copyright law only protected American citizens, as hapless British writers knew all too well. English law, however, often extended protection to Americans as well as British citizens. They had merely to be currently physically resident in an English jurisdiction (Mark Twain, for this reason, would vacation in Canada when his books were coming out in England) and their books had to be published in England first. In his literary nationality and commitments, then, it made sense, seemingly, for James to be on the fence, a detached observer.

To some extent, James' situation reflected a maturation of literary relations between England and America. American publishers had hitherto generally reprinted the works of English authors without payment. British publishers for their part kept aloof from their American brethren. This was now beginning to change. The Macmillans opened a New York branch office in 1869, and the deceased cofounder Daniel Macmillan's son Frederick at age twenty-one came to the American office in 1872. He told the thirty-some Henry Holt, "You Americans aren't publishers . . . you are only reprinters." Holt was spurred thereby to solicit Hardy in May 1873 for the publication of his books in the United States; he also arranged for Hardy to be serialized in the *New York Tribune*, which prompted the *New York Times* to commission a Hardy story. For these efforts—in a big change from the previous literary mugging of British authors in America—Hardy was paid.

The role of the fiction-serializing magazine, which had spread its influence across the Atlantic, was central in this. Harpers started an English version of its magazine in 1880 for which it got Hardy to do *A Laodicean*, which the European *Harpers* began serializing in December 1880. The following September the editor of the *Atlantic Monthly* sent out feelers to Hardy for a serial novel, too. Sometimes there were problems with the same serial novel running in both countries more or less simultaneously. *The Portrait of a Lady* had been printed both in the *Cornhill* and in the *Atlantic* in 1880, but the *Cornhill* ver-

A dogged-looking Anthony Trollope with a suggestion of the intensity that made fellow novelist Wilkie Collins describe him as "an incarnate gale of wind." Trollope, said Collins, "blew off my hat; he turned my umbrella inside out."

sion was printed first. Copies had then been shipped to the United States before the *Atlantic* came out, killing the sales of the *Atlantic*. So Hardy had to—and did—agree to a U.S. exclusive for the *Atlantic* on his novel *Two on a Tower* soon thereafter.

Having paying outlets for their fiction both in England and America differentiated Hardy and James from the previous generation of novelists writing in England. It helped sustain them financially given that, unlike, say, Dickens, their work was somewhat of a minority taste. "The multitude," James had observed to his brother in 1872, "has absolutely no taste . . . To write for the few who have is doubtless to lose money—but I am not afraid of starving." But to write for the "few" in England and also the "few" in America doubled the number of the "few" to whom one could sell books. Having two transatlantic audiences rather than only an English one made it easier for Hardy and James to survive as writers than it would have been in an earlier era.

The problem was that if, like James, one were only an observer and reporter of what one saw and not a moral cheerleader, like, say, Dickens, one might set down sad or tragic things just as they were. And one therefore might not even write a morally uplifting and/or pleasantly inconsequential happy ending to a story of the kind Victorian readers expected. James had begun his career as a novelist writing for the *Atlantic* of his friend William Dean Howells. When *The American* had worked its way gradually through the magazine's pages in 1876 only to culminate in the two lovers being torn asunder and Mlle. Cintre entering a convent, Howells protested. "I quite understand that as an editor you should go in for 'cheerful endings,'" James wrote back. A marriage would "have made a prettier ending, certainly; but I should have felt as if I were throwing a rather vulgar sop to readers who don't really know the world and who don't measure the merit of a novel by its correspondence to the same. Such readers assuredly have a right to their entertainment, but I don't believe it is in me to give them, in a satisfactory way, what they require." And *Daisy*

Miller, the book with which he first burst on the English literary scene in June 1878—through its publication in *Cornhill*—didn't exactly send people away chuckling at the death of its innocent heroine at the end.

Hardy faced the same problem. As early as December 1873, his American publisher Henry Holt wrote to tell him that "we can't make 'Blue Eyes' sell as it ought to. Its melancholy ending works . . . against its popularity . . . No appreciative reader can regret the admirable consistency of its conclusion. At the same time your most appreciative readers and especially your publishers and bankers may be justified in hoping that the next conception you think worth while to work out may be a more cheerful one." Leslie Stephen told Hardy that at the end of his 1880 *The Trumpet-Major*, "the heroine married the wrong man," and Hardy in his cheery way said that that was what generally happened, to which Stephen replied, "Not in magazines." After the 1874 *Far from the Madding Crowd*, indeed, at the end of which Bathsheba Everdene and Gabriel Oak marry, Hardy's major novels would invariably end with the hero or heroine being hanged or disgraced, or otherwise dying disagreeably. It was this kind of unrelenting determination to show the reader how grim things could be in the real world that made it desirable for writers like Hardy or James to have as many overseas audiences as possible to expand the necessarily limited audience to which they could appeal at home.

Hardy's work aroused additional antagonism because of its sometimes explicit—by contemporary standards—treatment of sex. "May I suggest that Troy's seduction of the young woman will require to be treated in a gingerly fashion, when, as I suppose must be the case, he comes to be exposed to his wife?" Stephen inquired of Hardy with respect to *Far from the Madding Crowd*, as it began to wind its way through *Cornhill* in 1874. "I mean that the thing must be stated but that the words must be careful—excuse this wretched shred of concession to popular stupidity; but I am a slave." Hardy was always quick to be helpful in this connection, writing to Evans' publisher, John

Blackwood, in April 1877, "I will just add that, should there accidentally occur any word or reflection not in harmony with the general tone of the magazine, you would be quite at liberty to strike it out if you chose." This on the chance that the latter might be able to offer him magazine room for his new serial, *The Return of the Native*. How far editors would go is clear from what Stephen apparently did to Chapter 18 of *Far from the Madding Crowd*, which in Hardy's manuscript described a view at Farmer Boldwood's of "the buttocks and tails of half a dozen warm and contented horses standing in their stalls." In the *Cornhill* publication of the novel, this view became one of the "backs and tails of half-a-dozen warm and contented horses," but then it was still not permissible to say in a novel that a woman had had a miscarriage. In his boldness in such matters, Hardy differed from James, who later criticized *Tess of the d'Urbervilles* to Robert Louis Stevenson for its frank sexuality and poor style, leading Hardy to remark acidly: "How indecent of those two virtuous females to express their mental nakedness in such a manner."

Yet there was a curious kinship between James and Hardy, both solitary in the end, neither of them, in contrast to all the previous leading male Victorian writers, parents. James not only felt like an observer but also acted the part of one. Dressed impeccably, with his beard, one contemporary said later, making him look like an Elizabethan sea captain, James in the late 1870s discovered clubs and dining out. Why had Trollope wanted to move to London? To be near "the clubs, and the dinner parties of the metropolis." James delighted in the Athenaeum Club, where he found, he told his sister, in the "drawing room, at 5 o'clock in the afternoon—all the great chairs and lounges and sofas filled with men having afternoon tea—lolling back with their laps filled with magazines, journals, and fresh Mudie books, while amiable flunkies in knee-breeches present them the divinest salvers of tea and buttered toast." It was the great age of the dinner party, which had replaced the ball as a suitable middle-class occupation in an increasingly stuffy middle-class society. By the first week of June 1879, James had dined out 107 times during the "past winter."

And, above all, as sitting at dinner tables and in drawing rooms allowed him to do, he observed and then noted—"I heard some time ago," he jotted in a notebook in early 1879, "that Anthony Trollope had a theory that a boy might be brought up to be a novelist as to any other trade. He brought up—or attempted to bring up—his own son on this principle, and the young man became a sheep farmer in Australia. The other day Miss Thackeray (Mrs. Ritchie) said to me that she and her husband meant to bring up their little daughter in that way." The idea became the story "Greville Fane," itself, if nothing else, a sign of how the novel-writing trade had become so routine and domesticated that it could presumably be "taught."

The next month, the attentive James ear was bent again. No walking the streets of London for hours late at night for first-hand encounters with the London poor, like Dickens. "Mrs. Kemble told me last evening the history of her brother H.'s engagement to Miss T.," he recorded. Mrs. Kemble's selfish, penniless sibling, it appeared, had been beloved years before by the daughter of the wealthy George Thackeray, the Master of King's College, Cambridge, and a distant relative of the author. The girl had been forbidden to marry Kemble, who was after her for her money. Kemble left her when it was clear the marriage could not occur, breaking her heart—and then resumed his suit when the old man died. Into one of the Jamesian notebooks went a record of the tale. With the events transposed to the New York City of his youth, the tale—*Washington Square*—began appearing in the June 1880 edition of *Cornhill*.

Hardy's distancing went beyond James', paradoxically, though he did marry. The alienation showed itself in his abhorrence of personal contact. Until he died, he would walk in the actual roadways of his Dorchester despite the need to dodge carts and carriages in order to keep from coming in contact with his fellow citizens on the sidewalk. Even as a child he hated being touched, and when he grew up his servants were strictly instructed not to assist him in donning his coat. Anny Thackeray had, in keeping with her father's practice and Dickens', advised Hardy that if he would be an author, then he must live in London. He and his wife tried it for a year in 1878; they were sick, the house leaked and was a mess, he suffered nervous attacks and so in June 1881 they moved back to Dorset—for good—after that, with trips up to London in spring and summer only for "the season."

But Hardy's literary position was in some respects more precarious than that of James, for he developed an openly alienated, vengeful attitude toward the society of which he was a part. In *Tess of the d'Urbervilles*, *Jude the Obscure*, and *The Return of the Native*, his characters were the victims of circumstances both so tragic and yet often so arbitrary as to reveal Hardy's underlying bitterness and lack of faith in the benevolence of the universe, summed up perhaps best in his memorable phrase about Tess being merely the sport of the President of the Immortals. "The tragical conditions of life imperfectly denoted [*sic*] in The Return of the Native & some other stories of mine I am less & less able to keep out of my work," he wrote somewhat wistfully to John Addington Symonds in 1889. "I often begin a story with the intention of making it brighter & gayer than usual; but . . ." His stance bewildered contemporaries. "What has Providence done to Mr. Hardy that he should rise up in the arable land of Wessex and shake his fist at his Creator?" Edmund Gosse was to ask in the January 1896 *Cosmopolis*.

Uniquely among the major Victorian male writers, Hardy withdrew to the countryside—Dorsetshire—to get away from his fellow men. As he chronicled the destruction of the rural landscape by the relentless forces of industrial capitalism, he could not escape the bitter sense that a heartless indifference ruled the universe. He was perhaps the more bitter for his having once believed so strongly. One should not forget that until he was twenty-five he still thought of entering the ministry— and then lost his faith. In addition, he had contracted an unhappy marriage in 1874, the year after his staunch friend and literary mentor Horace Moule slit his throat. Then, too, Hardy's literary success uprooted him from the rural artisan class of his father without making him accepted by the London upper class which he yearned to please. His wife, who was from a higher social class than her husband, once remarked apropos of dealing with Hardy's relatives that it was injurious to have too much to do with "the peasant class." Hardy, it seems, could feel at home nowhere. "I," he brooded in 1889, "am in a sense exiled."

Of course, in style and willingness to oblige his editors, he remained old-fashioned. And so, paradoxically, did the overall plan of his novels, even though in tone and theme they might seem bleak. Hardy created as the geographical setting for his major novels beginning with *Far from the Madding Crowd* an imaginary "Wessex," following the pattern of a series of interrelated novels initiated by Bulwer and Thackeray and followed by Trollope in his *Barchester* and *Palliser* novels. Like their novels, too, in his the same or related characters turned up in several novels, beginning with *The Return of the Native*, for example, in which the cousin of Bathsheba Everdene from *Far from the Madding Crowd* appears.

Yet it was increasingly a different era, with different sensibilities and different tastes. Wilkie Collins, with his nefarious villains and damsels in distress, was not yet losing his audience and his popularity, but he lived, he thought, in an era that was a "period of 'decline and fall' in the art of writing fiction." He had begun taking laudanum as a painkiller for persistent rheumatic gout some twenty years before. By the time of his final illness, his daily dosage was two tablespoonfuls, enough to kill twelve ordinary men, opined a surgeon familiar with his case. Collins paid the price in hallucinations that matched the terrors of his stories. Visions of a woman, who was sometimes a "shapeless monster, with eyes of fire and big green fangs," pursued him. Sometimes a throng of ghosts seemed to be trying to push him down the stairs when he tried to go up to bed. And when Hawthorne's son visited Collins sometime around 1880, he found the aging writer confused and unsure about the great masterpiece of his caller's father: *"The Scarlet Letter* is one of the greatest novels," he quoted Wilkie as saying. "Even the second volume, where most novelists weaken, is fine; and the third fulfils the splendid promise of the first." He appeared somewhat shaken, said Hawthorne, on discovering the American masterpiece to be, after all, but a single slim volume. "Very bent, and gnarled and gnome-like," Edmund Yates found Collins at a dinner in 1888, "dreadfully crippled." The next year Collins was dead.

Or there was the case of Trollope. Like his hero Thackeray, he suffered a waning popularity in his declining years. The once best-selling novelist who had regularly commanded £2,500 a novel at his peak got only £1,200 for his *Is He Popenjoy?* in 1877, £1,000 for *The Duke's Children* a year later and for *Ayala's Angel* in 1880 only £750, albeit with a modest proposed increase from sale to the newspapers. He could at least take comfort from the fact that the status of the novelist in general was by now eminently well established. Forster did a notable life of Dickens in 1874, and Macmillan in 1878 asked Trollope to do a life of Thackeray for their new *English Men of Letters* series, the undertaking in itself a sign of the new prestige of authors.

But then Trollope, too, passed from the scene. Gathered to read after dinner from a new comic novel in November 1882, a circle of Trollope relatives laughed their way through the story—until, looking over when she realized Trollope was silent, his niece saw that he couldn't move. It was a stroke. Within little over a month he was dead. "He delivered us from the marvels, senseless accidents, cat's-cradle plots of old romance, and gave us, to the best of his ability, a faithful picture of the daily life of the upper and middle classes," said Bernard Shaw, and so he had. Stalwart, determinedly antisensationalistic—"I do believe that no girl has risen from the reading of my pages less modest than she was before," Trollope once wrote with sincere pride, but the comment aptly defined the limits to which his art had reached.

Marian Evans' time was also passing. To be sure, she had replaced Dickens as a national literary institution. "Tears came into my eyes," Blackwood wrote to her upon receipt of a letter from Marian Evans in late 1876 telling him how grateful she was for all his encouragement through the years, "and I read the passage at once to my wife who was sitting beside me when I received the letter. I look upon such expressions coming from you, as the very highest compliment that a man holding the position I do could receive, and I shall keep the letter for my children as a memorial that their father was good for something in his day."

Her works had had overtones of religion yet she was no longer a believer, an appealing mix for a devout but ever more skeptical age. "You never think or feel you are reading fiction," said the awed reader at John Blackwood's firm, for whom Evans' work did not rank "as Novels but as second Bibles." "Such books are worth nine tenths of the Sermons ever preached or published." So, too, doubtless felt a woman who told Evans she had copied part of *Romola* into her New Testament. Some attended the Pops concerts to which she and Lewes went in order to see her. There were those who rushed up to kiss her hand when the opportunity presented itself, and one man anxiously sent a stamped, self-addressed postcard begging for reassurance of Evans' condition after he dreamed that she was ill. "It is something known, lived through and unalterable, that my life has flung itself at her feet—and not been picked up—only told to rise and make itself a serviceable place elsewhere.—So be it—so it is," gushed Edith Simcox, an overwrought literary groupie who literally fell at—and kissed—Evans' feet, and who dedicated a copy of her first book to Evans "with idolatrous love." And then there was Elma Stuart, who lovingly preserved a handkerchief into which Evans had cried. The Sunday gatherings at the Priory took on an appreciably reverential tone. "On Sunday I hope to attend service at the Priory," Dickens had noted dryly in 1870. Whereas he had made the novelist almost a family member,

Almost alone of the major Victorian male writers, Thomas Hardy did not find London congenial as a permanent residence. He therefore moved back to his native Dorset for good in 1881, ultimately settling into Max Gate, the house depicted here, which Hardy, drawing on his architectural training, designed himself.

albeit also a performer, Evans made the novelist a guru. And she had been very aware of her exalted status. When she was compared in a French review to Miss Mulock, a contemporary novelist, she had bristled privately in 1860 that "the most ignorant journalist in England would hardly think of calling me a rival of Miss Mulock—a writer who is read only by novel readers, pure and simple, never by people of high culture . . . we belong to an entirely different order of writers [sic]." Ah, "high culture"—a long way from Dickens' unpretentious efforts at entertainment and instruction—and a foreshadowing of the twentieth-century attitude toward "high" literature to come.

And then, on November 30, 1878, Lewes died, and Evans was utterly bereft. Within a short time she was looking for help to John Walter Cross, a tall red-bearded man who had befriended them nine years before, taken charge of managing their investments, found them a new country home, and livened their country days with what Lewes called "an apparatus for *Lawn Tennis.*" Within two years of Lewes' death she and Cross had married (he was forty to her sixty). A letter came from her brother Isaac congratulating her on entering the married state, his first communication to her since he had broken off contact twenty-three years before when he learned she was living with Lewes. Evans and Cross journeyed happily abroad to Venice and took a new house at Cheyne Walk in Chelsea. On December 19 when Edith Simcox came to visit, Evans mentioned a sore throat. It turned rapidly serious, and within four days, she was dead.

"Does it not seem now as if all our really great names were leaving us, and what is more, without much prospect as yet of any to take their place," asked George Gissing in 1881 when Carlyle in turn died. "Where are the novelists to succeed Thackeray, Dickens, George Eliot? What poetry will follow upon Tennyson and Browning when they, as must shortly be the case, leave their places empty? Nay, what *really great* men of any kind can honestly be said to have given tokens of their coming?"

The problem was perhaps not quite so simple as that. Or, rather, if the great men and women were leaving, perhaps, so, too, was that peculiar confidence with which, for all its turmoil and vicissitudes, the high Victorian era had been accompanied. On a slumberous summer afternoon in 1877, Henry James was left alone to contemplate London after *le tout monde* had vanished for grouse hunting and "the season" had come to an end—in Greenwich not even a decent meal was to be had. He liked the great order and majesty of London and what it stood for, of course. "I know that when I look off to the left at the East India Docks, or pass under the hugely piled bridges, where the railway trains and the human processions are for ever moving, I feel a kind of imaginative thrill. The tremendous piers of the bridges, in especial, seem the very pillars of the Empire."

But all was not as it seemed. A disastrous worldwide agricultural depression in the 1870s flooded the world market with the huge wheat crops of the American Midwest for the first time and severely damaged English agriculture. A series of such shocks to the vanishing rural England chronicled in *Middlemarch* and *The Mill on the Floss* hastened the dispossession from the rural landscape of families like Tess Durbeyfield's and the breakup of the estates inhabited by the great magnates like Trollope's Duke of Omnium, which depended, ultimately, on the rents from those same dispossessed families. Agricultural depression in Ireland spurred the organization of the Irish National Land League, acting against landlords. In 1882 there were twenty-six murders related to the unrest, and Trollope's last novel, the posthumously published 1883 *The Landleaguers*, fictionally chronicled the troubles.

Fenians murdered the English Secretary for Ireland in broad daylight in Dublin in 1882, and Irish terrorists began blowing up public buildings in England when the British government retaliated by suspending the right to trial by jury and other civil liberties. Even Henry James could not ignore such turmoil. He wrote *The Princess Casamassima*, a novel dealing with revolutionary violence, in 1884, descending to the information-gathering techniques of a Zola, for once, to get his material. ("I have been all the morning at Millbank prison (horrible place) collecting notes for a fiction scene," he wrote a friend. "You see I am quite the Naturalist.") Imperial rivalries stirred in Africa, and in 1882 Gladstone invaded Egypt. And the appearance of James' own *Daisy Miller* in *Cornhill* from June to July 1878, the work that first won James recognition in England as a fiction writer, signaled the irruption on the European scene of a new, powerful force—the coming of the Americans—at just the time when England was slowly beginning to doubt its own continued ascendancy. Or so James thought. Americans living on the Continent and passing through London, he said,

> have declared with assurance that the continental nations have ceased to care a straw for what England thinks, that her traditional prestige is completely extinct and that the affairs of Europe will be settled quite independently of her action and still more of her inaction. England will do nothing, will risk nothing; there is no cause bad enough for her not to find a selfish interest in it—there is no cause good enough for her to fight about it. Poor old England is defunct.

Against such a troubled, unsteady backdrop the calm certainties and moralistic admonitions of a writer from another era such as Marian Evans could only seem old-fashioned to many in the new generation. Indeed, as if in a passing of the mantle, serialization of *The Portrait of a Lady* had begun in *Macmillan's Magazine* in October 1880, two months before Evans' death. James was, of course, the natural heir to Evans, his technique of detailed psychological study having been heavily influenced by her lengthy works of inner portraiture. He was concerned, true, with form in a way, or to an extent, that none of the English writers were, calling *Middlemarch* "a mere chain of episodes, broken into accidental lengths and unconscious of the influence of a plan." He wrote likewise that "'Far from the Madding Crowd' gives us an uncomfortable sense of being a simple 'tale,' pulled and stretched to make the conventional three volumes ... Almost all novels are greatly too long."(!) (He also said cuttingly of Hardy's novel that "everything human in the book strikes us as factitious and insubstantial; the only things we believe in are the sheep and the dogs.") Some critics have maintained that James modeled Isabel Archer in part after Gwendolen Harleth in *Daniel Deronda*. He had twice visited Marian, evidently hoping for some kind of ritual blessing. Alas, the visits occurred under inauspicious circumstances. The first time James arrived to find that one of Marian's relatives had fainted dead away. (James, with perhaps uncharacteristic celerity, dashed off for a doctor.) On the second he was taken by a neighbor, who proffered a two-volume edition of *The Europeans* James had sent her. But Lewes thrust the volumes after James as he left, saying, "Ah, those books—take them away, please, away, away!"

Neither James nor Hardy was particularly concerned to affront their readers, though they might do so as a by-product of their way of writing. A deliberate, outright affront to the sensibilities of the Victorian novel-reading public that spoke directly of the new era—and threatened the portals of Mudie's and W. H. Smith's with something that might not perhaps be "select"— would be left to George Moore.

The son of an Irish landowner, Moore, like James, had lived in Paris for years, where he became a close friend of Manet and soaked up the influences of Baudelaire and Zola before returning to England. He had been an admirer of Miss Braddon, too, but his real hero was Zola, who was, he said later, "the beginning of me" and who had already graphically depicted the life of a prostitute in his 1880 *Nana*. Where James' challenge to the "traditional" Victorian novel was indirect, the 1883 *A Modern Lover*, Moore's first novel, was the story of a "good" lower-class girl who overcame her scruples about posing nude in order to help a struggling young artist. Moore was a crusader for the new era of naturalism that was sweeping Europe, the Europe of Ibsen and Zola, holding up a magnifying glass, whether in

The exterior of the grand W. H. Smith headquarters in London in 1901.

painting, drama, or fiction, to a life determined by the environment and the often cruel inevitabilities of scientific law.

Two ladies, however, wrote in to Mr. Mudie to protest the nude scene in *A Modern Lover*; Mudie did not circulate the book, and W. H. Smith put the novel on "limited circulation," which meant that practically speaking it was dead. Moore then went to see Mudie to protest the withholding of *A Modern Lover*, so he claimed later. "Then am I to understand," Moore reported having asked the great man, "that the entire opinion of the press is to be set aside, and that it is the taste of two ladies in the country that controls the destinies of English literature?" "I cannot undertake to discuss that question," he quoted the former liberal as blandly replying, "All I can say is that we must consult the wishes of our customers." That was that.

Moore was not, of course, the first to protest censorship by the circulating libraries. "Nothing will induce me to modify the title," Wilkie Collins raged, when Mudie's asked Bentley in 1873 to change the title of Collins' *The New Magdalen*. The author, who called Mudie's and W. H. Smith the "twin tyrants of literature," angrily responded: "His proposal would be an impertinence if he were not an old fool." Collins fumed that "the serious side of this affair is that this ignorant fanatic holds my circulation in his pious hands. Suppose he determines to check my circulation—what remedy have *we*? What remedy have his subscribers?"

The new novels by men like Moore were seen as a political and social challenge to the existing order, as Dickens' had been some sixty years before. In May 1888 Mr. Samuel Smith, MP for Flintshire, offered arguments in the House of Commons in support of his motion that "This House deplores the rapid spread of demoralizing literature in this country, and is of opinion that the law against obscene publications and indecent pictures and prints should be vigorously enforced, and, if necessary, strengthened." What he had in mind, Smith made clear, were English translations of Émile Zola. "These novels were only fit for swine." Surely England did not want "to stand still while the country was wholly corrupted by literature of this kind. Were they to wait until the moral fibre of the English race was eaten out, as that of the French was almost." (A diplomatic touch, the "almost.") "France, today, was rapidly approaching the condition of Rome in the time of the Caesars." Zola was influential—and detested by all right-thinking people. Hardy's own wife, indeed, worried lest her husband be "hand-in-glove with Zola."

French novels, with their telltale yellow covers, had long been regarded in England as dangerously "adult," inasmuch as they dealt frankly with sexuality and adultery, subjects largely off-limits to the writer who wanted Mudie's patronage. Even Thackeray thought *Madame Bovary* "a bad book." Indeed. "A heartless, cold blooded study of the downfall and degradation of a woman." "Novels in England are written to be read by boys and girls," said the *Fortnightly Review* accurately in 1871, "novels in France are not." And then along came *Zola*—even worse than Balzac!

But it was more and more a new era in publishing, one dominated by publishers like the cosmopolitan and German-Jewish William Heinemann, who began his publishing career in 1890 and eventually was to bring England countless translations of old and new works, including the great Russian novelists. Or there were J. M. Dent, the foul-tempered, abusive, penurious ex-binder who, beginning in 1904, produced the Everyman's Library cheap reprints ("I don't know how it is," he told a subordinate in puzzlement, "but when we get anybody who is any good he always leaves us."); the classical scholar Algernon Methuen Marshall Stedman (he dropped the "Marshall Stedman" in 1899), publisher of Kipling, Conrad, and Robert Louis Stevenson ("Goodbye, my boy; mind and make the next one human!" he always said encouragingly to one lesser writer); the small, bearded John Lane, publisher of the influential 1890s magazine of aestheticism *The Yellow Book*, whose initial art editor was Aubrey Beardsley, and distant cousin to and employer of Allen Lane, founder in 1935 of Penguin paperbacks; and the straw-boatered, morning-suit-wearing Fisher Unwin, who by 1900 was the country's biggest publisher of novels. They were beginning to publish in one- and two-volume editions, too.

And it was not just Zola people were turning to but other foreigners—like the Russians. In the December 1887 *Fortnightly Review* Matthew Arnold praised the vibrancy of Tolstoy's *Anna Karenina*, declaring that "the famous English novelists have passed away and left no successors of like fame." (*War and Peace*, like *Crime and Punishment*, appeared serially in *Ruskii Vestnik*, a St. Petersburg journal, in 1865, with *Anna Karenina* following in 1875—except Tolstoy, being after all a count, and not merely a money-hungry, middle-class English author, simply stopped writing it in the midst of the story—and after he reached the first ten chapters of Part III the serial was suspended until 1876.) The solemn-looking, bespectacled young Constance Garnett, whose grandfather had been a naval architect in Russia for Tsar Nicholas I and who taught herself Russian when she became pregnant, published her first translation (of Goncharov's *A Common Story*) in 1893. Thereafter her translations of the great Russian classics in a slightly musty tone that she thought reflected accurately the period style of the work she was translating became famous. The Russian novel: the September 1888 *Westminster Review* also saw it on the ascent and remarked on "the decline of our native novel." The Russians treated deep religious and philosophical matters— and adultery, in *Anna Karenina*—with a familiarity and ease shocking to a sheltered English public.

The old ways and the old firms suffered. Chapman and Hall almost went under in 1880 (Trollope briefly joined the board of directors in 1880 as part of an effort to stabilize it) under the lackadaisical guidance of Frederic Chapman, whom Dickens had thought such a fool. The firm sold their "Select Library of Fiction" to Ward, Lock & Co. in 1881, and Chatto & Windus, founded in 1855, bought the reprint rights from

Chapman and Hall for *The Way We Live Now* in the mid–1870s. In a symbolic passing of the publishing torch to a new generation, they published three of Trollope's last novels. Thank God for the standard collected editions Chapman and Hall had started publishing. "If it weren't for Dickens," the secretary of the firm said to the managing director of the firm in 1902, "we might as well put up the shutters to-morrow." In 1898 the house of Bentley, which had first published *Oliver Twist* in their magazine sixty years before, was sold to Macmillan and Company for £8,000 after the grandson of the founder, an antiques enthusiast, relinquished his interest in the firm to pursue his avocation of meteorology. John Blackwood had died in 1879, while George Smith in 1868 had finally sold off the non-publishing branches of Smith, Elder. He then focused his literary efforts on producing the monumental multivolume *Dictionary of National Biography* in 1882 under Leslie Stephen's editorial guidance after Stephen quit *Cornhill*.

Ironically, the country's most impressive living novelist simply withdrew further into his literary shell amidst evidence of this new atmosphere that he had surely helped to create. In a way, it was surprising. If James had inherited Evans' mantle as master psychologist, Hardy to some extent inherited her role as prophet, for he certainly did not view himself as a mere entertainer, whatever he had once said to Stephen about wishing to be simply a good serial writer. "Ever since I began to write," he noted in early 1891, "I have felt that the doll of English fiction must be demolished, if England is to have a school of English fiction at all." And his grim view of life seemed admirably suited to describing what was happening to England or at least to its countryside. Decline—Hardy made it his theme in his 1891 *Tess of the d'Urbervilles*, where the d'Urbervilles decline from a grand past as the English countryside and its social order are ravaged by an out-of-control capitalism that ultimately destroys Tess. Her fall ran parallel to what Hardy felt had been what he called "the decline and fall of the Hardys."

The century's last real "Victorian" novelist finally shut up shop. "The popular vehicles for the introduction of a novel to the public have grown to be, from one cause and another, the magazine and the circulating library; and the object of the magazine and the circulating library is not upward advance but lateral advance," he wrote feelingly in an 1891 essay. "The magazine in particular and the circulating library in general do not foster the growth of the novel which reflects and reveals life. They directly tend to exterminate it by monopolising all literary space." He knew whereof he spoke, of course. By one editor he had been compelled to rewrite a scene in *Tess* in which Angel Clare carried a dairymaid across a stream in his arms to one in which he transported her in a wheelbarrow, while in the American version of his 1895 *Jude the Obscure* Jude and Sue Bridehead's children became their siblings to spare American readers any indecency.

Hardy had evolved a partial solution to this problem—in keeping with his long-expressed public willingness to accommodate the wishes of magazine editors—by either altering or deleting "offensive" incidents from the serial magazine versions of his stories and then restoring them when the novel was published in book form. In this way, the multiplicity of formats that had come into existence by the latter part of the nineteenth century—three-decker, serial magazine, one-volume reprint, collected works edition, and foreign editions for the Continental audience—helped an avant-garde writer like Hardy obtain some protective coloration, just as did having two transatlantic markets. "I wish I could send you the real copy of the story I have written for Harpers'" magazine, he wistfully wrote a fellow novelist in February 1895, of *Jude the Obscure*, "as the form in which it is appearing there is a conventionalized one, in several points."

But now even that was not enough. No, the *Pall Mall Gazette* still found *Jude* full of "dirt, drivel, and damnation"; Mrs. Oliphant found it full of "grossness, indecency, and horror"; while the *Bookman* in New York called parts of the book reminiscent of watching "some foul animal that snatches greedily at great lumps of putrid offal." An outraged Australian reader burnt a copy of *Jude* and sent Hardy the ashes, and in June of 1896 the Bishop of Wakefield wrote to W. H. Smith and announced that he had burned *Jude* in a bonfire, whereupon Smith withdrew the book from his bookstalls. *Jude*, said some, was influenced by Zola! Hardy protested, not altogether truthfully, that he had "read in Zola very little." All the abuse was too much. To have *Jude* of all novels attacked was particularly mortifying, perhaps, because of its chronicle of a poor boy struggling to better himself through learning—the story of Hardy's life. Hardy announced that he was quitting the novel to return to his first love, poetry.

On the surface, as this outcome perhaps implied, all still appeared bright and rosy for the old-fashioned novel. By the early 1890s, the now gigantic enterprise of W. H. Smith stocked some 300,000 volumes, and Smith had entered the advertising business as well—cocoa, cold remedies, Bovril, concert notices, and other advertisements all filled the railway stalls. "Mr. W. H. Smith's bookstalls," said Henry James glowingly, are "a feature not to be omitted in any enumeration of the charms of Paddington and Euston. It is a focus of warmth and light in the vast smoky cavern; it gives the idea that literature is a thing of splendor, of a dazzling essence, of infinite gas-lit red and gold." At the great W. H. Smith headquarters on the Strand a paternalistic order throve in which company-sponsored excursions along the Thames benefitted workers not only in the main newspaper and book division but also those to be found in the "cap department, for issuing the caps marked with the name of the firm; a card room, for supplying the packs of playing-cards sold at railway stations; a rug-room, for railway rugs and straps; a string-room, for supplying the many wheels of cord used in tying parcels; and a sweet-smelling collection of old tea-chests, used for packing books." Smith himself, with no naval experience, had risen to become First Lord of the Admiralty in 1877—just as W. S. Gilbert was writing *H.M.S. Pinafore*. The writer used Smith as the basis for the comic

From a Photo. by]　AGE 21.　[*Bowen & Carpenter.*

From a Photo. by]　AGE 32.　[*Stereoscopic Co.*

From a Photo. by]　AGE 40.　[*Fred. Hollyer.*

From a Photo. by]　AGE 50.　[*Barraud.*

THOMAS HARDY.
BORN 1840.

THOMAS HARDY, who was born at a Dorsetshire village, was educated as an architect in his native place, at the same time giving much attention to literary studies. At twenty-one he came to London, where he continued to study design under Sir Arthur Blomfield, A.R.A., and modern languages at King's College. At twenty-two he gained several prizes and medals for designs, and also wrote much poetry which he never published. At thirty-one he wrote his first novel, "Desperate Remedies," and at thirty-four "Far from the Madding Crowd," his masterpiece, in which the humours and pathos of agricultural life are displayed in a manner which has had no equal.

A write-up of Thomas Hardy from the Strand Magazine *in the 1890s. An example of the new literary culture of celebrity at a time when movie stars and television personalities did not yet exist.*

opera's nautically challenged Admiral Sir Joseph Porter. As Smith passed among the undergraduates at Oxford to receive an honorary degree, they burst into "Stick close to your desk and never go to sea," etc.

As for Mudie's, when Mudie himself died in 1890, said the *Times* in a sonorous obituary, he left behind "a business which has now for many years been regarded almost in the light of a national institution." The regular provision of "Mudie's unnumbered volumes" to a middle-class household, wrote Trollope in his 1881 *Ayala's Angel*, "had been almost as much a provision of nature as water, gas, and hot rolls for breakfast." Most of his employees had started with the company as boys and remained ever since. "To be engaged at Mudie's was regarded by many of the staff as practically equal to being in a government position," observed a man who joined the firm around 1900. It was said in a not uncharacteristic story that the last request of the firm's dying chief binder was to be buried as near as possible to Mr. Mudie. And so the manager still continued to work away at his correspondence on a high stool with a quill pen as the century dwindled down, descending to help on the busy Saturday mornings when customers stocked up on reading for the weekend. When an employee came to bid Mudie's son, now head of the business, farewell, he found the boardroom table covered with piles of gold sovereigns—it was pay day—"each pile being somebody's monthly salary."

Mudie had even reorganized his company into a limited liability enterprise in 1864, and in a move uniting both production and distribution, sold 50 percent of the ownership to a group of major publishers that included John Murray, Richard Bentley, and others. This meant power, even arbitrary power. "I have just heard on very good authority," Daniel's son Frederick Macmillan was to write to budding novelist Mrs. Humphry Ward in November 1884, "that Mudie has a very strong objection to books lettered in black and as he is a rather crotchety person he is just as likely as not to buy as few as possible of Miss Bretherton if we stick to the black letters." The Macmillan firm accordingly relettered the cover of her new novel to suit the old man.

But Mudie had written to fellow Mudie shareholder (as well as, of course, publisher) George Bentley in fervent if largely unpunctuated prose that same year,

> I will only say—for the present and that in the strictest confidence (which I know you will kindly keep) that we find by careful analysis of figures extending over 2 or 3 years that not one in twelve of the 3 vol novels pays its way. We are not alone. Other libraries feel the difficulty arising from the over production and over pressure of this class of books.

Certainly there was an increase in the output of novels—from 516 in 1873 to 755 by 1886 to 1,315 in 1894. In 1881 there were 3,400 who responded to the English census that they were editors, authors, or journalists, by 1891 6,000, and by 1901, 11,000. Compared to the steady income that Trollope could count on by writing his given amount each day, as one contemporary observer wrote in 1887, "now the novel-market is not only affected, like all others, by the prevailing depression, but the pay is becoming excessively precarious and speculative." The circulating libraries, in fact, had been providing an artificial living for lots of novelists who would otherwise have been unable to get by. As a character in George Gissing's 1891 *New Grub Street* put it, "An author of moderate repute may live on a yearly three-volume novel ... But he would have to produce four one-volume novels to obtain the same income; and I doubt whether he could get so many published within the twelve months. And here comes in the benefit of the libraries; from the commercial point of view the libraries are indispensable. Do you suppose the public would support the present number of novelists if each book had to be purchased?" The writers needed the libraries, and the libraries wanted three-deckers. Ergo, the authors wrote three-deckers, even if the logic of such

W. H. Smith, pioneer in "railway novels," whose cheap prices, flashy covers, and convenient one-volume format appealed to the rail traveler. Appointed First Lord of the Admiralty in 1877, the un-nautical Smith was immortalized by W. S. Gilbert, then at work on H.M.S. Pinafore, in the song, "Stick to your desks / And never go to sea. . . ."

a system perhaps churned out more novels—and supported more novelists—than it reasonably should have. "England," the *Daily News* had observed as far back as 1871, was a "Paradise of inefficient and unknown novelists."

Was it this overproduction that led to promotions like the Balsam Fir Soap Company letting the world know apropos of an 1888 best seller by Mrs. Humphry Ward that "we have purchased an edition of the Hyde Park Company's *Robert Elsmere*, and also their edition of *Robert Elsmere and the Battle of Belief* ... These two books will be presented to each purchaser of a single cake of Balsam Fir Soap"? "While Parisian novels pass into their 80th edition, second editions [of English novels]," wrote a contemporary, "are becoming extremely rare, as a third is phenomenal and a fourth miraculous."

Cheap reprints like those of the railway library now appeared much more rapidly after publication than they had before, cutting into Mudie's profit from the resale of used books from its circulating library. Reprints were cheaper, too. In the 1880s Macmillan dropped the usual price of six shillings for hardcover reprints to two shillings in paper and cardboard. In the meantime the increasing number of free libraries hurt the borrowing of new volumes at profit-making libraries like Mudie's. Moreover, tastes were changing. The popular nautical novelist W. Clark Russell (favorite reading of Dr. Watson and his creator, Conan Doyle) had worried when he started his literary career soon after the midcentury that "the great masses of readers—those who support the circulating libraries—are ladies. Will it be possible to interest ladies in forecastle life and in the prosaics of the cabin?" Perhaps. *"East Lynne,"*—which dealt in murder, adultery and divorce—"in my humble judgment, ought to be placed in every girl's hands as soon as she has arrived at an age when she may find that life has for her unsuspected dangers," said one observer about the sensation novel that had been something of a scandal years before. And now George Moore found that when Mudie's turned down his new novel, *A Mummer's Wife* (it had a controversial scene in which a man entered a room with a woman—and then *closed the door*), he could simply get it published, as he did, in 1885, in a one-volume edition—and see it go into five printings. Times were changing.

In June 1894, Mudie's and Smith issued a public announcement stating that they would no longer pay any more than four shillings a book for new acquisitions and that publishers had to ensure that the time between initial publication of a book and its republication in a cheap edition was at least one year. It was a bombshell. Even the *New York Times* mentioned Smith and Mudie's decision on the front page of its July 1, 1894, Sunday edition. (On an inside page there appeared, in appropriate counterpoint, Chapter XXV—"continued"—of Miss Braddon's *Thou Art the Man*). "This at once will drive out of the field a swarm of amateur novelists whose work is taken now only because the price paid by the libraries more or less secures the publisher against initial expenses, even if the books are failures," said the *Times*, echoing Gissing's analysis in *New Grub Street*. "It seems clear that the grotesque and injurious institution of three-volume editions is on its last legs."

Meanwhile, the supremacy of the English novel was being challenged by the new prestige and authority of English drama. In June 1889, there was presented "for seven performances only" at the National Theatre a new play called *A Doll's House*. It was an eye-opener, the run having to be extended to twenty-four performances after the furor it created. Educated, affluent audiences were returning to the theater, and the 1890s saw a revitalized English stage, with the production of *Arms and the Man* (1894), *The Devil's Disciple* (1897), *Lady Windermere's Fan* (1892) and *The Importance of Being Earnest* (1895). In the latter play, when the governess Miss Prism first told Cecily, after her charge slighted "the three-volume novels that Mudie sends us," that she herself once wrote a three-volume novel, the audience must have roared. Especially since Miss Prism, in a Wildean dig at Mudie's carefully inoffensive formula for "select" novels, then noted innocently that "the good ended happily, and the

A typical W. H. Smith railway bookstore, through which cheap reprints of novels became widely available a year or so after their initial three-volume publication and distribution through circulating libraries like Mudie's. You could rent books to take with you on the train, dropping them off—like rental cars—at your destination.

bad unhappily. That is what Fiction means." Likewise, the new popularity of the short story, as practiced by Kipling, Conrad, Robert Louis Stevenson, James, and others, eclipsed the novel. The *Strand Magazine*, which began publication in 1891 and rose to a monthly circulation of 500,000, popularized in the short stories it printed a character as popular as Pickwick had once been—Sherlock Holmes.

Mudie's and W. H. Smith had pulled the plug on the three-decker. While publisher William Heinemann suggested as a last-minute rescue measure that the libraries institute a differential price system (subscribers would be charged more for "good" books than for "bad" ones), Smith and Mudie held firm. And, lo and behold, the three-decker format and the price of thirty-one shillings six pence so long artificially maintained largely by Smith and Mudie's collapsed almost overnight. The first edition of the much-reviled *Jude the Obscure* was published in November 1895 in one rather than the hitherto customary three volumes. In 1894 184 three-deckers were published, in 1895 there were 52, in 1896, 25, and by 1897 there were just four. The three-decker was dead.

There were mourners, of course, the publishers, the authors who had depended on it, naturally, and then, also, the sentimentalists. "I dreamed for many years of building a veritable three-decker out of chosen and long-storied timber—teak, green-heart, and ten-year-old oak knees—each curve melting deliciously into the next that the sea might nowhere meet resistance or weakness; the whole suggesting motion even when, her great sails for the moment furled, she lay in some needed haven—" went an eloquent elegy that played on the symbolic connotations of the three-decker's naval heritage. "A vessel ballasted on ingots of pure research and knowledge, roomy, fitted with delicate cabinet-work below-decks, painted, carved, gilt and wreathed the length of her, from her blazing stern-galleries outlined by bronzy palm-trunks, to her rampant figure-head— an East-Indianman worthy to lie alongside *The Cloister and the Hearth*."

So mourned Rudyard Kipling, whose elegant lament for the old three-deckers seemed to suggest they were emblematic of the passing of the Empire as, perhaps, in some sense they were. But he had not built such a three-decker—and, significantly, it did not affect his career negatively. Did the leisurely three-decker really suit a world of motorcars, telephones, electric lights and elevators? The popular novelist Hall Caine wrote wistfully of having been a reader years before for "a publishing house of the old days, half office, half study; a workshop where books might be made, not turned out by machinery." This was all before publishers moved to the suburbs, before the publishing houses grew so large, when there had still been some collegiality, and a less hurried pace. *Autre temps, autre moeurs.* "The Sale dinner," wrote a biographer of John Murray in 1891, "has all but succumbed during the past decade . . ." So, too, "the country booksellers. . . . are dying out."

Perhaps not inappropriately, shortly before the death of the three-decker came the death, all but forgotten, of Thackeray's mad wife, Isabella, after her long years of madness and confinement; her daughter Anny, with her at the end, noted a final peace. Theresa Reviss, the model years before for Thackeray's juvenile Becky Sharp, had meanwhile announced herself "compromised" by an incautious Lord Chancellor who took her out on his yacht, for which she was rewarded (or silenced) by being set up in an Italian villa. She then married respectably, and was last rumored, having resurfaced in London as the Countess de la Torre, an old lady in her eighties, to be under the disapproving eye of the London police for the neglect of her cats. Only the ghosts lingered. An acquaintance passing 142 Strand with the now aged publishing firebrand John Chapman chanced to remark on Marian Evans' passion for Herbert Spencer. A hand gave his arm "an eloquent squeeze," and Chapman whispered, "You know, she was very fond of me!" Like some unshakable curse, the literary vultures descended anew on the Reverend Arthur Nicholls, long retired and living with his second wife (who patiently tolerated a portrait of Charlotte Brontë over her

Memorandum of Agreement

Dated Jan 20 · 1879.

BETWEEN

Henry James Eq

AND

MACMILLAN AND CO.

FOR THE PUBLICATION OF

'Daisy Miller', 'The Europeans,'
'The American', & 'French Poets'

$\frac{1}{2}$ Profits

The full text of the "half-profits" contract between Henry James and his publisher,
Macmillan, for the first publication of Daisy Miller, The Europeans, The

Memorandum of Agreement made this 20th

day of _January_ 18_79_, between _Henry James Jun._

Esq.

on the one part, and Messrs. MACMILLAN and Co. on the other part.

It is Agreed that the said Messrs. MACMILLAN and Co. shall

publish at their own risk and expense "_Daisy Miller_" _and other_

stories

the copyright of which shall be the joint property of ___Henry___

James Jun.ᵉ Esq. and Messrs. MACMILLAN and Co. in the

proportions stated below, and after deducting from the produce of the sale

thereof all the expenses of printing, paper, boarding, advertising, trade allow-

ances, and other incidental expenses, the profits remaining of every edition

that may be printed of the work during the term of legal copyright are to

be divided into _two equal_ parts, _one part_ to be paid to

the said _Henry James Jun.ᵉ Esq._

and the other to belong to Messrs. MACMILLAN and Co.

The books to be accounted for at the trade-sale price, twenty-five

as twenty-four, unless it be thought advisable to dispose of copies or of

the remainder at a lower price, which is left to the discretion of Messrs.

MACMILLAN and Co.

Accounts to be made up annually to Midsummer, delivered on or

before October 1, and settled by cash in the ensuing January.

It is further agreed that "French Poets & Novelists"
"The Europeans" and "The American" shall be published
on the above terms

Macmillan & Co:

Henry James jr

American, *and a volume of critical essays. The brevity is characteristic of an era
when "gentleman's agreements"—often merely handshakes—still ruled publishing.*

hearth). A much-respected antiquarian book dealer and his associate offered to acquire Charlotte's letters and intimated that they would then donate them to the South Kensington Museum for use by all the world—and promptly sold the letters to private purchasers across the globe.

The three-decker was dead, the writers who sustained it and, increasingly, the public that had devoured it, were gone. It was the turn of a younger, more self-conscious, more sophisticated—and ironical—generation, one of whom showed some of her writing to that same Mrs. Lynn Linton who had written for the *Westminster Review* so many years before and sold her family's Gad's Hill house to Dickens. "I have had your sketch," Mrs. Linton now wrote to the youthful correspondent who had favored her with her fiction, "I am out of young society now, but are such people as Sant and Feo possible in modern drawing rooms? Would a man on first introduction eat that half sandwich, drink out of the same cup, go home unasked in the same hansom, and squeeze the ungloved hand of a girl of good birth and morals? In earlier times he would have—perhaps—treated a loose woman with this familiarity—but a good girl—a lady? . . . You are clever, and I think *have it in you*," wrote the woman who had published her first novel in 1846, "but yours is so far outside my sphere of thought and social knowledge, that I can scarcely judge of your truthfulness of presentation. It's not my world as I knew it that you give."

It certainly was not.

In 1901 George Smith died. In 1917 his firm would be absorbed by the firm of John Murray, which had published Jane Austen and Lord Byron so many years before. In 1904 the former *Cornhill* editor and Thackeray son-in-law Leslie Stephen died, and his daughter moved out of his house into new quarters in the no longer fashionable district of Bloomsbury where Thackeray's Amelia Sedley had lived years before. Together with the son of a friend of Anny Thackeray's, a young man named Lytton Strachey, Stephen's daughter would—along with her brothers and a young, distant relative of Macaulay's named

E. M. Forster—form the nexus of a new movement in English fiction.

"We were full of experiments and reforms," she wrote as she later recalled the coming of a new day in literature. "We were going to do without table napkins . . . we were going to paint; to write; to have coffee after dinner instead of tea at nine o'clock." The mixture of measured whimsy and self-deprecating irony signaled the coming of a nervier, edgier, more self-conscious age and sensibility.

Everything was on trial.

Everything . . .

So spoke Virginia Woolf with the voice of modernity—and with it the days of the great Victorian novel were gone forever.

SELECTED BIBLIOGRAPHY

Ackroyd, Peter. *Charles Dickens*. New York: HarperCollins, 1992.

Adrian, A. A. *Mark Lemon: First Editor of Punch*. London and New York: Oxford University Press, 1966.

Allen, Walter. *The English Novel*. Harmondsworth: Penguin, 1973.

Allingham, B., and D. Radford, eds. *William Allingham: A Diary*. Harmondsworth: Penguin, 1985.

Alston, Robin. "The British Book Trade: 1701 to 1800." In *Publishing History* 16.

Altick, Richard D. *The English Common Reader*. Chicago and London: Chicago University Press, 1957.

_____. *Lives and Letters*. New York: Alfred A. Knopf, 1965.

_____. *The Presence of the Past*. Columbus: Ohio State University Press, 1991.

_____. *Writers, Readers and Occasions*. Columbus: Ohio State University Press, 1989.

Anesko, Michael. *Friction with the Market*. New York: Oxford University Press, 1986.

Ardis, Ann. *New Women, New Novels*. New Brunswick, N.J., and London: Rutgers University Press, 1990.

"The Art of Novel Writing," *The Gentlemen's Magazine* 9, new series (1872).

Barker, Juliet. *The Brontës*. London: Weidenfeld and Nicolson, 1994.

Bell, Aldon. *London in the Age of Dickens*. Norman, Okla.: University of Oklahoma Press, 1967.

Bell, Mackenzie. *Half Hours with Representative Novelists of the Nineteenth Century*. London: Routledge, 1927.

Bentley, Nicholas, et al. *The Dickens Index*. Oxford and New York: Oxford University Press, 1988.

Bertram, James. *Some Memories of Books, Authors and Events*. London: Archibald Constable & Co., 1893.

Besant, Walter. "The Rise and Fall of the 'Three-Decker'." *Dial* 17 (October 1, 1894).

Betham-Edwards, Matilda. *Mid-Victorian Memories*. London: John Murray, 1919.

Bleackley, Horace. *Jack Shepard*. Edinburgh and London: W. Hodge & Co., 1933.

Bliss, Trudy, ed. *Jane Welsh Carlyle: A New Selection of Her Letters*. New York: Macmillan, 1950.

Booth, Bradford A. "Trollope and 'Little Dorrit'." *The Trollopian*, no. 4 (March 1948).

Briggs, A., ed. *Essays in the History of Publishing*. London: Longmans, 1974.

Brightfield, Myron. *Victorian England in Its Novels (1840–1870)*. Los Angeles: University of California Library, 1971.

Brown, Lucy. *Victorian News and Newspapers*. Oxford: Clarendon Press, 1983.

Browne, Edgar. *Phiz and Dickens*. London: James Nisbet & Co., Ltd., 1913.

Burns, Wayne. *Charles Reade*. New York: Bookman Associates, 1961.

Butt, John, and Kathleen Tillotson. *Dickens at Work*. Fair Lawn, N.J.: Essential Books, 1958.

Campbell, James. *Edward Bulwer-Lytton*. Boston: Twayne Publishers, 1986.

Carlisle, Janice. *The Sense of an Audience*. Athens, Ga.: University of Georgia Press, 1981.

Carter, John, ed. *New Paths in Book Collecting*. London: Constable & Co., 1934.

Cecil, Lord David. *Early Victorian Novelists.* Indianapolis, Ind.: Bobbs-Merrill, 1935.

Charavat, William. *The Profession of Authorship in America, 1800–1870.* New York: Columbia University Press, 1992.

Chase, Mary Ellen. *Thomas Hardy from Serial to Novel.* Minneapolis: University of Minnesota Press, 1927.

Church, A. J. "Authors and Publishers." *Nineteenth Century* (May 1907).

Cohen, J. R. *Charles Dickens and His Original Illustrators.* Columbus: Ohio State University Press, 1980.

Colby, Robert A. *Fiction with a Purpose.* Bloomington and London: Indiana University Press, 1967.

_____. "Goose Quill and Pen." In *Innovators and Preachers.* Joel Wiener, ed. Westport, Conn.: Greenwood Press, 1985.

_____. "The Librarian Rules the Roost." *Wilson Library Bulletin* 26 (April 1952).

_____. "That He Who Rides May Read." *Wilson Library Bulletin* 27 (Dec 1952).

Colby, Robert A., and Vineta Colby. *The Equivocal Virtue.* Hamden, Conn.: Archon Books, 1966.

Collins, A. S. *The Profession of Letters, 1780–1832.* New York: E. F. Dutton & Co., 1928.

Collins, Philip. "'Agglomerating Dollars with Prodigious Rapidity': British Pioneers on the American Lecture Circuit." In James R. Kincaid and Albert Kuhn. *Victorian Literature and Society.* Colombus: Ohio State University Press, 1984.

_____. "Dickens's Public Readings: The Kit and the Team." *The Dickensian* 74, no. 384, part 1 (January 1978).

_____. Introduction to *Sikes and Nancy and Other Public Readings.* New York: Oxford University Press, 1983.

_____, ed. *Dickens: Interviews and Recollections.* 2 vols. London: Macmillan, 1983.

Collins, Wilkie. *My Miscellanies.* New York: Harper & Bros., n.d.

"The Commerce of Literature." *Westminster Review* (April 1852).

"The Condition of Authors in England, Germany, and France," *Fraser's Magazine* (March 1847).

Coolidge, A. C. *Charles Dickens as Serial Novelist*. Ames, Iowa: Iowa State University Press, 1967.

Cross, Nigel. *The Common Writer: Life in Nineteenth-Century Grub Street*. Cambridge and New York: Cambridge University Press, 1985.

Cruse, Amy. *After the Victorians*. London: G. Allen & Unwin, 1938.

_____. *The Victorians and Their Books*. London: G. Allen & Unwin, 1935.

Cunliffe, John. *Leaders of the Victorian Revolution*. New York: Russell & Russell, 1963.

Curwen, B. *A History of Booksellers*. London: Chatto & Windus, 1873.

Daiches, David, and John Flower. *Literary Landscapes of the British Isles*. New York and London: Paddington Press Ltd., 1979.

Daryl, Philip. *Public Life in England*. London and New York: Routledge, 1927.

David, Paul B. *The Lives and Times of Ebenezer Scrooge*. New Haven: Yale University Press, 1990.

Davies, J. A. *John Forester: A Literary Life*. Leicester: Leicester University Press, 1983.

De la Mare, Walter, ed. *The Eighteen-Eighties*. Cambridge: The University Press, 1930.

Devey, Louisa. *Life of Rosina, Lady Lytton*. London: Swan Sonneschien, Lowrey & Co., 1887.

Dickens, Charles. "The Guild of Literature and Art." *Household Words* (May 10, 1851).

Dodds, John W. *The Age of Paradox*. London: Victor Gollancz Ltd., 1953.

Drabble, Margaret. *A Writer's Britain: Landscape in Literature*. New York: Alfred A. Knopf, 1979.

_____, ed. *The Genius of Thomas Hardy*. New York: Alfred A. Knopf, 1976.

Dunleavy, Janet. *George Moore*. Lewisburg, Pa.: Bucknell University Press, 1973.

Edel, Leon. *Henry James: The Conquest of London*. New York: Avon Books, 1978.

_____. *Henry James: The Middle Years*. New York: Avon Books, 1978.

_____. *Henry James: The Untried Years*. New York: Avon Books, 1978.

Edel, Leon, and Lydall Powers. *The Complete Notebooks of Henry James*. New York: Oxford University Press, 1987.

Edwards, P. D. "Trollope Changes His Mind: The Death of Melmotte in the Way We Live Now." *Nineteenth-Century Fiction* 18 (1963).

Eliot, George. *Selected Critical Writings*. Oxford and New York: Oxford University Press, 1992.

Ellis, S. M. *The Solitary Horsemen*. Kensington: The Cayme Press, 1927.

_____. *Wilkie Collins, Le Fanu and Others*. New York: R. R. Smith, 1931.

_____. *William Harrison Ainsworth and His Friends*. London: John Lane Company, 1911.

"English Novels." *Fraser's Magazine* (October 1851).

Exman, Eugene. *The House of Harper*. New York: Harper & Bros., 1967.

Fahnestock, Jeanne R. "Geraldine Jewsbury: The Power of the Publisher's Reader." *Nineteenth-Century Fiction* 28, no. 3 (December 1973).

"False Morality of Lady Novelists." *The National Review* (1859).

Feather, John. *A Dictionary of Book History*. London and New York: Croom Helm, 1986.

_____. *A History of British Publishing*. London and New York: Croom Helm, 1988.

Feltes, Norman. *Modes of Production of Victorian Novels*. Chicago: University of Chicago Press, 1986.

Fielding, K. J. "The Monthly Serialisation of Dickens's Novels." *The Dickensian* 54, no. 324 (January 1958).

_____. "The Weekly Serialisation of Dickens's Novels." *The Dickensian* 54, no. 326 (September 1958).

Flint, Kate. *The Woman Reader, 1837–1914*. Oxford: Clarendon Press; New York: Oxford University Press, 1993.

Ford, George. *Dickens and His Readers*. Princeton: Princeton University Press, 1955.

Forster, John. *The Life of Charles Dickens*. London: Dent, 1966.

Fraser, Rebecca. *The Brontës*. New York: Ballantine Books, 1988.

Garrett, Peter. *The Victorian Multi-Plot Novel*. New Haven: Yale University Press, 1980.

Gary, Franklin. "Charlotte Brontë and George Henry Lewes." *PMLA*, 51 (June 1936).

Gash, Robert. *Robert Surtees and Early Victorian Society*. Oxford: Clarendon Press; New York: Oxford University Press, 1993.

Gaskell, Elizabeth. *Life of Charlotte Brontë*. Harmondsworth: Penguin, 1975.

Gerin, Winifred. *Anne Thackeray Ritchie*. Oxford and New York: Oxford University Press, 1981.

_____. *Charlotte Brontë*. Oxford: Clarendon Press, 1967.

_____. *Elizabeth Gaskell*. Oxford: Clarendon Press, 1976.

_____. *Emily Brontë*. Oxford: Clarendon Press, 1971.

Gettman, R. A. *A Victorian Publisher: A Study of the Bentley Papers*. Cambridge: Cambridge University Press, 1960.

Gittings, Robert. *Thomas Hardy's Later Years*. Boston: Little, Brown, 1978.

_____. *Young Thomas Hardy*. Boston: Little, Brown, 1975.

Glendinning, Victoria. *Anthony Trollope*. Harmondsworth: Penguin, 1992.

Glyn, Jenifer. *Prince of Publishers*. London and New York: Allison & Busby, 1986.

Goldberg, Michael. *Carlyle and Dickens*. Athens, Ga.: University of Georgia Press, 1972.

Gordon, John D. "Reading for Profit: The Other Career of Charles Dickens." New York: New York Public Libary, 1958.

Gordon, Lyndall. *Charlotte Brontë*. London and New York: W. W. Norton & Co., 1995.

Griest, Guinevere L. *Mudie's Circulating Library and the Victorian*

Novel. Bloomington: Indiana University Press; London: David & Charles, 1970.

Gross, John. *The Rise and Fall of the Man of Letters*. New York: Collier Books, 1970.

Grubb, Gerald. "Dickens's Pattern of Weekly Serialization." *Journal of English Literary History* 8 (1942).

_____. "The Editorial Policies of Charles Dickens." *PMLA* 58 (1943).

Haight, Gordon. "Dickens and Lewes." *PMLA* 71, no. 1 (March 1956).

_____. *George Eliot*. New York: Oxford University Press, 1968.

_____. "George Eliot's Royalties." *The Bookseller* (October 2, 1954): 1140–1141.

_____, ed. *The George Eliot Letters*. New Haven: Yale University Press, 1954–1978.

_____. *Selections from George Eliot's Letters*. New Haven: Yale University Press, 1985.

Hall, N. John. *Trollope*. Oxford: Clarendon Press; New York: Oxford University Press, 1991.

_____. *Trollope and His Illustrators*. London: Macmillan, 1980.

Hall, N. John, ed., with Nina Burgis. *The Letters of Anthony Trollope*. Palo Alto, Calif.: Stanford University Press, 1983.

Halperin, John. *Trollope and Politics*. London: Macmillan, 1977.

Hamer, Mary. *Writing by Numbers: Trollope's Serial Fiction*. Cambridge and New York: Cambridge University Press, 1987.

Hanson, Lawrence, and Elisabeth Lawrence. *Necessary Evil: The Life of Jane Welsh Carlyle*. London: Constable & Co., 1952.

Harden, Edgar. *The Emergence of Thackeray's Serial Fiction*. Athens, Ga.: University of Georgia Press, 1979.

_____, ed. *The Letters and Private Papers of William Makepeace Thackeray*. A supplement to Gordon N. Ray, *The Letters and Private Papers of William Makepeace Thackeray*. New York and London: Garland Publishing, Inc., 1994.

Hardy, Thomas. "Candour in English Fiction." *The New Review* 2, no. 8 (January 1890).

Harvey, John. *Victorian Novelists and Their Illustrators*. New York: New York University Press, 1971.

Hayward, Arthur. *The Day of Dickens*. London: Routledge, 1926.

Hepburn, James. *The Author's Empty Purse and the Rise of the Literary Agent*. London and New York: Oxford University Press, 1968.

Herring, Paul. "The Number Plans for Dombey and Son." *Modern Philology* 68 (1970): 151–187.

"Hints on the Modern Governess System," *Fraser's Magazine* 30 (November 1844).

Hollingsworth, Keith. *The Newgate Novel*. Detroit, Mich.: Wayne State University Press, 1963.

House, Madeline, and Graham Storey, eds. *The Letters of Charles Dickens*. Pilgrim ed. Oxford: Clarendon Press, 1965.

"How We Get Our Newspapers." *All the Year Round* (December 25, 1875).

Hughes, Douglas, ed. *The Man of Wax*. New York: New York University Press, 1971.

Hughes, Linda, and Michael Lund. *The Victorian Serial*. Charlottesville, Va.: University Press of Virginia, 1991.

Huxley, Leonard. *The House of Smith, Elder*. Privately printed, London, 1923.

Innis, B. A. "The English Press in the Nineteenth Century." *The University of Toronto Quarterly* 15, no. 1 (October 1945).

Jack, Ian. *English Literature, 1815–1832*. Oxford: Clarendon Press, 1963.

Jacobson, Marcia. *Henry James and the Mass Market*. University, Ala.: University of Alabama Press, 1883.

James, Elizabeth. "An Insight into the Management at Railway Bookstalls in the Eighteen Fifties." *Publishing History* 10 (1981).

James, Henry. *Collected Travel Writings: Great Britain and America*. New York: Library of America, 1993.

James, Louis. *Fiction for the Working Man*. London and New York: Oxford University Press, 1963.

Jefferson, John G. *Novels and Novelists: From Elizabeth to Victoria*. London: Hurst and Blackett, 1858.

Johnson, Edgar. *Charles Dickens: His Tragedy and Triumph.* New York: Simon & Schuster, 1952.

_____. *Sir Walter Scott.* New York: Macmillan, 1970.

Jones, Annabel. "Disraeli's Endymion: A Case Study." In Asa Briggs, ed. *Essays in the History of Publishing.* London: Longmans, 1974.

Jones, Linda. "James Grant on Magazine Day." *Victorian Periodical Review* 7, no. 1 (March 1974).

Keating, P. J. *The Haunted Study.* London: Secker & Warburg, 1989.

Kellet, E. E. "Mudie's." *The Spectator* (July 16, 1937).

Kipling, Rudyard. "The Old Three-Decker." *Saturday Review* 78 (July 14, 1894).

Klancher, Jon. *The Making of English Reading Audiences, 1790–1832.* Madison: University of Wisconsin Press, 1987.

Knight, Charles. *Passages of a Working Life During Half a Century.* London: Bardbury and Evans, 1864, 1865.

Lackington, James. *Memoirs of the First Forty-five Years of James Lackington.* New York: Garland Publishing, Inc. Reprinted, 1974.

"The Lady Novelists." *Westminster Review* (October 1852).

Lansbury, Coral. *The Reasonable Man: Trollope's Legal Fiction.* Princeton: Princeton University Press, 1981.

Larken, Geoffrey. "The Shuffling Scamp." *Brontë Society Transactions* 15, no. 5, part 80 (1970).

Lauterbach, C. E., and E. S. Lauterbach, "The Nineteenth-Century Three-Volume Novel." In *Papers of the Bibliographical Society of America* 11 (1957).

Laver, James. *Hatchards of Piccadilly.* London: Hatchards, 1947.

Lehmann, Rudolph C. *Charles Dickens as Editor.* New York: Sturgis & Walton Company, 1912.

Levine, George. *The Boundaries of Fiction.* Princeton: Princeton University Press, 1968.

Ley, J. W. T. *The Dickens Circle.* London: Chapman and Hall, 1918.

Lonoff, Sue. "Charles Dickens and Wilkie Collins." *Nineteenth-Century Fiction* 35, no. 2 (September 1980).

Lund, Michael. "Novels, Writers, and Readers in 1850." *Victorian Periodical Review* 17, nos. 1 and 2 (spring and summer 1984).

Lytton, Edward Robert Bulwer, Earl of. *The Life, Letters, and Literary Remains of Edward Bulwer, Lord Lytton*. London: K. Paul, Trench, 1883.

"The Manufacture of Novels." *The Spectator* (August 31, 1901).

Marchand, Leslie. *The Athenaeum*. Chapel Hill: University of North Carolina Press, 1941.

Mason, Leo. "William Harrison Ainsworth." *The Dickensian* 35, no. 251 (summer 1939).

Maurer, Oscar. "Anonymity vs. Signature in Victorian Reviewing." *Studies in English* 27, no. 1 (June 1948).

_____. "'My Squeamish Public': Some Problems of Victorian Magazine Publishers and Editors." *Studies in Bibliography* 12 (1959).

Mauskopf, Charles. "Thackeray's Attitude Towards Dickens's Writings." *Nineteenth-Century Fiction* 21, no. 1 (June 1966).

Maxwell, Sir Herbert. *Life and Times of the Rt. Hon. W. H. Smith*. Edinburgh and London: William Blackwood and Sons, 1893.

Maxwell, W. B. *Time Gathered*. London: Hutchinson, 1937.

Mclean, Ruari. *Victorian Book Design and Colour Printing*. London: Faber & Faber, 1972.

McMaster, R. D. *Trollope and the Law*. Houndmills, Basingstoke, Hampshire: Macmillan, 1986.

Millgate, Michael. *Thomas Hardy*. New York: Random House, 1982.

Millgate, Michael, and Richard Purdy, eds. *Collected Letters of Thomas Hardy*. Oxford and New York: Clarendon Press, 1978–1988.

Moore, George. *Literature as Nurse, or Circulating Morals*. Sussex: The Harvester Press; Atlantic Highlands, N.J.: Humanities Press, 1976.

Morgan, Charles. *The House of Macmillan*. London: Macmillan, 1943.

Mumby, Frank A. *Publishing and Bookselling*. London: J. Cape; New York: R. R. Bowker, 1949.

Mumm, S. D. "Writing for Their Lives: Women Applicants to the Royal Literary Fund, 1840–1880." *Publishing History* 27 (1990).

My First Book. Introduction by Jerome K. Jerome. London: Chatto & Windus, 1897.

Nowell-Smith, S. H., ed. *Letters to Macmillan*. London and Melbourne: Macmillan; New York: St. Martin's Press, 1967.

Oliphant, M. O. *Annals of a Publishing House*. Edinburgh: William Blackwood & Sons, 1897.

Olsen, Donald J. *The City as a Work of Art*. New Haven and London: Yale University Press, 1986.

Patten, Robert. *Dickens and His Publishers*. Oxford: Clarendon Press; New York: Oxford University Press, 1978.

_____. *George Cruikshank's Life, Times and Art*. New Brunswick, N.J.: Rutgers University Press, 1992–1996.

_____. "Pickwick Papers and the Development of Serial Fiction." *Rice University Studies* (1975).

Pearl, Cyril. *The Girl with the Swansdown Seat*. Indianapolis, Ind.: Bobbs-Merrill, 1955.

Peters, Catherine. *The King of Inventors*. Princeton: Princeton University Press, 1991.

Peters, Margot. *Unquiet Soul*. New York: Pocket Books, 1976.

Phelps, Gilbert. *The Russian Novel in English Fiction*. London: Hutchinson, 1956.

Phillips, Walter C. *Dickens, Reade and Collins: Sensation Novelists*. New York: Columbia University Press, 1919.

Plant, Marjorie. *The English Book Trade*. London: G. Allen & Unwin, 1974.

Pollard, Arthur. *Mrs. Gaskell*. Manchester: Manchester University Press, 1965.

Pollard, Graham. "Serial Fiction." In *New Paths in Book Collecting*. John Carter, ed. London: Constable & Co., 1934.

Ray, Gordon, *The Buried Life*. New York: Haskell House, 1974.

_____. *Thackeray*. New York: McGraw-Hill, 1955–1958.

_____, ed. *The Letters and Private Papers of William Makepeace Thackeray.* Cambridge: Harvard University Press, 1945–1946.

Redding, Cyrus. *Fifty Years' Recollections.* London: Charles J. Skeet, 1858.

Rigby, Elizabeth. "Jane Eyre and Vanity Fair." *Quarterly Review* (December 1848).

Rosa, Matthew. *The Silver-Fork School.* New York: Columbia University Press, 1936.

Rose, Phyllis. *Parallel Lives.* New York: Alfred A. Knopf, 1983.

Rowell, George. *The Victorian Theatre, 1792–1914.* Cambridge and New York: Cambridge University Press, 1978.

Sadleir, Michael. "Aspects of the Victorian Novel." *Publishing History* 5 (1979).

_____. *Bulwer and His Wife.* London: Constable & Co., 1933.

_____. *The Evolution of Publishers Binding Styles, 1770–1900.* London: Constable & Co., 1930.

_____. *Nineteenth-Century Fiction.* New York: Cooper Square Publishers, 1968.

_____. "The Northanger Novels: A Footnote to Jane Austen." The English Association, pamphlet no. 68 (November 1927).

_____. "Yellow-backs." In *New Paths in Book Collecting.* John Carter, ed. London: Constable & Co., 1934.

Schacterle, Lance. "Oliver Twist and Its Serial Predecessors." *Dickens Studies Annual* 3 (1974).

Schmidt, Barbara Quinn. "Novelists, Publishers and Fiction in Middle-Class Magazines: 1860–1880." *Victorian Periodicals Review* 17 (1984): 142–153.

_____. "The Patron as Businessman: George Murray Smith." *Victorian Periodicals Review* 16, no. 1 (spring 1983).

"Sensational Novels." *Fortnightly Review* (April 1863).

Shattock, Joanne, ed. *Oxford Guide to British Women Writers.* Oxford and New York: Oxford University Press, 1993.

Shattock, Joanne, and Michael Wolff, eds. *The Victorian Periodical Press.* Leicester: Leicester University Press; Toronto: University Press of Toronto, 1982.

Showalter, Elaine. *A Literature of Their Own.* Princeton: Princeton University Press, 1977; Virago 1978.

Smith, George. "Charlotte Brontë." *Cornhill Magazine* (December 1900).

Speare, M. E. *The Political Novel.* New York: Oxford University Press, 1924.

Spedin, James. *Publishers and Authors.* London: J. R. Smith, 1867.

Spencer, Jane. *The Rise of the Woman Novelist.* Oxford and New York: B. Blackwell, 1986.

Srebrnik, Patricia. *Alexander Strahan, Victorian Publisher.* Ann Arbor: University of Michigan Press, 1986.

Steig, Michael. *Dickens and Phiz.* Bloomington: Indiana University Press, 1978.

Stetz, Margaret. "Life's 'Half-Profits': Writers and Their Readers in Fiction of the 1890's." In *Nineteenth-Century Lives.* L. Lockridge, J. Maynard, and D. Stone, eds.

Stevenson, Lionel. "Dickens's Dark Novels, 1851–1857." *Sewanee Review* 51 (1943).

_____. "The Rationale of Victorian Fiction." *Nineteenth-Century Fiction* 27, no. 4 (March 1973).

Storey, Gladys. *Dickens and Daughter.* London: F. Muller, 1939.

"Suggestions About Gift-Books." *Fraser's Magazine* (February 1852).

Super, R. H. *The Chronicler of Barsetshire.* Ann Arbor: University of Michigan Press, 1990.

Sutherland, John. "The British Book Trade and the Crash of 1826." *The Library* 9, no. 2, 6th series (June 1987).

_____. "Chips Off the Block: Dickens's Serialising Imitators." In Joanne Shattock, ed. *Dickens and Other Victorians.* Houndsmills, Basingstoke, Hampshire: Macmillan, 1988.

_____. "Cornhill's Sales and Payments: The First Decade." *Victorian Periodicals Review* 19, no. 3 (fall 1986).

_____. "Dickens, Reade and *Hard Cash.*" *The Dickensian* 81, no. 405, part 1 (spring 1985).

_____. "The Fiction Earning Patterns of Thackeray, Dickens,

George Eliot and Trollope." In *Browning Institute Studies* 7 (1979).

_____. "Henry Colburn Publisher." *Publishing History* 19 (1986).

_____. "The Institutionalization of the British Book Trade." In Robin Myers and Michael Harris, eds. *Development of the British Book Trade*. Oxford: Oxford Polytechnic Press, 1981.

_____. *The Life of Walter Scott*. Oxford, England, and Cambridge, Mass.: Blackwell, 1995.

_____. *Mrs. Humphry Ward*. Oxford: Clarendon Press; New York: Oxford University Press, 1990.

_____. *The Stanford Companion to Victorian Fiction*. Palo Alto, Calif.: Stanford University Press, 1989.

_____. *Thackeray at Work*. London: Athlone Press, 1974.

_____. *Victorian Fiction: Writers, Publishers, Readers*. Houndsmills, Basingstoke, Hampshire: Macmillan, 1995.

_____. *Victorian Novelists and Publishers*. Chicago: University of Chicago Press, 1976.

Taylor, John T. *Early Opposition to the English Novel*. New York: King's Crown Press, 1943.

Terry, R. C. *Victorian Popular Fiction, 1860–80*. London: Macmillan, 1983.

"The Three-Decker." *The Saturday Review* (July 28, 1894).

Tillotson, Geoffrey, and Kathleen Tillotson. "Writers and Readers in 1851." In *Mid-Victorian Studies*. London: University of London, Athlone Press, 1965.

Tillotson, Kathleen. *Novels of the Eighteen-Forties*. London: Oxford University Press, 1961.

Tinsley, W. *The Random Recollections of an Old Publisher*. London: Simpkin, Marshall, Hamilton, Kent & Co.; Bournemouth: Bright's Ltd., 1900.

Todd, Janet, ed. *Dictionary of British Women Writers*. London: Routledge, 1989.

Trollope, Anthony. *An Autobiography*. Oxford and New York: Oxford University Press, 1980.

Turner, Michael. "Reading for the Masses: Aspects of the Syndication of Fiction in Great Britain." In Richard Landon, ed. *Book Selling and Book Buying*. Chicago: American Library Association, 1978.

Uglow, Jenny. *Elizabeth Gaskell*. New York: Farrar Straus & Giroux, 1993.

_____. *George Eliot*. New York: Pantheon, 1987.

Vann, J. Donn. *Victorian Novels in Serial*. New York: Modern Language Association of America, 1985.

"A Visit to Mudie's." *Pall Mall Gazette* (March 11, 1884).

Vizetelly, Henry. *Glances Back Through Seventy Years*. London: K. Paul, Trench, Trubner & Co., 1893.

Wall, Stephen, ed. *Charles Dickens*. Harmondsworth: Penguin, 1970.

Waugh, Arthur. *A Hundred Years of Publishing*. London: Chapman and Hall, 1930.

Wiener, Joel. "Edmund Yates: The Gossip as Editor." In Joel Wiener, ed. *Innovators and Preachers*. Westport, Ct.: Greenwood Press, 1985.

Williams, Charles P. "The Personal Relations of Dickens and Thackeray." *The Dickensian* 35, no. 250 (spring 1939).

Williams, Merryn. *Thomas Hardy and Rural England*. London: Macmillan, 1972.

Wilson, Charles. *First with the News: The History of W. H. Smith, 1792–1972*. New York: Doubleday, 1986.

Winnifrith, Tom. *The Brontës and Their Background*, 2d ed. Houndsmills, Basingstoke, Hampshire: Macmillan, 1988.

Wise, Thomas, and J. Symington, eds. *The Brontës: Their Lives, Friendships and Correspondence*. Oxford: Blackwell, 1933.

Wolff, R. L. *Sensational Victorian*. New York: Garland Publishing, Inc., 1979.

INDEX

PHOTOGRAPHY CREDITS

Grateful acknowledgment is made to the institutions listed below for permission to reproduce the images herein.

By courtesy of the Trustees of the Boston Public Library, 135

By permission of the British Library, 103, 246–247

© British Museum, 7, 21, 155

Courtesy of the Brontë Society, 58–59, 64, 81, 116

Courtesy of the Dickens House Museum, London, 150, 170–171, 185

The Thomas Hardy Memorial Collection, Dorset Country Museum, Dorchester, Dorset, 225

Courtesy of the National Portrait Gallery, London, 69, 97, 109, 123

Henry W. and Albert A. Berg Collection, The New York Public Library, Astor, Lenox, and Tilden Foundations, 19, 49, 73, 88–89

General Research Division, The New York Public Library, Astor, Lenox, and Tilden Foundations, 14, 128, 165, 176–177, 181, 192–193, 199, 237

Print Collection, The New York Public Library, Astor, Lenox, and Tilden Foundations, 28